Allied Health Professions – Essential Guides

Managing and Leading in the Allied Health Professions

Edited by

Robert Jones

and

Fiona Jenkins

Series Foreword by
Penny Humphris

Foreword by
Professor Donald M. Berwick

Radcliffe Publishing
Oxford • Seattle

Radcliffe Publishing Ltd
18 Marcham Road
Abingdon
Oxon OX14 1AA
United Kingdom

www.radcliffe-oxford.com
Electronic catalogue and worldwide online ordering facility.

British Library Cataloguing in Publication Data

A catalogue record for this book is available from the British Library.

ISBN-10 1 85775 706 8
ISBN-13 978 1 85775 706 4

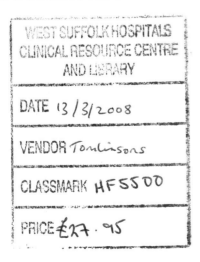
Typeset by Anne Joshua & Associates, Oxford
Printed and bound by TJ International Ltd, Padstow, Cornwall

Contents

A watershed in professional independence: development of autonomy   35
Clinical autonomy   37
Clinical diagnosis   37
Landmarks in the development of a profession   38
The rise of competence and decline of the profession?   41
AHP management: the future?   43
References   43

4   Allied Health Professions management and organisation: what
    structure?
    Fiona Jenkins and Robert Jones   45

    Introduction   45
    The research   47
    Conclusion   66
    References   68

5   Introducing our assessment *Tool* for evaluating ANP management
    structures
    Robert Jones and Fiona Jenkins   70

    Introduction   70
    Application of the *Tool*   71
    Scoring system: assessment *Tool* for AHP management models   71
    Conclusion   72

6   Using organisation as a strategic resource to build identity and
    influence
    Rosalie Boyce   85

    Introduction   85
    Healthcare 'down under': system and policy context   86
    The Australian allied health workforce   87
    Organisational restructuring and the development of 'allied health'   88
    Evaluating allied health organisational models   89
    Leadership and allied health organisation   93
    From organisation to identity through cultural change   94
    Regional and national initiatives in allied health organisation and
        influence   95
    Future vision: a National Allied Health Alliance   96
    Conclusions   97
    References   98

7   Leadership in the Allied Health Professions
    Christina Pond   100

    Introduction   100
    The leadership concept: a brief history   100
    Leadership and emotional intelligence   103
    Leaders and followers   104
    Leadership and management   105

List of figures

List of tables

List of boxes

Series foreword

The NHS, the biggest organisation in the UK and reputedly the third largest in the world, is undergoing massive transformation. We know that effective leadership is essential if the health service is to achieve continuous improvement in the services it offers. It needs people from all types of backgrounds – clinical and managerial – to step up and take on leadership roles to shape the future of health improvement and health care delivery.

Leaders are needed at every level of the health service. The concept of leadership only coming from the top and being defined by position and title is now out of date. It is much more about ways of thinking and behaving and individuals seeing themselves as having the potential to make a real difference for patients. Effective leadership is about working in partnerships and teams to develop a vision for the future, set the direction, influence those whose input is needed and deliver results – a high quality, safe, timely and accessible health service for all.

Allied health professionals operate in every setting in which health care is delivered. You have unparalleled opportunities to help patients to lead their own care and to see how services to patients, clients and carers can be improved across entire patient pathways, crossing traditional professional and organisational boundaries to improve patients' experiences. You have the potential to make a difference by leading improvement and managing services and resources well.

There are already many outstanding leaders in the NHS in the allied health professions making a real difference to services. Two of them had the vision for this series of books and have worked with formidable energy and commitment to make them a reality. Robert and Fiona have both made a considerable investment in their own professional and personal development and delivered substantial improvements in the services for which they are responsible. They have increased their awareness, skills and knowledge and taken on leadership roles, putting into practice many of their ideas and learning. They have worked tirelessly to spread their learning and skilfully persuaded a great many academics and practitioners to contribute to these books to provide a rich collection of theories, tools, techniques and insights to help you.

This series of books has been written to encourage and support many more of you to embark on or to continue your development, to enhance your leadership and management skills, knowledge and experience and to give you confidence to take on new roles and responsibilities. I am sure that many of you, who have not previously considered yourselves as leaders will, when you have read these books, reconsider your roles and potential and take the next steps on your journeys.

Penny Humphris
Director of the NHS Leadership Centre
August 2006

Foreword

In many ways, the term "Allied Health Professional" encodes a culture. The code raises questions: "Allied" to what? In what way "Professional"? Why "Health" and not "Health Care"? Would it be waggish to ask if, say, physicians are also "Allied Health Professionals"? Or, does the term solidify some notion that physicians are "Core" Health Professionals, and the rest pasted on?

I ask these questions, not in a contentious mood, but in an effort to re-raise a point I first heard from Dr. (Ph.D., not M.D.) W. Edwards Deming, a great teacher in the modern quality movement: "The job of a leader," he said, "is to redraw the boundaries of a system."

No one observing health care today, whether in the UK or the US, can doubt that something important is amiss. The profiles of problem vary among developed nations. In the UK, at least until recently, the issues have been mostly about the quality of service in the NHS – consistency, access, dignity, reliability, and coordination. In the US, all of these matter too, but they occupy second seat to the concert-master issue: cost. Naïve critics of care argue for changes in incentives and market structures, in an effort to wring better performance from these troubled systems. In my opinion, they ignore one of the other main lessons of the modern quality movement: that performance is a property of the system itself, as embedded in the design of the care system as, say, the top speed of a particular automobile is embedded in, is a property of, the design of that automobile. If you want a higher top speed, you don't offer your automobile "incentives"; you redesign it.

That is where Dr. Deming's call to leaders has its traction – in the quest for sound redesigns. Trying to get better performance from an existing system within its historic rules and norms is not enough. To achieve truly new performance requires breaking the fetters of assumption, habit, and time-worn structures. It requires raising new and uncomfortable questions. It demands new thinking as far from the *status quo* as a race car is from a jalopy, or as an airplane is from a tank.

In the health care systems of western nations, the confining habits, beliefs, and norms – those that restrict the potential of performance – often become codified in roles. Job descriptions, professional norms, boundaries among professions, certification and licensure requirements, and professional education and acculturation themselves too often become rituals to defend the *status quo*, though masquerading, of course, as forms of excellence and "the right way" to think and act.

"It is the job of leaders to redraw the boundaries of a system." In finding the silos and boundaries, good leaders can help their people discover latent possibilities they would not otherwise have seen. "Why is this a rule?" they may ask. "Who says it must be this way?" "Why did we build this fence instead of a highway?" "Why do we compete, when cooperation seems better?"

Mindful about the threat of assumptions, and hopeful about the potential for thinking fresh about roles, relationships, and inter-professional boundaries, my alarm systems turn "orange" at the term "Allied Health Professionals." What I would like to see in the exploration of this term is a level of open-mindedness, ambition, and energy that can tear down walls that do not serve our patients well, not shore up divisions.

That – to redraw the boundaries – is potentially the most promising and exciting task for these authors and those in the publications that will follow in Radcliffe Publishing Limited's new 'Allied Health Professions – Essential Guides' series. Correctly undertaken, this set of supports for leaders will help them think in fresh and even (in the best sense) aggressive ways about what health care in the future should become. We do not just need leaders now; we need leaders *of change*.

Few professionals are better prepared to engage this worthy exploration than Robert Jones and Fiona Jenkins. They are respected in their therapy fields, and have extensive track records of innovative and capable leadership. They are the type of optimistic, clear, honest, and bold leaders that mark the NHS at its best. Those characteristics can be seen perhaps best in the breadth of authorship in this book. Collecting the ideas and instruction of contributors from many nations and in a wide range of roles, Rob Jones and Fiona Jenkins have shown the open-mindedness and curiosity that can be a front door to "redrawing the boundaries."

I do not believe that the chronic health care crises of either my country or that of Jones and Jenkins will yield to any single idea for redesign – no one magic answer. But I have a sense approaching certainty that, as we find at last a route out of the thicket of excess cost and unreliable care, one crucial asset will be a set of new ways – perhaps entirely new ways – to think about the distribution of roles, responsibilities, credentials, training, and opportunity for the health care workforce as a whole. When that happens, the wisdom and insights of these authors will prove invaluable, and, I hope, the questions raised for me by the term, "Allied Health Professional," will have the most hopeful answers.

- Question: "Allied to what?" Answer: "Allied in the continual pursuit of the relief of suffering for those we serve."
- Question: "In what way 'Professional'?" Answer: "In the willingness to subordinate self-interest and prior assumptions to the pursuit of continual improvement in our effectiveness as a team. In the willingness to redraw the boundaries in the *status quo*."
- Question: "Why 'Health' and not 'Health Care'?" Answer: "To broaden the base of our capacity to serve."
- Question: "Are physicians, too, 'Allied Health Professionals'?" Answer: "Of course. Why would you even bother to ask? We are all on the same team."

Professor Donald M. Berwick MD, MPP, FRCP, KBE
President and CEO Institute for Health Care Improvement
Clinical Professor of Paediatrics and Health Care Policy
Harvard Medical School
August 2006

Preface

There is a wide literature available on the theory and practice of management and leadership. However, to date there has not been a specific publication on Management, Leadership and Development in the Allied Health Professions. With so many fundamental and radical changes and upheavals taking place at such a rapid pace in the National Health Service (NHS) at present, we believe it is the right time for a series of books in this field. Our series 'Allied Health Professions – Essential Guides' – of which this is the first book – is intended for Allied Health Professions managers and aspiring managers, leaders, clinicians, researchers, educators and students and also for non-AHP registrants within the Health Professions Council. The series will also be valuable and of interest for doctors, nurses, pharmacists, optometrists, other professionals working in management and leadership roles and general managers within the NHS.

The books are set in the context of structural, organisational and management changes within the NHS and wider health and social care settings today, encompassing theory and practice and the many changes, policy and practice developments, innovations and new ways of working. All of these and other issues are discussed and set in the context of the NHS in the 21st century and Allied Health Professionals within it.

All of the contributors to this volume, *Managing and Leading*, have recognised expertise nationally and internationally and are widely experienced in their fields. The text is not a continuous narrative, but a collection of subjects closely related and linked into the whole; we have not attempted to adjust the style of individual authors. Although each chapter stands alone in its own right, there are major themes which bring the different aspects together. We would like to thank all of our contributors for sharing their knowledge, experience and expertise. It was a privilege to work in close collaboration with them all.

AHPs must be proactive and responsive to the many changes taking place, to see the upheavals as opportunities, transforming them into positive steps towards the improvement of our services. There is no 'best, right or only one way' of management and leadership; our aim, and that of all our contributors, has been to indicate various approaches and provide an in-depth and wide range of information, which we believe will enhance the evidence base, knowledge, understanding and skills to support managers, leaders and clinicians to manage and lead their services sensitively, effectively and efficiently and by so doing provide the best quality service possible for our patients and service users.

Robert Jones and Fiona Jenkins
August 2006
www.jjconsulting.org.uk

About the editors

Dr Robert Jones PhD, MPhil, BA, FCSP, Grad Dip Phys, MHSM, MMACP.
Head of Therapy Services, East Sussex Hospitals NHS Trust; Physiotherapy Registrant; Member Health Professions Council 2001–2006.

Robert is a Senior Manager and Head of Therapy Services in secondary and primary care, with contracts in the independent sector, working at executive board level. He has extensive experience in strategic, operational and change management with a PhD in Management and MPhil in Social Policy and Administration. Robert is a Fellow of the Chartered Society of Physiotherapy and former CSP chair, vice president and council member. He completed a one year secondment to the Commission for Health Improvement as AHP consultant and has also contributed to a number of DH working groups. He has detailed knowledge and expertise in statutory and professional regulation and is a recent member of the NHS Information Authority Project Board and National QAA Steering Group. Robert has lectured at international and national levels on, for example, management, information management, service improvement and modernisation and he has a wide range of publications in these areas. He is an external lecturer and Honorary Fellow at the University of Brighton and a Governor of Moorfields Eye Hospital NHS Foundation Trust.

Robert has led a wide range of service improvements and innovations, some of which are national exemplars.

Fiona Jenkins MA (dist.), FCSP, Grad Dip Phys, MHSM, NEBS Dip (M), PGCO.
Head of Physiotherapy South Devon Health Services, and Service Improvement Lead.

Fiona manages and leads a physiotherapy service that covers acute care, primary care and a care trust. Additionally, she holds a role of service improvement lead. A Fellow, former council member and vice president of the Chartered Society of Physiotherapy, Fiona has led a large number of multidisciplinary service improvement and modernisation projects across South Devon, one of which has attracted national research funding and has been used by the DH as an exemplar. Her current areas for service improvement include: physical and sensory disability, Long Term Conditions National Service Framework, musculoskeletal and stroke services redesign. She has successfully introduced several new and extended roles within her large cross-organisational staff team. She has lectured both nationally and internationally on a wide range of management topics. Her MA is in management, with a particular interest in the management and organisation of Allied Health Professions services. In 2004 Fiona received a Department of Health award for innovative thinking. Fiona is currently undertaking research for a PhD in management.

Both Fiona and Robert successfully completed the INSEAD NHS/Leadership Centre Clinical Strategists' programme at the business school in Fontainebleau,

France. They have continued to work with INSEAD on the development of teaching cases for use on future MBA programmes. They were Modernisation Agency Associates and have worked collaboratively on service improvement, modernisation and joint national and international presentations and lectures.

List of contributors

Dr Rosalie A. Boyce PhD, M Bus., BSc, Grad Dip Dietetics, Grad Dip Health Admin
Research Fellow, University of Queensland, Australia
Visiting Professor, Sheffield Hallam University, UK

Professor Norma Brook FCSP BSc(Hons), Pg Dip, Dip TP, Grad Dip Phys
Former President of Health Professions Council

Professor Jon Chilingerian PhD
Brandeis University
Heller School for Social Policy and Management
United States
Healthcare Management Initiative
INSEAD
Fontainebleau
France

Professor Bridgit Dimond MA, LLB, DSA, AHSM, **Barrister-at-law**
Emeritus Professor of the University of Glamorgan

Dr Sally French PhD, MSc(Psych), MSc (Soc), BSc, Dip TP, MCSP
Associate Lecturer
Open University

Professor Mattia Gilmartin PhD, RN
Senior Research Fellow
Healthcare Management Initiative
INSEAD
Fountainebleau
France

Professor Ann Moore PhD, FCSP, FMACP, Grad Dip Phys, Cert Ed, Dip TP, ILTM
Professor of Physiotherapy and Director of the Clinical Research Centre for Health
Professions
University of Brighton

Christina Pond MBA, BSc(Hons)
Former Director of Team and Network Leadership Development
NHS Leadership Centre

Professor Amanda Squires PhD, MSc, FCSP
Senior Programme Development Manager
Healthcare Commission

Professor John Swain PhD, MSc, BSc, PGCE
Professor of Disability and Inclusion
University of Northumbria

List of abbreviations

A&C	Admin and Clerical
ACAS	Advisory, Conciliation and Arbitration Service
AfC	Agenda for Change
AHA	Area Health Authority
AHP	Allied Health Profession
AHPs	Allied Health Professions and Allied Health Professionals
AHPA	Allied Health Professions Australia
AHPCA	Allied Health Professions Council of Australia
BMA	British Medical Association
CEO	Chief Executive Officer
CG	Clinical Governance
CHI	Commission for Health Improvement
CHRE	Council for Healthcare Regulatory Excellence
CIP	Cost Improvement Programme
COT	College of Occupational Therapists
CPD	Continuing Professional Development
CPSM	Council for Professions Supplementary to Medicine
CRHP	Council for Regulation of Healthcare Professionals
CSP	Chartered Society of Physiotherapy
CV	Curriculum Vitae
DA	District Administrator
DCA	Department of Constitutional Affairs
DCP	District Community Physician
DDA	Disability Discrimination Act
DET	Disability Equality Training
DGH	District General Hospital
DGM	District General Manager
DH	Department of Health
DHA	District Health Authority
DHSS	Department of Health and Social Security
DMT	District Management Team
DMU	Directly Managed Unit
DoH/DH	Department of Health
EBP	Evidence-based Practice
ECDL	European Computer Driving Licence
EI	Emotional Intelligence
EPR	Electronic Patient Record
ESP	Extended Scope Practitioner
EWTD	European Working Time Directive
FHSA	Family Health Services Authority
GBM	Green Belt Movement
GMC	General Medical Council

GMS	General Medical Services
GP	General Practitioner
GPSI	General Practitioner with Special Interest
HC	Health Circular
HCA	Health Care Assistant
HPCA	Health Professions Council of Australia
HCS	Health Care Scientists
HCPs	Healthcare Professionals
HEI	Higher Education Institution
HMSO	Her Majesty's Stationery Office
HN	Health Notice
HOSC	Health Overview and Scrutiny Committee
HPC	Health Professions Council
HR	Human Resources
ICP	Integrated Care Pathway
ICU	Intensive Care Unit
IM&T	Information Management and Technology
IPR	Individual Performance Review
ISO	International Standards Office
IT	Information Technology
IWL	Improving Working Lives
KSF	Knowledge and Skills Framework
LDP	Local Development Plan
LEO	Leading in Empowered Organisations
LREC	Local Research and Ethics Committee
MA	Modernisation Agency
MD	Medical Director
MDT	Multidisciplinary Team
MOH	Ministry of Health
NAHBC	National Allied Health Benchmarking Consortium
NAHBPC	National Allied Health Best Practice Consortium
NAHCC	National Allied Health Casemix Committee
NHS	National Health Service
NICE	National Institute for Health and Clinical Excellence
NMC	Nursing and Midwifery Council
NP-fIT	National Programme for Information Technology
NSF	National Service Framework
NVQ	National Vocational Qualification
OR	Operating Room
OT	Occupational Therapy
PALS	Patient Advisory Liaison Service
PAS	Patient Administration System
PBC	Practice-based Commissioning
PbR	Payment by Results
PCG	Primary Care Group
PCRN	Primary Care Research Network
PCT	Primary Care Trust
PDP	Personal Development Plan
PEC	Professional Executive Committee

PFI	Private Finance Initiative
PI	Performance Indicator
PLG	Professional Liaison Group
PRP	Performance-related Pay
R&D	Research and Development
RCA	Root Cause Analysis
RCN	Royal College of Nursing
RGN	Regional General Manager
RN	Registered Nurse
RHA	Regional Health Authority
RMT	Regional Management Team
RSDU	Research Support Development Unit
SALT	Speech and Language Therapy
SARRAH	Services for Rural and Remote Allied Health
SFI	Standing Financial Instructions
SHA	Strategic Health Authority
SLA	Service Level Agreement
SS	Social Services
SWOT	Strengths, Weaknesses, Opportunities, Threats
TQM	Total Quality Management
UMT	Unit Management Team
WDC	Workforce Development Confederation
WTE	Whole Time Equivalent

List of books in this series

Chapter 1

Management in the Allied Health Professions: an overview

Robert Jones and Fiona Jenkins

Introduction

The structure, organisation and management of the Allied Health Professions (AHPs) in the National Health Service (NHS) is – in common with the service as a whole – on a continuum of far-reaching and challenging redesign and high-impact change. AHP managers have wide-ranging roles and responsibilities within extremely complex environments. Their work materially affects the level, efficiency and effectiveness of service provision, alternatives available and evenness and equity of services across many specialty and organisational boundaries: primary, secondary and tertiary care and others, for example, social services, education, voluntary and independent sectors.

The key focus of this chapter is to introduce some important concepts and functions of management and the manager, relating this to Allied Health Professions management. There is a close link between this and Chapters 2 to 6. In Chapter 2, the changing structure, organisation and management of the NHS are outlined from an historical perspective through to recent NHS policy initiatives. Chapter 3 focuses on the evolution and significance of professionalisation of the Allied Health Professions and the relevance of this to their management. In Chapter 4 the roles, responsibilities and duties of AHP managers in the context of NHS structure and organisation are explored in depth. We set out a framework for assessing possible management structures for AHPs in Chapter 5. In Chapter 6 Rosalie Boyce discusses Australian AHP management arrangements and the inter-relationship between the Allied Health Professions which could have a significant bearing on possible future arrangements for the UK and other health systems.

As readers will be only too aware the NHS in 2006 is undergoing another period of significant change. The third book of this series, which is focused on the 'big picture' for health professions includes a chapter contributed by Pat Oakley who further develops many of the themes in this book and explores in detail the implications of this latest round of radical restructuring and new policy initiatives and implementation.

Allied Health Professions

The term 'Allied Health Profession' was first coined in *Meeting the Challenge: a strategy for the Allied Health Professions* in 2000[1] to describe the 13 professions comprising:

- art therapists
- drama therapists
- music therapists
- dietitians
- occupational therapists
- orthoptists
- orthotists
- paramedics
- physiotherapists
- podiatrists
- prosthetists
- radiographers (diagnostic and therapeutic)
- speech and language therapists.

The Health Professions Council (HPC), the regulator for the AHPs and healthcare scientists in the UK, lists 13 professions which in addition to the above include operating department practitioners, clinical scientists and biomedical scientists, almost 170 000 registrants.[2] A further large group of staff – not regulated by the HPC – working under the umbrella of AHPs and within their management remit includes assistants and technical instructors; the staffing within all these professions and occupational groups represents a significant percentage of the 1.3 million staff employed in the NHS. After nursing and healthcare assistants the AHPs are the second largest staff group within the NHS. It is incumbent on the NHS and AHPs themselves to ensure the highest quality of management capability in terms of expertise, skills, knowledge and competence in order to optimise the use, effectiveness and efficiency of this complex and essential workforce and maximise the impact and benefit of all resources within their remit.

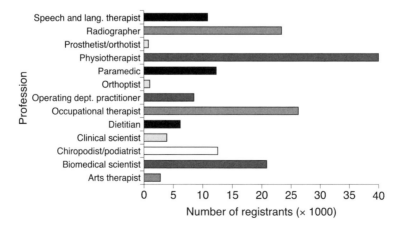

Figure 1.1 Number of HPC registrants

In 2004 the DH[3] summarised the contribution of the AHPs as providing patient-centred care with expertise working across a range of health and social services, promoting good health, treating those who are acutely ill and caring for those with long-term conditions. However, the Department also recognised AHPs as having roles that:

> . . . have too often been undervalued or neglected.

In 1997[4] the Chief Executive Officer of the NHS, Sir Alan Langlands, in his 'Foreword' to a review of therapy services in the NHS, stated:

> Therapy services are an integral part of the Health Service and provide an important and valuable service to patients.

Meeting the Challenge: a strategy for the Allied Health Professions[1] emphasised the roles and contributions of AHPs in the provision of modern high-quality patient care:

> Delivering the NHS Plan will require changes in the way in which all NHS staff, including those in the AHPs, work. Members of these professions are central to the modernisation programme we have set in train . . . 'Meeting the Challenge' sets out how we want to see the role of the AHPs developed and supported, building on real accounts of the work which they do.

The main purpose of this strategy was to support and develop the AHPs in contributing to delivery of the priorities for the NHS as set out in the NHS Plan[5] and the NHS Improvement Plan.[3]

Despite this, the scope, spectrum and contribution of AHP services are often not well understood and therefore AHP services are not always used to the optimum benefit of service users and the NHS as a whole. AHP services offer critical contributions to the NHS and operate in a wide range of environments. This complexity is affected by organisational, operational and regulatory factors.

An important aspect of the AHP manager's role is to ensure that the positive and wide-ranging contributions of their services, including consultant, specialist and extended scope practitioner posts and the many other facets of modernisation and service improvement, are widely recognised and understood by commissioners, directors and managers, all other service providers and the service users as essential and integral to high-quality healthcare service provision.

The expertise, experience and skills of AHPs are essential to, for example:

- clinical assessment and diagnosis
- working in primary, secondary, tertiary and palliative care in a wide range of locations, including social services, education, the voluntary and independent sectors
- the planning, development and implementation of evidence-based modern services
- critical care
- facilitating safe and speedy discharge from hospital
- teaching the skills needed to prevent readmission to hospital
- enabling patients to return to home, work and leisure as soon as possible
- providing rapid intervention for acute conditions as part of the multi-disciplinary team

- providing rehabilitation
- assessing for provision of appropriate equipment
- providing support and training for carers
- networking widely with other agencies in the provision of collaborative, partnership and cross-boundary services
- providing health improvement/education.

There are many possible objectives for AHP services whether managed on a multi- or unidisciplinary basis and dependent on a wide range of factors such as: type of service provider; location; population served; demographic background; size and profile of teams and so on. Examples of objectives which might be regarded as appropriate and common to AHP services might be, for example:

- to provide high-quality assessment and care based on individual needs using established professional standards, ethical practice, National Guidelines and evidence base while ensuring value for money for commissioners and service users
- to ensure patient and public involvement in planning and development of services and the availability of user information in appropriate formats
- to respond to changing patterns of healthcare provision, working flexibly in partnership and collaboration with all agencies
- to achieve best possible outcomes for all service users
- to ensure effective and efficient clinical and managerial practices, guided by good communication, clinical governance, evidence-based practice, clinical audit and outcome measurement
- to ensure continuing professional and personal development for all staff, ensuring all staff are respected and their contributions valued
- to work closely and collaboratively with all other disciplines
- to work within and contribute positively to the strategies and policies of the employing organisation and to contribute to the objectives of the organisation as a whole, also taking a proactive role in relevant government policies
- to maintain strong links with universities, professional and regulatory bodies and trade unions
- to ensure that information management and technology (IM&T) is sensitive to clinical service and managerial needs – that data is accurate, timely, relevant and for identified purposes
- to ensure a positive approach to service improvement and modernisation, including flexibility in working practices and responsiveness to the needs of service users, including a proactive approach to National Service Frameworks.

This list of possible contributions and objectives is not exhaustive.

Management and the manager

'Management' was defined by French and Saward[6] as:

> The task of ensuring that a number of diverse activities are performed in such a way that a defined objective is achieved – especially the task of creating and maintaining conditions in which desired objectives are achieved by the combined efforts of a group of people (which include the person carrying out the management).

In some ways we are all managers in that we all have some choice about the use of our time and whether or not to do one thing or another. However, as Mullins[7] put it:

> We are concerned with management as involving people looking beyond themselves and exercising formal authority over the activities and performance of other people.

The question, 'What is a manager?', is difficult to answer with a single definition, as Locke[8] stated:

> . . . because there are as wide a variety of management jobs in the economy as there are definitions in the extensive academic literature.

However, some broad definitions may be helpful as a foundation from which to examine the management responsibilities of senior AHP managers. Efficient management involves understanding what factors influence management effectiveness, as well as being able to manage and monitor what is happening. A wide range of good-quality information is required to support effective decision making and actions:

> . . . being able to measure these factors, setting targets that we wish to achieve and being able to monitor progress towards these targets . . . if you can't measure what is happening, then you can't manage it.
>
> Bullas[9]

Henry Mintzberg[10] set out a basic description of managerial work, defining the manager as: 'The person in charge of an organisation or one of its sub-units'.

Besides chief executive officers this definition would include company vice-presidents, bishops, foremen, hockey coaches and prime ministers. In answer to the question 'What do managers have in common?' Mintzberg cites an important starting point as: that all managers are vested with formal authority over an organisational unit.

The manager's job has been described in terms of various roles or organised sets of behaviours (*see* Table 1.1).

Mintzberg's 10 roles for the manager are discussed in *Understanding Organizations*.[11] These are interpersonal roles which are figurehead, leader and liaison; informational roles, that is, monitor, disseminator and spokesman; and finally decisional roles which are entrepreneur, disturbance handler, resource allocator and negotiator. Handy suggested that the mix of roles varied from job to job as well as in the hierarchy of the organisation. Top jobs had more 'leading roles' but every management job had some elements of all three roles. Handy himself uses more colloquial descriptions of the three sets of roles which are leading, administrating and fixing. All of these are central to the management of AHP services in the NHS. Barnard, in his classic work *The Functions of the Executive*,[12] set out the functions of the executive – by which he meant all kinds of managers – as being the maintenance of organisational communication, the securing of essential services from individuals in the organisation and the formulation and definition of purpose, that is, planning. Again, these three functions are essential components in the management of AHP services in integrating the whole and in finding the best balance between conflicting forces and events. Planning and

Table 1.1 The roles of the manager

Role	Mintzberg's definition	Handy's description
Interpersonal roles	Figurehead	
	Leader	(Leading)
	Liaison	
Informational roles	Monitor	
	Disseminator	(Administrator)
	Spokesman	
Decisional roles	Entrepreneur	
	Disturbance handler	(Fixing)
	Resource allocator	
	Negotiator	

Adapted from Handy (1999)[11]

control are seen by Armstrong[13] to be the two key managerial activities. He recognises the importance of the part played by management techniques in managerial skills, procedures and activities.

Kotter[14] describes the roles of managers as: planning, organising structure, resources, controlling and problem solving. Leadership is an integral part of management but does not replace it (*see* Chapter 7).

Two 'popular' answers to the question, 'What is a manager?' are mentioned in *The Practice of Management* by Drucker.[15] One is that 'Management is the people at the top' – the term 'management' being little more than a euphemism for 'the boss'. The other one defines a manager as someone who directs the work of others and who, as the slogan puts it, 'does his work by getting other people to do theirs'. All of these definitions and answers shed some light, but they are inadequate because they do not wholly explain what management is or what managers do. These two questions can only be answered by:

> . . . analysing management's function. For management is an organ; and organs can be described and defined only through their function.
> Drucker[15]

Øvretveit[16] defines management as the work of: 'getting the best match between needs and resources, over the short, medium and long term'.

Drucker[17] likened the manager to the conductor of a symphony orchestra. As conductor, the manager is the one through whose effort, vision and leadership the various instrumental parts, that are so much noise by themselves, become the 'living whole of music'.[11] On the other hand he likened the manager to a doctor – the manager is the first recipient of problems. The manager's role is therefore to identify the symptoms in any situation; to diagnose the disease or cause of the trouble; to decide how it might be dealt with, through a strategy for health; and 'to start the treatment'. Koontz, O'Donnell and Weihrich[18] suggest that the basic functional areas of management are: planning, organising, staffing, leading and controlling.

The importance and impact of relevant organisational structure and systems fit for specific purposes to the facilitation of economic, effective and efficient management and operational performance are often underestimated or over-looked, particularly with respect to the AHPs. Without appropriate organisational structures and systems in place to support strategic initiatives and operational management, performance will deteriorate and clinical service provision will suffer. 'It is important to have clearly defined decision-making processes which are efficient.'[19]

Structures and systems are the anatomy and physiology of an organisation; together they define what the organisation can do, and define what capabilities it has.

Mintzberg[20] sees the challenge as:

> Not so much in trying to comprehend all the possible dimensions of organisational structure as in developing the ability to focus on those dimensions which are currently important to the organisation's evolution.

He describes the 7-S framework, in which the central idea is that organisational effectiveness stems from the interaction between several factors.

- **Systems:** These are all the procedures, formal and informal, which make the organisation function. This is possibly the dominant variable in the '7-S' model. It relates for example to budgeting systems, information, and training.
- **Style:** The power of style is how it is managed. One element is how the managers spend their time, another is symbolic behaviour of the 'top team'.
- **Staff:** There are two main aspects relating to staff. At one end of the spectrum

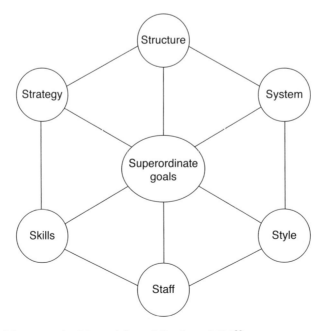

Figure 1.2 7-S framework. Adapted from Mintzberg 1995[20]

are appraisal systems, pay scales and formal training programmes. At the other end of the spectrum are morale, attitude, motivation and behaviour.
- **Skills:** This factor captures crucial attributes. Skills can be divided into 'current' skills and 'new' skills as these are acquired.
- **Strategy:** This relates to the actions that an organisation plans in response to or anticipation of changes in its external environment. Strategy is how an organisation aims to improve its position. Importantly strategy should precede structure.
- **Structure:** The central issue relating to the structure of an organisation is how to divide up the tasks, how to co-ordinate them and how to make the whole thing work.
- **Superordinate goals:** These are guiding concepts – a set of values and aspirations, often unwritten, going beyond the conventional formal statement of corporate objectives.

This framework outlines the importance of organisational structure, but commends attention to the other 'S' factors if an organisation is to succeed.

The Allied Health Professions manager

An essential element of management is co-ordinating the activities of staff and guiding their efforts towards the goals and objectives of the organisation. To achieve the maximum effectiveness of AHP interventions and co-ordinated service provision for users across all boundaries, an overview with good communication is necessary. AHP managers are responsible for ensuring the optimum use of limited workforce and all other resources; they act as catalysts to initiate and develop new fields of service, and widen provision, forging stronger links with a wide range of agencies both inside and outside the NHS.

The roles, responsibilities and duties of AHP managers are wide-ranging and complex whether they manage unidisciplinary services, such as speech and language therapy and podiatry, or multiple services such as all the therapies or various other combinations of services both in and outside of the AHPs (*see* Chapter 4).

During the last 30 years the roles of AHP managers have evolved, reflecting the many government-initiated reforms and policy changes; developments in working practices and service changes (*see* Chapter 2); changes in structure, management, and the workforce; weakening of the traditional power-base of the professions and new regulatory mechanisms; the increasing knowledge and power of the consumer or service user through easier and widening communication, choice and more involvement; the drive towards collaborative and partnership working and many other approaches to modernisation and service improvement.

There is a paucity of published literature relating to the management roles of AHPs either as individual professions or as a group. Jones[21] researched the job content of AHP managers through an empirical study of senior physiotherapy managers in England and Wales; the main purpose of this questionnaire survey was to investigate the job content of this group of managers. He identified 27 different roles which could be broadly subdivided into key function areas (*see* Box 1.1).

Box 1.1 The key function areas of an AHP manager

- Strategic management
- Human resource management
- Operational management
- Budget and resource management
- Information management
- Education pre- and postgraduate
- Research and development
- Clinical and professional leadership and consultancy

Of these roles, human resource (HR) management included the greatest range of tasks. This aspect involved recruitment and retention, performance management, appraisal and staff development, grievance and disciplinary policy management, management of HR policies and HR administration work and staff deployment. Clearly there is a strong connection between good people management and high-performing organisations; it is often said that when staff leave their employment they are leaving their manager not their job. Human resource management is a crucial element of the AHP manager's role.

Berry[22] conducted a postal questionnaire survey of AHP managers to examine the management of therapy professions. The work of these managers was analysed and the results of the survey compared with the results reported by Jones.[21] Berry grouped together the main tasks from the list cited by Jones and made comparison between her own findings and those of the earlier research. Berry indicated that the responsibilities and duties of senior AHP managers remained wide-ranging, verifying the previous research.

> It can be seen that although there has been a slight decrease in responsibility in some areas – notably quality assurance and service development – in all other areas responsibility has remained the same or increased.
>
> Berry[22]

Jones[23] subsequently undertook a further questionnaire survey of senior AHP managers in England. The results showed that the majority of senior AHP managers were still managing unidisciplinary services only. However, the broadening of the span of control and remit of these managers was gaining momentum, with 36% managing multiple services. The findings indicated the widening scope of management work in the context of the NHS reforms leading up to 2000. The Jones and Berry research was further developed by Jenkins, relating to management arrangements for AHPs in 2004–05 and is presented in Chapter 4.

Within AHP services many professional and managerial decisions are synonymous with one another. Decisions are in their broadest sense concerned with clinical matters, for example, the development of AHP consultant, extended scope practitioners and clinical specialists or advanced practitioner posts; advising on service developments and improvements; implementing government policies and guidelines in the context of AHP services; the development of seven-day-a-week working; cross-boundary working collaboratively with social services and education services and a multitude of others. Professional accountability cannot be divorced from the control of resources deployed in providing effective patient care. Senior AHP managers and the professional heads of individual disciplines accountable to them are the professional and clinical heads of service, with an overall management function, and the amalgamation of these strands is essential to maximising effectiveness and efficiency.

Effectiveness and efficiency

A core component of the role of the AHP manager is to ensure provision of effective and efficient services. Value for money is demanded in relation to public services, industries and businesses of all types, including the NHS, and in common with other services this requirement is central to the management of AHPs. Optimum value for money for patients and taxpayers is attainable only through maximising effectiveness and efficiency within the services and it is the management of an effective and efficient service – in all its aspects – that is the core of the AHP manager's job.

Effectiveness and efficiency are two quite different though related concepts. Effectiveness relates to the clinical outcomes of service provision taking into account evidence-based clinical practice whilst efficiency is concerned with maximising the outputs from a given set of inputs and is linked to the necessary balance between the resources needed to achieve the aims and objectives of the service.

Table 1.2 Some factors influencing effectiveness and efficiency

Effectiveness	*Efficiency*
Availability of staff expertise	Regular monitoring of inputs, outputs and throughput
Clinical evidence to support interventions	
Use of clinical guidelines and protocols	Use of data to provide timely, accurate and relevant information
Care pathways	Redesign service in light of new evidence
Clinical outcome measures	
Clinical audit	Service benchmarking
Appropriate equipment/facilities	Ongoing staff mix monitoring
Patient/Public involvement (PPI)	Budget monitoring
Complaints and plaudit monitoring	Workload planning and monitoring
Strong collaborative and partnership working	Absence management
	Caseload prioritisation
Clinical supervision	Capacity planning
Peer review	
Staff education and training	
Staff continuing professional development and personal development plans	

Table 1.3 Efficiency factors in AHP services

Staff time spent treating patients	Planning and scheduling the working day
Caseload adjustment	Comparison of staff caseloads
Avoidance of unnecessary overtime	Prioritising problems
Maximising use of skills (teaching other carers)	High-quality clinical assessment
Thorough record-keeping systems	Patient discharge at appropriate time
Monitoring changes in referral	Accessibility of appropriate equipment
Optimum skill mix appropriate to task	Monitoring objectives (goals) and outcomes
Caseload priority when staff absent	Waiting list times
Intervention priority of most urgent patients	Monitoring patient non-attendance (DNA rates)
Use of appropriate appointment systems	More control for service users
Home care programmes	Optimum use of space
Time tabling of most frequently used equipment	Relevant postgraduate education and training
Planning travel to other units	Simple and relevant paperwork systems
Most effective use of highly skilled staff	Monitoring staff absence
Monitoring of overtime, 'on-call' and travel costs	Analysis of activity statistics
Pattern of service use by referrers	Average numbers of interventions within episodes of care
Evidenced-based practice	Collaborative and partnership working
Interdisciplinary working	Capacity planning

An effective service could be defined as providing excellent outcomes for service users. An efficient service provides effectiveness with the least level of resource input.

Management goals are set for the whole service or individual sub-units of the service. Once goals have been set and agreed the manager must ensure that measurement of the goals is undertaken.[9] The effectiveness of the service as a whole is calculated by the summation of the effectiveness of all its parts. An important task for the AHP manager is to work towards the development of the relevant outcome measures which are necessary to achieve the balance of resources needed for the agreed and optimum use of finances.

> The greater the outputs from a given set of inputs, the greater the efficiency.
>
> Brookes[24]

For AHP services resource inputs can be described in terms of:

- **revenue spending:** staffing, travel costs, consumables, utilities, etc.
- **capital spending:** buildings, facilities and equipment.

The tasks of the manager require the efficient use of resources in order to provide optimum clinical outcomes, that is, service effectiveness, which has many contributing factors.

There are many factors involved in achieving efficiency and we would suggest the list of examples in Table 1.3. This list is not exhaustive and not in priority order.

Management of quality

The New NHS: modern, dependable[25] stated that the new NHS would have 'quality at its heart'. In this context, it is an important aspect of the AHP managers' role to ensure best possible quality of healthcare provision for service users. Quality of healthcare must focus on the process as well as clinical decision making and an appropriate definition should point to a broad vision of quality improvement within organisations. As the DH[25] put it: 'doing the right things, for the right people at the right time and doing them right first time'.

In July 2004, the DH published *Standards for Better Health*,[26] which set out the 24 core standards that 'describe the level of service which is acceptable and which must be universal'. The Healthcare Commission[27] undertakes assessments and checks compliance with these core standards throughout the NHS.

Maxwell[28] described six essential components of a quality service.

1 **Appropriateness:** The service or procedure is what the population or individual actually needs. This is different from demand if demand is taken to mean a willingness on the part of the consumer to pay for the service. Need is professionally identified.
2 **Equity:** There is a fair share for the population.
3 **Accessibility:** Service is not compromised by undue limits of time or distance.
4 **Effectiveness:** The intended benefit is achieved for the individual or the population.
5 **Acceptability:** Services are provided to satisfy the reasonable expectations of the patient, providers and the community.
6 **Efficiency:** Resources are not wasted on one patient or service to the detriment of another.

Picker Institute research[29] into patients' and carers' perspectives cites eight parameters against which they judge quality:

1 Respecting patients' views, preferences and expressed needs.
2 Access to care.
3 Emotional support.
4 Information, communication and education.
5 Co-ordination of care.
6 Physical comfort.
7 Involvement of family and friends.
8 Continuity and transition.

Quality issues require organisations, managers and their staff to take account of both the patients' and clinicians' perspectives in the provision of high-quality standards of service.

Morris[30] indicated that there is no 'universal' definition of what quality in healthcare is, but that quality is a major issue. However, she offers a definition of quality based on the idea of value for money and recognising that the consumer of healthcare services is not necessarily the purchaser of them:

> Quality in healthcare is the total package of features and characteristics in healthcare service or product and the way in which it is provided, that bear on its ability to satisfy the agreed need of the consumer and the agreed requirements of the purchaser within the constraints imposed by professional judgement, at lowest cost, and whilst minimising wastes and losses.[30]

The provision of high-quality clinical services is integral to the role of AHP managers, whether they manage uni- or multidisciplinary services. The management of clinical governance, incorporation of the evidence base into clinical and managerial practice, based on up-to-date research, clinical audit, outcome measurement, standard setting and service monitoring, for example, are all essential elements of the role of the AHP manager.

Accountability

A further responsibility of the AHP manager is to be accountable for the service provision within the terms laid down by the employer and jointly agreed. To be accountable is to be required by a specified person, group or organisation to report to and justify (give account for) actions in relation to specified matters. Accountability for an AHP service, in common with many other NHS services, is multifactorial.

The AHP manager, as professional and clinical head of service, has three main strands of accountability.

- To the patient.
- As an agent for the employer – or purchaser of service in external contracts.
- For the management and leadership of services.

> The traditional organisation of AHPs has stressed functional organisation and the integrity of a profession-centred approach to maximise clinical expertise.
>
> Jenkins[31]

The AHP is accountable to his/her patients for high standards of therapeutic practice and behaviour. Despite the imperative for the clinician to gain informed consent, service users may sometimes not be in a position or be inclined to require that the AHP justifies actions on specified matters relating to practice. The AHP manager is often the first arbiter in professional matters within the service and is the individual to whom the staff are accountable; in this the AHP manager acts as agent for the employer. There are numerous activities for which the staff are accountable to the AHP manager, for example, undertaking clinical caseloads; attending relevant ward rounds, case conferences and meetings; incorporation into clinical practice of the evidence base; keeping full and accurate clinical records; and the collection of statistical information. In turn, the AHP manager is accountable to the employer for the provision of effective and efficient services.

Accountability cannot be divorced from the control of the resources deployed in effective care.

In some circumstances, employers have opted for a system of 'split' account-ability whereby the manager is accountable to one officer managerially and another professionally. However, unless the 'ground rules' and procedures are clearly set out and agreed by all parties, confusion, ineffective and inefficient management and leadership may result as professional and managerial decisions are often synonymous with one another. Accountability impinges on both professional and managerial aspects and the two are inextricably linked.

In conclusion

Management is an active process based on theoretical foundations. It has many facets, the most important of which is unerring patient focus. The challenge is enlightened governance: changing behaviour, making things happen, facilitating change and transformation and improving quality. It is about good leadership, team working, involving all, having proper facilities and design. The manager works with people helping their development in reaching objectives and achieving results as well as being involved with processes, systems and strategy.

> . . . Indeed, all the research into how managers spend their time reveals that they are creatures of the moment, perpetually immersed in the nitty-gritty of making things happen.[32]

References

1 Department of Health. *Meeting the Challenge: a strategy for the allied health professions*. London: HMSO; 2000.
2 HPC. *Annual Report*. London: Health Professions Council; 2005.
3 Department of Health. *The NHS Improvement Plan: putting people at the heart of public services*. London: HMSO; 2004.
4 Department of Health. *Providing Therapists' Expertise in the New NHS: developing a strategic framework for good patient care. Part 1*. Brighton: Practices made Perfect; 1997.
5 Department of Health. *The NHS Plan: a plan for investment, a plan for reform*. London: HMSO; 2000.
6 French D, Saward H. *A Dictionary of Management*. London: Pan Reference; 1984.
7 Mullins LJ. *Management and Organisation Behavior*. 6th ed. Harlow: Prentice Hall; 2002.
8 Lock D, editor. *Handbook of Management*. 3rd ed. London: Gower; 1992.
9 Bullas S. *Managing Hospital Quality and Cost*. Harlow: Longman; 1994.
10 Mintzberg H. *The Strategy Process: concepts, contexts and cases*. London: Sage Publications; 1988.
11 Handy C. *Understanding Organizations*. 4th ed. London: Penguin Business Books; 1999.
12 Barnard C. *The Functions of the Executive*. 1938. In: Koontz H, O'Donnell C, Weikrich M, editors. *Management*. London: McGraw-Hill; 1984.
13 Armstong M. *A Handbook of Management Techniques*. London: Kogan Page; 1986.
14 Kotter J. *Leading Change*. Boston: Harvard Business School Press; 1998.
15 Drucker P. *The Practice of Management*. London: Pan; 1968.
16 Øvretveit J. *Therapy Services: organisation, management and autonomy*. Reading: Harwood Academic Publishers; 1992.
17 Drucker P. *Innovation and Entrepreneurship*. London: Pan; 1985.
18 Koontz H, O'Donnell C, Weikrich H, editors. *Management*. London: McGraw-Hill; 1984.

19 Leatt P, Shortell SM, Kimberley JR. *Health Care Management: organizational design and behaviour*. 4th ed. Albany: Delmar Publishing; 2000.
20 Mintzberg H, Quinn JB, Voyer J, editors. *The Strategy Process*. Harlow: Prentice Hall; 1995.
21 Jones R. *Management in Physiotherapy*. Oxford: Radcliffe Medical Press; 1991.
22 Berry M. *Management of the Therapy Professions in the National Health Service of the 1990s*. MBA thesis; 1994.
23 Jones R. *An Investigation into the Development of a Computerised Information System for NHS Physiotherapy Services in England: an action research study*. PhD thesis; 2000.
24 Brookes R, editor. *Management Budgeting in the NHS*. Keele: Health Service Manpower Review; 1986.
25 Department of Health. *The New NHS: modern, dependable*. London: HMSO; 1997.
26 Department of Health. *Standards for Better Health: national standards, local action*. London: HMSO; 2004.
27 Healthcare Commission. *Criteria for Assessing Core Standards*. London: Healthcare Commission; 2005.
28 Maxwell RJ. Quality assessment in health. *BMJ*. 1984; **288**(1): 470–1.
29 Edgman-Levitan S, Cleary PD. What information do consumers want and need? *Health Affairs*. 1996; **15**(4): 42–56.
30 Morris B. Quality in healthcare. In: JJ Glynn and DM Perkins, editors. *Managing Healthcare*. London: Saunders Co. Ltd; 1995.
31 Jenkins F. *Management Arrangements for the Allied Health Professions within the National Health Service in England: a research study*. MA dissertation; 2005.
32 Crainer S. *Key Management Ideas: thinkers that change the management world*. 3rd ed. Harlow: FT Prentice Hall; 1998.

Chapter 2

Evolution of structure, organisation and management in the NHS

Robert Jones and Fiona Jenkins

Introduction

The NHS has undergone a process of continuous and substantial change during the last 30 years, which has impacted significantly on its structure, organisation and management. An appreciation of the historical perspective through a review of major landmarks in this process is essential to an understanding of how NHS management arrangements have evolved and how this impacts on the AHPs in the 21st century.

Early reorganisation

The first major reorganisation of the NHS – since its inception on 5 July 1948 – took place on 1 April 1974, the aim of which was to:

> . . . provide a fully integrated service in which every aspect of health care could be provided by the health professions.
>
> DHSS[1]

The resulting arrangements introduced management teams at regional, area and district levels. A common feature was consensus decision making with the aim of promoting centralisation, the medical profession maintaining its autonomy.

This method of management had competing rationales for its introduction. Fox[2] describes these as unitary and pluralistic, the unitary rationale being based on the premise that parties involved in the decision-making process have objectives that do not fundamentally conflict with each other, which assists the consensus process. By contrast the pluralistic rationale allows for the existence of legitimately differing interests within organisations, where parties may have conflicting priorities and makes consensus more difficult, as parties have to negotiate and compromise.[3]

The overarching aim of the process was to reach agreement by consensus within management teams. Some commentators later criticised consensus decision making as being slow, weakening accountability and producing weak decisions, particularly Sir Roy Griffiths in his report to the Department of Health[4]. However, Kogan's research for the Royal Commission on the NHS in1978[5,6] found strong support for the view that consensus management was generally successful and this was echoed by Elcock and Haywood.[7]

As a result of the 1974 reorganisation and the development of the DHAs as key accountable bodies, management posts were gradually introduced for the AHPs at district level and in the case of physiotherapy, for example, there were 180 such district management posts out of the 206 DHAs in England and Wales.[8]

A platform for change: *Patients First*

In December 1979, the newly elected Conservative government under the premiership of Margaret Thatcher published a consultative document *Patients First*[9] in response to the Royal Commission on the NHS[6] which had been set up by the previous Labour government. It was the aim of *Patients First* to simplify the organisational structure of the NHS and to incorporate some of the Royal Commission recommendations. An important objective of *Patients First* was to move responsibility for making decisions closer to the locality for which services were being provided. A major recommendation was that the District Health Authorities (DHAs) should become the key accountable bodies in the new structure. They would be responsible for planning and service provision. The arrangement of DHAs in the NHS until 1 April 1991 derived largely from the recommendations of *Patients First* and the consequent DHSS Circular HC(80)8[10] which set out the government's intentions following the consultation period after the publication of *Patients First* – removal of the Area tier of management, bringing decision making as near to the patient as possible; the simplification of professional consultative machinery and that unit management be based on hospitals – which were all incorporated in a further reorganisation which took effect on 1 April 1982. *Patients First* was the platform for the wide-ranging series of changes which would be introduced throughout the next two decades.

General management: the Griffiths Report

For several years the government had been dissatisfied with consensus manage-ment in the NHS. A year after the 1982 reorganisation, general management was introduced following the publication of the 'National Health Service Management Inquiry' – the Griffiths Report[4] – and the subsequent Health Circular HC(84)13.[11]

In answer to a written question about the control of manpower in the NHS the Secretary of State – Norman Fowler – replied:

> I have today established an independent NHS Management Inquiry into these matters. Health Authorities in England have a revenue budget of almost nine billion pounds; employ about a million people; and spend almost 75% of their revenue on pay. The government needs to be satisfied that these considerable resources are managed efficiently and give the nation value for money. The inquiry will be led by Mr Roy Griffiths, Deputy Chairman and Managing Director of J. Sainsbury PLC.
>
> Hansard[12]

The Griffiths Inquiry was unique in the history of official investigations into the workings and management of the NHS: the team comprised only four members and there were no medical interests represented, in contrast with the many bodies which had previously reported to successive Secretaries of State on various aspects of the NHS. The report *Management Arrangements for the Reorganised*

National Health Service – the Grey Book[1] is one example where the committees were large (having more than 15 members).

Griffiths in his letter to the Secretary of State attached to his Report stated:

> We were asked by you in February to give advice on the effective use and management of manpower and related resources in the National Health Service; to inform you as our inquiries proceeded; and to advise you on progress by the end of June. It was emphasised that we had not been asked to prepare a report, but that we should go straight for recommendations on management action.
>
> DHSS[4]

The way was thus prepared by the Secretary of State for an innovative and radical series of changes in the organisational structure and management of the NHS.

The introduction of general management into the NHS involved the setting and attainment of objectives and targets for the organisation. There was to be a system of reviews and performance indicators (PIs) to support this in order to promote a greater degree of accountability and responsibility by doctors and managers in the running of the service. Doctors were to manage their own budgets and financial systems would be put in place to support this. The Griffiths Report emphasised the importance of obtaining value for money, making effectiveness and efficiency the key focus throughout and the dominant power base within the NHS was to be the general management function rather than the previous consensus management approach.

The report concluded that there was a lack of drive in the NHS because at each level of management there was no one person held accountable for action; decisions were delayed or avoided, leading to an inefficient service. The main findings of the team were that there was no real continuous evaluation of performance, precise management objectives were rarely set, little measurement of healthcare output took place, and clinical and economic evaluation of practices was uncommon. One of the most significant observations was the identification that a clearly defined general management function was absent from the service.

> . . . it still lacks any real continuous evaualtion of its performance against criteria . . . there is little measurement of health output; clinical evaluation of particular practices is by no means common and economic evaluation of these practices extremely rare.
>
> DHSS[4]

A telling passage from the report simplistically sums this up:

> If Florence Nightingale were carrying her lamp through the corridors of the NHS today she would almost certainly be searching for the people in charge.[4]

Figure 2.1 shows the NHS management structure before implementation of the Griffiths Report. Figure 2.2 shows the management structure as proposed in the Griffiths Report. The Health Circular HC(84)13[11] charged health authorities with the task of establishing the general management function and identifying general managers.

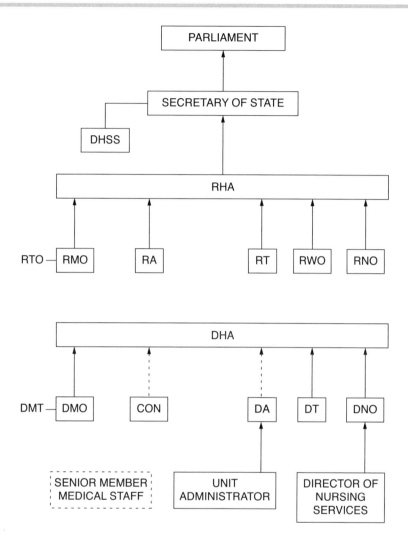

Solid lines indicate management accountability
Dotted lines indicate professional accountability

RMO – Regional Medical Officer
CON – Consultant
RA – Regional Administrator
RNO – Regional Nursing Officer
RWO – Regional Works Officer
RTO – Regional Team of Officers
DMT – District Management Team

DMO – District Medical Officer
GP – General Practitioner
RT – Regional Treasurer
DA – District Administrator
DT – District Treasurer
DNO – District Nursing Officer

Figure 2.1 Management structure pre-Griffiths

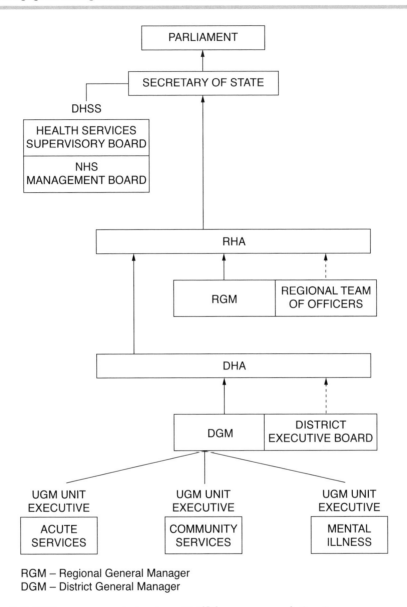

RGM – Regional General Manager
DGM – District General Manager

Figure 2.2 NHS management structure (Griffiths recommendations)

The introduction of the philosophy and structures of general management as recommended in the Griffiths Report:

> . . . laid down the foundations of a management culture of command and obedience that increased the responsiveness of the NHS to political direction. It gave the managers new skills and powers in planning and managing clinical services, and a growing confidence in exercising them. And it created a climate of opinion and practice that finally enabled the government to implement its plans for the internal market . . .
>
> Butler[13]

In the section of the report entitled 'general observations', Griffiths outlined in detail the 'advantages of the general management process'. In its advocacy of general management, the team was damning of functional management in that the advantages of the functional specialities were offset by the need to establish the general management process effectively. Consensus management methods were vigorously criticised as being responsible for the making of 'lowest common denominator decisions', which were seen as weak and of poor quality. NHS management was thought to be reactive and passive rather than proactive, and there was a lack of management data on activity and consumer views. Much of the report was about changes which were needed in attitude, understanding and expectations, as well as the style of management.

The Secretary of State was advised by Griffiths that he should set up and chair a Health Service Supervisory Board and a full-time NHS Management Board which would be responsible for determining the objectives and direction for the service, approving overall budget and resource allocations, making strategic decisions and monitoring performance.

The Management Board would be the executive arm of the Supervisory Board and would have responsibility: 'to plan implementation of the policies approved by the Supervisory Board; to give leadership to the management of the NHS; to control performance; and to achieve consistency and drive over the long term'.[4]

The recommendation to set up the NHS Management Board was a totally new departure in the organisation of the service and would be crucial to the implementation of general management. Below Management Board level, Griffiths advised that the appointment of general managers should be made at RHA, DHA and Unit levels. These posts would carry responsibility for improving the efficiency of the organisation and the appointments could be made either from within the NHS or from outside. General managers could, therefore, come from any background, such as the armed forces or business.

RHA and DHA chairs were to be given greater freedom to organise the management structure of the authorities. Responsibility for making decisions was to be moved closer to the localities for which services were being provided – echoing *Patients First* – in this, the units would play a key role. All day-to-day decisions were to be taken in the units of management and each Unit would be given a total budget and be required to develop management budgets involving doctors who would be expected to relate workload and service objectives to financial and manpower allocations, in order to 'sharpen up the questioning of overhead costs'.[4] The report also contained recommendations on personnel, manpower, conditions of service, information and levels of decision making.

Implementation of the Griffiths Inquiry created a radical and far-reaching culture change in the organisation and management of the service, despite the Griffiths team's view that the NHS was in no condition to undergo another restructuring. The Royal Commission on the NHS (Merrison Report, 1979)[6] while making recommendations for reform, had also expressed the plea that there should be no more major upheavals in order to enable the NHS to settle down following the 1974 reorganisation. However, despite this, the reorganisation which took place in 1982 brought about major changes in the senior management levels of the Service and were followed two years later by the implementation of the Griffiths recommendations. These in turn laid the foundation for the government White Paper *Working for Patients*,[14] the consequent Health Service Bill enacted in 1990 and the Resource Management Initiative.

General management was defined by Griffiths as:

> The responsibility drawn together in one person, at different levels of the organisation, for planning, implementation and control of performance . . .
>
> DHSS[4]

He claimed that the advantages of a general management process were:

- providing the necessary leadership to capitalise on existing high levels of dedication and expertise
- bringing about a constant search for major change and cost improvement
- securing proper motivation of staff
- ensuring that the professional functions were effectively geared towards the overall objectives and responsibilities of the general management process
- making sense of the process of consultation.

It was the Unit general management (UGM) function which would at that time be the source of a dilemma concerning the organisation and management of AHP services.

AHP management

In Districts where there were District AHP Managers, service was provided, managed and co-ordinated across Unit and specialty boundaries. Postholders were generally responsible for managing the District AHP budgets, personnel, equipment and facilities; budgetary resources, staff and equipment could usually be moved across Unit boundaries. In some health authorities, Designated District AHP managers were appointed to advise District management teams on AHP matters; such designates had no managerial responsibility, as confirmed by DS 331/75, 'Designation of Therapists'.[15] In some HAs, there were no District or Designated District AHP managers and in these authorities, management of AHP services happened on a piecemeal and fragmented basis

The District AHP managers for their specific services were the professional leaders, both managerially and clinically. The head was responsible for input into the annual District planning cycle, implementation of DHSS, RHA and DHA policies, making sure that AHP functions were geared into the overall objectives of the organisation and for a wide range of managerial, administrative and consultancy duties.

Clinical leadership and management were important aspects of the District AHP manager's role. Postholders were clinical heads of clinical services, the leaders and professional directors whose major concerns were for patient care. The day-to-day work of the District AHP managers consisted largely of actions and decisions about patients and clinical matters, there being an inextricable link between these clinical and managerial roles.

General management and AHP management

Under the Griffiths proposals, the Units of management were to be the focus for the impact of general management. UGMs were to be accountable for drawing together planning, implementation and control of performance, and would have overall responsibility for the total unit budget. One objective of Unit management was to bring decision making closer to the patients than had previously been the case.

Before the advent of Griffiths, the majority of DHAs had chosen to employ District AHP managers. With the move towards basing management structures at Unit rather than District level, a question would arise about the level at which AHP services were to be managed:

> For some activities, it would clearly be widely uneconomic to have each Unit with its own department. Also it seems that some functions needed a District presence so that uniformity of policy and practice can be ensured.
>
> Dixon[16]

As well as the important factors concerning the economics of managing AHPs and uniformity of service provision across all Units within a District, there would be many other matters of concern to AHPs and general managers alike. When the Griffiths Report was published, District AHPs had been undertaking most of these duties and responsibilities and had been doing so for some years.

The UGM would be accountable for the overall planning, service provision and performance of the Unit. It might, therefore, be argued that UGMs would need full managerial control over the AHPs. However, it was the type and level of this control, the managerial relationship between them and the proposed organisational structures that raised questions for general managers and AHPs alike.

The 1990 NHS and Community Care Act

In January 1988, the Prime Minister revealed in a BBC television interview that a review of the NHS was in progress. The review was:

> Tightly controlled within the bosom of the government led by the Prime Minister herself . . . the other original members of the group were Nigel Lawson (Chancellor of the Exchequer), John Major (Chief Secretary to the Treasury), Mr John Moore (Secretary of State for Social Services), Mr Tony Newton (Minister of State for Health) and Sir Roy Griffiths (Deputy Chairman of the NHS Management Board).
>
> Brown[17]

It undertook no formal consultation and had no published terms of reference and although submissions were received privately, no list of those consulted was ever published:

> The review group functioned, in effect as a Cabinet committee and its initial objective was primarily political; to change the NHS in ways that would still the chorus of discontent about its funding while maintaining, and preferably advancing, the broad thrust of government policy for the public services.
>
> Butler[13]

The NHS and Community Care Act[18] received the Royal Assent in June 1990 and encompassed the most radical shake-up of the NHS since its inception. The legislation took effect on 1 April 1991 and was based on the three White Papers *Working for Patients*[14], *Caring for People*[19] and *Promoting Better Health.*[20] *Working for Patients* and *Caring for People* dealt with reform of health and social care in the hospitals and community and *Promoting Better Health* proposed changes to Family Practitioner Committees which were under the legislation to become Family Health Service Authorities (FHSAs).

Boyce[21] commented, that from the late 1980s there had been a growing emphasis on structural reform in countries with publicly funded health systems; changes in the NHS at this time typified these developments.[22]

Working for Patients was born out of the need to review NHS funding:

> Each day we learn of new problems in the NHS – beds are shut, operating rooms are not available, emergency wards are closed, essential services are shut down in order to make financial savings . . . acute hospital services have almost reached breaking point . . . additional and alternative funding must be found, we call on the government to do something now to save our health service, once the envy of the world.
>
> Hoffenberg *et al*[23]

It did not address this issue, rather it recommended changing funding arrangements to be based on weighted capitation through which money would follow patients together with the introduction of an 'internal market' to bring about an element of competition into healthcare. The government wanted to create an atmosphere of managed competition in the NHS through market forces as a stimulus for the more efficient provision of health services.

The overall aims and objectives were summarised by Dennis[24] as:

> Giving better care and greater choice for the patient . . . That there should be greater cost-effectiveness on the part of the provider, with money to follow the patient . . .

Following *Working for Patients*[14] a series of associated papers were issued giving guidance on the implementation of many aspects of the reforms. A review of the imposed timetable for the enforcement of the reforms indicated an extremely rapid pace of implementation. In attempting to sustain the momentum of change, particularly in view of the political climate, many aspects of the reforms were implemented without adequate periods of development and consolidation. This restricted full evaluation of the long-term implications of the changes, as well as the necessary planning and preparation required to manage this crucial process of change.

Much of the philosophy which underpinned the reforms was developed from the work of Entoven.[25]

From the late 1980s there has been a growing emphasis on structural reform in countries with publicly funded health systems. Developments in international health service structure have been extensively reported and commented on – Ham *et al*,[26] Enthoven[27] and Day and Klein.[28] The changes that have occurred in the NHS have some similarities to other healthcare systems, for example the USA, Australia and Scandinavia.[22,29]

The impact of the so-called 'internal market' reforms led to redistribution and rationing of resources.[21] Internal market reforms introduced a competitive element into healthcare, with purchasers and providers competing for business. It was designed to emphasise financial management of clinical activity, the aim being to create linkages between clinical activity, decision making and financial consequences. The introduction of market philosophy into a publicly funded service was designed to improve efficiency, by producing 'managed competition' and 'regulated markets'. Critics of market reforms argue the inappropriateness of competition in a publicly funded healthcare system, producing inequality of services in different parts of the country, known as 'postcode lottery'.[30] They saw these as valid reasons to question the merits of this approach to the NHS.[28] Despite this view, global trends have ensured that market forces continue to influence publicly funded healthcare systems in several countries.[26,29]

Fundamental to the reforms was the concept of freeing DHAs from their responsibility for funding and managing the hospitals and units within their areas and the creation of a new role whereby they would be responsible for the purchase of care for their local population. As commissioning or purchasing authorities the Districts were empowered to look further afield for the provision of services if they so wished. The government's main aim was to increase competition throughout the NHS. Large GP practices were to be encouraged to become 'fundholders' with commissioning responsibilities. Acute hospitals were able to become self-governing trusts, which was designed to free them from the NHS management structure, though in practice the proposed 'freedom' never happened. Some concepts from the 1990s are re-emerging in a modified form, for example, with the creation of foundation trusts and practice-based commissioning.[31,32] Dennis[24] observed that the NHS changes were designed to give better care and greater choice for patients with greater cost-effectiveness on the part of the provider and money centred around patient activity rather than organisations. Whether these aims were achieved is debatable, as many years later patient choice is still on the agenda as a 'new' idea, as witness the 'Choose and Book' initiative.

The process change that took place after 1991 was labelled 'quasi-market transformation' by Kitchener and Whipp.[33] This described the replacement of government-run monopolistic state providers by competitive 'independent' ones. These authors commented that despite the near annual reorganisations that had taken place over the last 25 years in the NHS, this had had no effect on changing the clinical practice of staff.

Towards the 21st century: the 'New' Labour era

Under the Labour government which came into office in 1997, NHS reform was continued, further developing health policy, including development of primary care-led health services.

A 10-year plan for the NHS, *The NHS Plan: a plan for investment, a plan for reform*, was published by the DoH in 2000,[34] setting out strategy for the NHS. Fundholding by GP practices was abolished and primary care trusts (PCTs) were established with responsibility for commissioning and provision of primary care services. Regional Health Authorities were abolished and replaced by the 28 Strategic Health Authorities (SHAs). A further government document, *Shifting the Balance of Power: the next steps*, was published in 2002.[35] The main objective was to give greater decision making and power to patients and 'frontline' staff, underpinned by changes in organisational roles and relationships.

Zairi and Jarrar[36] pointed out the continuum of health policy from the 1980s into the 21st century, reflecting the importance attached by successive governments to the measurement and improvement of health service quality, and effectiveness and efficiency. This included performance monitoring against an increasing number of targets with the introduction of National Service Frameworks (NSFs) and guidelines to promote equity of standards.[37]

In 2004 the DH published *Standards for Better Health*,[32] outlining plans to continue NHS modernisation up to 2008. It included 24 core standards describing a level of service which is acceptable and must be universal for patients and service users of all ages.

The document set out three main themes: empowering patients and service users, increased emphasis on personalised care, and further devolution of decision making to local organisations.

Figure 2.3 sets out a pictorial overview of the structure and organisation of the NHS in pre-General Election 2005.

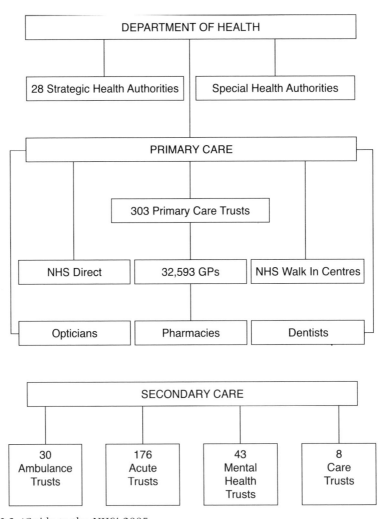

Figure 2.3 'Guide to the NHS' 2005

From 2005: the NHS – sink or swim?

Following the 2005 General Election and the re-election of the Labour government under the premiership of Tony Blair there was much speculation about future NHS structure, organisation, management and service provision. This speculation centred around the introduction of 'practice-based commissioning', increased use of the private sector, a substantial decrease in the number of PCTs and SHAs, with the separation of the commissioning and service provision functions and the introduction of contestability.

The Secretary of State for Health, in her introduction to *A Patient-led NHS*,[38] said:

> A patient-led NHS will be self-improving and sustainable over the long term. But it will only happen if we make reform a reality. Now is not the time to rest on our laurels; now is the time to step up the pace of reform.
>
> All of this gives us a chance, for the first time, to make real our founding values: a universal service, with equal access free at the point of use, with treatment based on clinical need not ability to pay. This is what we mean by a patient-led NHS: free for all and personal to each.

This agenda has been set out in the government White Paper *Our Health, Our Care, Our Say*.[39] The implications of this 'landmark' White Paper which is a watershed in NHS policy are fully explored and developed by Pat Oakley in *The 'Big Picture' for Health Professionals*, the third book in our series Allied Health Professions – Essential Guides.

Editor's note

As this book goes to press the NHS is going through a period of fundamental and dynamic transformation. These changes will require AHP managers to demonstrate a thorough understanding of policy development and its implications for service provision. Pat Oakley's chapter in the third book will provide the reader with an essential background and the knowledge required to understand the strategic direction and operational requirements which will enable them to effectively engage in the management process.

The major reforms eminating from this White Paper[39] include:

- review of the role of the NHS CEO
- decrease of SHAs from 28 to 10
- reconfiguration of PCTs from 303 to 152
- separation of commissioning and service provision roles and introduction of contestability
- stringency requirement to bring the NHS into sustainable financial balance.

Table 2.1 Major DH policy initiatives

Policy initiatives	Brief description
Reconfiguration of SHAs	Reduction in the number of SHAs following consultation.
Reconfiguration of PCTs	Reduction in number of PCTs following consultation. PCTs larger in size, with division of commissioning and provider roles. Debate regarding future provider function.
NHS funding	Significant growth in NHS funding until 2008. Serious cost pressures experienced, massive job losses as services required to achieve financial balance. Levels and sources of funding uncertain after 2008.
Agenda for Change	Remuneration and terms and conditions for the majority of NHS staff (including AHPs). Leading to blurring of professional boundaries, new roles, and new ways of working.
Consultant contract	Remuneration and terms and conditions package for hospital consultants.
GP contract	Remuneration and terms and conditions package for GPs.
Foundation trusts	Independent not-for-profit public benefit corporation with accountability to local communities rather than central government control.
Care trusts	Health organisations, merging health and social care into single organisations.
Children's trusts	Combining education, social care and health provision for children into single organisations.
Partnership trusts	One organisation providing mental health services across a wide area typically across a whole county.
Contestability	Diversity of health care service providers linked to patient choice and efficient use of resources.
Payment by results	The aim of the financial system to provide a transparent rules-based system for paying trusts. A new way of funding for health services whereby PCTs pay a standard tariff for a set of procedures, supports patient choice and diversity.
Choose and Book	Patient 'choice' of service providers for a range of hospital procedures.
Practice-based commissioning	Engaging practices and primary care professionals in commissioning services tailored to the needs of local communities. Process supported by PCTs.
Quality Outcome Framework	Part of the 2003 General Medical Services contract – a voluntary system of financial incentives for improving quality.
Workforce planning	Review of workforce and skill mix, linked with service requirements, developing new roles and re-profiling the workforce.
Connecting for Health	The national IT programme for the NHS.
Electronic staff record	IT-based workforce management system.

Table 2.1 (*cont.*)

Policy initiatives	Brief description
Hospital reconfigurations	Reprofiling of hospital provision, e.g. critical care hospital for population of 350–500 000. New community hospitals providing day surgery units (not traditional cottage hospitals).
Expert Patient Programme	Promotion of self-care using the skills and knowledge of patients to lead programmes.
Patient and public involvement	Engagement of service users in service development, evaluation and provision.
Management of long-term conditions	Improved care for patients with long-term medical conditions; intervention by the right person in the right place at the right time.
Improving Working Lives	Promotion of work–life balance and flexible working practices.
Regulation	Protection of the public through strengthened national regulations of the professions.

It is clear that as the NHS move toward the latter part of the first decade of the 21st century the change continues. Farrah[40] described the ongoing changes in the NHS:

> The system between practices, PCTs, Strategic Health Authorities and the Department of Health is a bit like a Newton pendulum.

Table 2.1 lists the major policy initiatives emanating from the DH. The impact of these developments has given rise to significant turbulence and uncertainty about the future of the NHS. How these issues are managed will determine the longer term viability of the NHS and whether it will sink or swim.

The changes that have taken place in the structure, organisation and management of the NHS over the last 30 years represent a series of synergistic events which are the foundation for the set of further radical reforms currently being introduced. An important concomitant has been the sea change which has in parallel taken place in the structure, organisation, management and contribution of the Allied Health Professions. AHP managers, their roles, responsibilities and the structures in which they work have evolved with the constantly changing NHS. It is unlikely that there will be a period of consolidation. Therefore, AHP managers will need to be aware of the impact that changing health structures are likely to have on their professions and position themselves to influence strategic decision makers or become decision makers themselves.

Reading list

Davies P, editor. *The Nuts and Bolts of Primary Care Provision*. Retford, Notts: NHS Alliance; 2006.

Department of Health. *The Expert Patient: a new approach to chronic disease management for the 21st century*. London: DH; 2001.

Department of Health. *Care Trusts: background briefing*; 2002. www.dh.gov.uk/publications.

Department of Health. *"Choose and Book": patient's choice of hospital and booking appointment – Policy Framework*. London: DH; 2004.

Department of Health. *The NHS Improvement Plan: putting people at the heart of public services*. London: DH; 2004.

Department of Health. *A Short Guide to NHS Foundation Trusts*. London: DH; 2005.

Department of Health. *Health Reform in England: update and next steps*. London: DH; 2005.

Department of Health. *Creating a Patient-led NHS: delivering the NHS Improvement Plan*. London: DH; 2005. www.dh.gov.uk/publications.

Department of Health. *Report and Responses to the Consultation on the Future Support Arrangements for Patient and Public Involvement in Health*. London: DH; 2005. www.dh.gov.uk/publications.

Department of Health. *The NHS in England: the operating framework for 2006/7*. London: DH; 2006. www.dh.gov.uk/publications.

Department of Health. *Implementing Payment by Results. Technical Guidance 2006/7*. Executive Summary. London: DH; 2006. www.dh.gov.uk/publications.

Department of Health. *Practice-based Commissioning: achieving universal coverage*. London: DH. www.dh.gov.uk/publications; 2006.

Department of Health. *Supporting People with Long Term Conditions to Self Care: a guide to developing local strategies and good practice*. London: DH. www.dh.gov.uk/publications; 2006.

Department of Health. *Health Reform in England: update and commissioning framework*. London: DH. www.dh.gov.uk/publications; 2006.

Jones R, Jenkins F, editors. *Allied Health Professions – essential guides*. Further books in this series. Oxford: Radcliffe Publishing; 2006/07.

Natpact. *Allied Health Professionals: self-assessment tool*. London: NHS Modernisation Agency/ Natpact; 2003.

NHS Alliance. *Choice and Access to AHP/PCP Care in the NHS*. London: DH; 2004. www.natpact.nhs.uk.

Øvretveit J. *Therapy Services: organisation, management and autonomy*. Reading: Harwood Academic Publishers; 1992.

Reader P. *The Future of Clinical Leadership in Primary Care Trusts: an NHS Alliance paper*. Retford: NHS Alliance; 2006.

Reader P. *The Future of Clinical Leadership in Primary Care and PCTs: a discussion paper*. Retford: NHS Alliance; 2006.

Wortham K, editor. *Engaging Clinicians in the New NHS*. Retford: NHS Alliance; 2003.

References

1 DHSS. *Management Arrangements for the Re-organised Health Service: The Grey Book*. London: HMSO; 1972.

2 Fox A. *Industrial Sociology and Industrial Relations*. Research Report No 3. Royal Commission on Trades Unions and Employers Association. London: HMSO; 1966.

3 Harrison S. Consensus decision making in the National Health Service – a review. *Journal of Management Studies*. 1982; **19**(4): 377–94.

4 DHSS. *National Health Service Management Inquiry: Griffiths Report*. London: HMSO; 1983.

5 Kogan M. *The Working of the National Health Service*. Research Paper No.1. Royal Commission on the NHS. London: HMSO; 1978.

6 DHSS. *The Royal Commission on the NHS – Merrison*. London: HMSO; 1979.

7 Elcock H, Haywood SC. *The Buck Stops Where? Accountability and control in the National Health Service*. Hull: University of Hull Institute of Health Studies; 1980.

8 Jones R. *Management in Physiotherapy*. Oxford: Radcliffe Medical Press; 1991.

9 DHSS. *Patients First*. London: HMSO; 1979.

10 DHSS. HC(80)8. London: HMSO; 1980.

11 DHSS. HC(84)13. London: HMSO; 1984.

12 Hansard. Written Answers in Hansard. **3 February**: 181; 1983.

13 Butler J. *Patients, Policies and Politics*. Milton Keynes: Open University Press; 1992.

14 DHSS. *Working for Patients*. London: HMSO; 1989.

15 DHSS. DS 331/75, *Designation of Therapists*. London: HMSO; 1975.

16 Dixon M. The organisation and structure of units. In: Wickings I, editor. *Effective Unit Management*. London: King's Fund; 1983.

17 Brown C. Clarke braced for Showdown over Health Review. *The Independent*. 1989; **30 January**.

18 *The NHS and Community Care Act 1990*. London: HMSO; 1990.

19 Department of Health. *Caring for People*. London: HMSO; 1989.

20 DHSS. *Promoting Better Health*. London: HMSO; 1987.

21 Boyce RA. Internal market reforms of healthcare systems and the allied health professions: an internal perspective. *International Journal of Health Planning and Management*. 1993; **8**(3): 201–7.

22 Saltman RB. Emerging trends in Swedish Health System. *International Journal of Health Services*. 1991; **21**(4): 615–23.

23 Hoffenberg R, Todd IP, Pinker G. Crisis in the National Health Service. *BMJ*. 1987; **295**: 1505.

24 Dennis K. What will it really look like? In: P Spurgeon, editor. *Health Service Management Theories: the changing face of the National Health Service in the 1990s*. London: Longman; 1991.

25 Enthoven AC. *Reflections on the Management of the National Health Service*. London: Nuffield Provincial Hospitals Trust; 1985.

26 Ham C, Robinson R, Benzeval M. *Healthcheck; healthcare reforms in an international context*. London: King's Fund Institute; 1990.

27 Enthoven AC. Internal market reform of the British National Health Service. *Heath Affairs*. 1991; **Fall:** 60–70.

28 Day P, Klein R. British healthcare experiment. *Health Affairs*. 1991; **Fall:** 39–59.

29 Harrison S. Working the markets: purchaser/provider separation in English healthcare. *International Journal of Health Services*. 1991; **21**: 625–35.

30 Coulter A. Fundholding general practices: early successes-but will they last? *BMJ*. 1992; **304**: 397–8.

31 Department of Health. *Keeping the NHS Local: a new direction of travel*. London: HMSO; 2003.

32 Department of Health. *Standards for Better Health: national standards, local action*. London: HMSO; 2004.

33 Kitchener M, Whipp R. Tracks of change in hospitals: a study of quasi market transformation. *International Journal of Public Sector Management*. 1997; **10**(1–2): 47–61.

34 Department of Health. *The NHS Plan: a plan for investment, a plan for reform*. London: HMSO; 2000.

35 Department of Health. *Shifting the Balance of Power: the next steps*. London: HMSO; 2002.

36 Zairi M, Jarrar YF. Measuring organisational effectiveness in the NHS: management style and structure best practice. *Total Quality Management*. 2001; **12**(7–8): 882–9.

37 Department of Health. *A First Class Service: quality in the NHS*. London: HMSO; 1998.

38 Department of Health. *A Patient-led NHS*. London: HMSO; 2005.

39 Department of Health. *Our Health, Our Care, Our Say: a new direction for community services*. London: HMSO; 2006.

40 Farrah M. The big story. *Health Service Journal*. 2004; **Oct 21**: 13.

Chapter 3

Devolopment and significance of the profession in AHP management

Robert Jones and Fiona Jenkins

Introduction

Many aspects of AHP management and leadership discussed throughout this series of books are closely linked with the professionalisation of these occupational groups. An understanding of the professionalisation process and what it is that constitutes a profession is helpful in clarifying the development of AHP management and leadership. In this chapter, the process of professionalisation and its relevance in the context of AHP management are explored. The chapter concludes with an overview of the currently diminishing role and 'power base' of the profession in the context of sea-changes taking place in the politics, structure, organisation, regulation and management of the NHS and the effect of this on AHP and NHS management, today.

The title 'health profession' embraces many of the occupational groups in healthcare provision; the AHPs are one such grouping. The growth of professionalisation and occupational development has had an important influence on the way in which AHP services have been managed in the NHS. The process of professionalisation is one important reason why most AHP services have been and still are managed by Allied Health Professionals. The introduction of general management into the NHS with the unitisation of services under the management of Unit General Managers (UGMs) – who could come from any background in or outside the NHS (*see* Chapter 2) – and the 1989 government White Paper *Working for Patients*[1] opened up debate about the most effective and efficient way to manage and provide AHP services.

What is a profession?

Exactly what constitutes a profession is a complex issue. The term may be used in both descriptive and evaluative senses. Friedson[2] distinguished between the structural element of professional status and that concerned with values, attitudes and behaviour – 'professionalism'.

There is a vast literature on the sociology of the profession, much of it American in origin. One of the earliest works on the topic was a study which concluded that a profession was a complex of characteristics[3] The acknowledged 'ideal' professions of law and medicine exhibited all or most of these features. The features to which they referred were:

- a technique acquired by prolonged and intellectual training which enabled them to provide a specialised service
- the development of an association which imposed tests of competence and required the observance of certain standards of conduct.

This model was conceived in the static terms of the definable characteristics or traits which 'accepted' professions possessed. However, Carr-Saunders and Wilson accepted that other occupational groups may have been in the process of developing some of these characteristics.[3]

Five attributes for a profession were proposed by Greenwood[4] as:

1 systematic theory
2 authority
3 community sanction
4 ethical code
5 a culture of professional knowledge, behaviour and ethos.

A developmental sequence of professionalisation was proposed by Wilensky[5] in which the first step was to start doing full-time the thing that needed doing, setting up a new area of practice recruited from other occupational groups. This would be followed by the establishment of training schools, which would lead directly to the consideration of standards and recognition in the community. The practitioners pushing for prescribed training, and the first ones to go through it would combine to form a professional association. Wilensky postulated that the next steps would be interoccupational conflict between the new practitioners and older established occupations in the same sphere, the definition of core tasks, efforts to gain support of the law for areas of practice and the prescription of an ethical code. This sequence was challenged on the grounds that in the UK the formation of professional associations had emerged before the founding of training schools, whether professionally run or university based.[6] Nevertheless, having accepted this reordering the pattern put forward by Wilensky, by Carr-Saunders and Wilson, and by Greenwood seems broadly to have been followed in the development of many of the AHPs, which stand up as professions or on a continuum of professionalisation when tested against these criteria. The claims of AHPs to full professional status turn largely upon the issue of autonomy and the extent of their freedom from control by the medical or other professions.

Development of autonomy: the early days

The roles of the AHPs and the provision of service were, for many years, extensively shaped by control over their practice by the medical profession. However, over the years there has been a steady and clear move away from this control and self-management has developed, leading to increasing clinical and therapeutic independence.

In the early days of the NHS, the influence of the medical profession in regard to the direction, prescription, training and supervision of the AHPs was very powerful. Official Ministry of Health memoranda issued in 1949, in the case of physiotherapy, for example, stated that physiotherapy should be prescribed and directed by a specialist (doctor).[7] These views were reinforced in 1951, when the

Report of the Committee on Medical Auxiliaries, The Cope Report,[8] was published.

In 1949, a series of eight committees were set up by Aneurin Bevan (Minister of Health). The committees were set up under the chairmanship of Mr V Zachary Cope MD. Cope's brief was to report on the supply and demand, training and qualification of certain medical auxiliaries employed in the NHS.

At the time AHP occupational groups were known as medical auxiliaries. The eight subcommittees, one for each occupational group, met separately under the overall co-ordination of Mr Cope and two Ministry officials. There were no plenary sessions, medical auxiliaries from different occupations being kept separate and always being outnumbered by doctors and Ministry officials. The medical auxiliary participants were Ministry nominees, and were not representatives from the professional associations, which were limited to giving evidence only.[9]

The report reaffirmed that AHPs were auxiliaries. Auxiliaries were defined as 'persons who assist medical practitioners (other than as nurses) in the investigation and treatment of disease by virtue of some special skill acquired through a recognised course of training'.[8] The dominant role of the medical profession was emphasised:

> In every hospital one consultant, preferably a specialist in physical medicine, should be given the oversight of a department . . . the general direction of studies in each School should be in the hands of a medical practitioner who should, wherever possible, be a specialist in physical medicine.[8]

Doctors were seen as taking the lead in the qualifying examinations; it was recommended that half of the examiners should be chosen from a panel of medical practitioner examiners. The idea that the auxiliaries should validate their own qualifications was dismissed as unsatisfactory. The reports also recommended that a statutory body be set up to undertake a review of educational standards, and to ensure that the demand for auxiliaries was matched by a well-trained supply. The statutory body envisaged would comprise a two-tier system in which medical auxiliaries would be in a minority on the policy-making council, but would be allowed a majority on the Supervisory Council. It is clear from this that the medical auxiliaries were officially regarded as being totally subordinate to the medical profession.

The proposals of the Cope Committee[8] were abandoned by the Minister of Health as a result of the occupational groups refusing to co-operate. Following the abandonment of the Cope Report, the Ministry of Health reopened discussion with the medical auxiliaries in 1954. For the first time, each profession was invited to nominate two delegates to the discussions which would encompass the possibility of a method of State Registration.

After years of debate and discussion, the Professions Supplementary to Medicine Bill was introduced into the House of Commons in 1959 and this led to the 1960 Act of Parliament[10] which provided for the registration of eight professions. These Allied Health Professions had won the status of Professions Supplementary to Medicine, which provided a statutory framework that allowed for the professions to have a degree of self-regulation for the protection of their patients.

In 1972, the Tunbridge Report[11] was published. The brief had been: 'to consider the future provision of rehabilitation services in the NHS, their organisation and development, and to make recommendations'.

The members of the Tunbridge Committee were all doctors. There was no representation from the remedial professions (as physiotherapy, remedial gymnastics and occupational therapy were known at that time). The report served only to reinforce the old dogma emphasising the dominance of the medical profession in the management, supervision and clinical role of AHPs. There were many statements throughout the entire report which argued for the continued dominance by the medical profession, for example, on the question of how rehabilitation departments should be organised and who should be in charge of them. The consultant would have overall managerial responsibility for the rehabilitation services, and would decide how the general day-to-day running of the rehabilitation department should be organised according to local circumstances:

> We recommend that delegation of responsibility for day-to-day treatment of patients should be permitted to members of the remedial professions, provided that they are always under the supervision of the appropriate consultant.[11]

The consultant in rehabilitation (with responsibility for remedial services) was to be responsible for planning the general programmes of rehabilitation for patients, organising facilities for the assessment of social, vocational and clinical aspects of disability, and the reasonable deployment of all remedial staff from the most senior therapist to assistant.

AHPs would have little, if any, managerial responsibility for even the day-to-day running of the departments in which they worked. Their clinical practice was dictated by the prescriptions laid down by consultants, who were to be in a position of control of rehabilitation services, even as far as AHP techniques and everyday practice were concerned.

So disappointed were the representatives from the remedial professions that they refused to endorse the report and instead wrote their own Statement by the Committee on the Remedial Professions.[12] The statement expressed the need for the provision of representation from the remedial professions on advisory committees at both regional and area levels, so as to ensure participation in policy formulation and decision making as these affected their activities. The need for research was acknowledged, as were the differing roles of AHPs.

A watershed in professional independence: development of autonomy

As a result of the disquiet caused by the Tunbridge Report, a Working Party, under the chairmanship of Mr EL McMillan, was set up in 1973 by Sir Keith Joseph, the Secretary of State for Social Services. It was to make recommendations on the future role of the remedial professions in relation to other professions and to the patient, and on the pattern of staffing and training needed to meet this.[13] The Working Party comprised one senior member of each of the three so-called remedial professions, a representative from the CPSM, and four members from the DHSS. The Scottish Home and Health Department was represented at the meetings by an observer. The problem areas considered by the Working Party included:

- misuse and waste of professional skills
- dissatisfaction with career and salary structure
- shortage of trained therapists
- inadequate support from clerical, secretarial and portering staff
- problems of overlapping of responsibilities, not only between the remedial professions themselves, but also between them and other professions.

The Working Party recognised that in NHS hospitals the remedial professions had very limited managerial responsibilities associated with their clinical duties. These professions were often represented at management and policy-making levels by nursing or medical colleagues. McMillan acknowledged that senior members of the remedial professions 'may organise their own departments though often this is within a framework set by a consultant'.[13]

On the relationship between the remedial professions and the medical profession, the McMillan Report saw the doctor as the 'key figure' in carrying primary clinical responsibility for the patient; however, the report spelled out clearly the Working Party's concern that frequently this was interpreted as requiring the doctor to prescribe and supervise in detail the therapy provided. In criticising these practices, the report noted that too often 'therapists' were given insufficient scope to exercise their skills to the best possible advantage of the patient. McMillan drew attention to the scarce opportunities for members of the remedial professions to take on managerial roles or to receive appropriate management training. The recommendations would profoundly affect the development of clinical relationships between the therapy and medical professions, as well as the organisation and management of AHP services. The report stated:

> Only a few doctors would be skilled in the detailed application by therapists of particular techniques . . . We attach the greatest importance to the doctor/therapist relationship. We think it follows that the therapist can operate more effectively only if given greater responsibility and freedom within a medically orientated team . . .

McMillan also recommended that the nature and duration of treatment should be for the therapist to determine. An important recommendation in the report about the management and organisation of the remedial professions was that they should co-ordinate, organise and administer their own services. This was 'in keeping with the principle that professional people are more properly managed by members of their own profession'.[13]

Furthermore, this approach was strengthened by the recommendation that there should be an AHP at District level with management responsibilities for hospital and community services. These bold recommendations marked a watershed in the development of AHP services. It was the first time that such recommendations had appeared in an official report or government document and would pave the way, together with the other recommendations, for the development of self-management and clinical responsibility and constitute a significant 'stepping stone' along the continuum of professional organisation.

Clinical autonomy

A further important development in the process of professionalisation was the growing recognition of the rights and responsibilities of AHPs in clinical differential diagnosis and the control of their own clinical interventions. The DHSS issued a code of practice in September 1977, Health Services Development – Relationship between the Medical and Remedial Professions HC(77)33.[14] This, arguably the most important official document published in the context of the development of autonomy within the three remedial professions, recognised their rights to make their own decisions on prescribing appropriate forms of intervention for patients referred to their services. HC(77)33 also gave formal recognition of the right to alter or terminate treatment, when appropriate in their professional judgement, paving the way for recognition of the same rights for the AHPs as a whole. If an AHP were to accept detailed prescriptions of treatment from doctors rather than a note of the medical diagnosis, reason for referral and information concerning relevant contraindications, that practitioner would be accepting the doctor's knowledge of AHP practice as being greater than his/her own.

However, the doctor, in referring patients, was not seen as handing over total control but, in asking for treatment by an AHP practitioner, was asking for the expertise of another qualified professional.

The circular also stated that the therapist had a duty and a consequential right to decline to perform any therapy which his/her professional training and expertise suggested was actively harmful to the patient.

The McMillan Report, which had resulted from sustained pressure by the remedial professions, had foreshadowed much of the contents of HC(77)33. The circular represented a further step in the developing independence and responsibility of AHPs, both by its recognition of current practice and by making positive recommendations concerning future relationships. The level of clinical autonomy for AHPs, which the circular recognised and protected, followed on from the developments taking place in the management and organisation of District AHP services in the NHS.

Clinical diagnosis

An integral part of AHP practice – clinical diagnosis – is a rigorous method of history-taking, clinical examination and assessment. Clinical diagnosis allows conclusions to be drawn concerning possible causes of the patient's problems, enabling appropriate intervention, if required. The term 'clinical diagnosis' is used rather than medical or pathological diagnosis. Medical diagnosis (the doctor's prerogative although there is often an input by AHPs), encompasses clinical diagnosis together with medical test findings, X-rays, biopsies, etc., while pathological diagnosis can only be made at post-mortem examination. The concept of clinical diagnosis underlies the clinical independence of the AHP in deciding appropriate action to be taken. Although the doctor may give a medical diagnosis, the AHPs' independent professional role is acknowledged. This represents an important marker of AHP autonomy, recognising their distinct contribution to patient care within a discrete body of knowledge and skill.

The AHP carries legal responsibility for his/her practice. A doctor's signature on a piece of paper does not offer any immunity from legal proceedings in the event of malpractice; such a signature does not protect the AHP, who must act in accordance with his/her own professional judgement.

Patients or clients are referred to AHPs from a wide range of sources including, for example, self-referral, social services and the education services. In all such instances, it is regarded as good practice for the AHP to liaise with the patient's doctor. It is also relevant that AHPs undertake a significant workload which is not the subject of referral, in, for example, health improvement and education, ergonomic, workplace assessment, keep fit and so on.

Landmarks in the development of a profession

Occupational therapy and physiotherapy are two examples of longer established Allied Health Professions. Macdonald *et al*[15] suggested that occupational therapy could trace its origins to treatment through occupation to before written records, with some reference made during the period of magic (before 600 BC).

Physiotherapy is taken as an example of the development of a profession illustrating the connection with related professions, including medicine. In the 1880s, Swedish remedial gymnasts came to this country and were, as Wickstead, historian of the early years of the profession of physiotherapy, writes, 'freely employed by the progressive members of the medical profession for "medical rubbing"'.[16] The immigration of Swedish masseuses led to British women taking up this work as an alternative to, or in addition to, nursing and midwifery. In 1894, an organisation called the Society of Trained Masseuses was established by a small group of nurses and midwives dedicated to medical rubbing and determined to protect it from the massage scandals that were common at the time. By 1896 this Society was inviting patronage from eminent doctors and was seeking medical assistance in qualifying its students. Certificates of competence were presented to students when they reached a satisfactory standard. The Society soon contrived a code of conduct for its members and thus at this early stage in its development the Society had accorded with three of the stages in the natural history of professionalisation.

- The founding of an association based on training.
- Examinations of competence.
- An ethical code.

In 1900, the name of the Society was changed to the Incorporated Society of Trained Masseuses. Although the medical profession had recognised the Society of Trained Masseuses, the founders realised at an early stage that they had no public or legal status and no legal hold over its members. Therefore, application was made for incorporation under the Companies Act without the use of the word 'limited', as the omission of this word indicated incorporation as a professional and not as a business organisation.

In 1905, male nursing orderlies of the Royal Medical Corps were allowed to take the examinations of the Society, but were not at that stage admitted to membership. Male masseurs could not become Members as membership carried with it the right to membership of the Trained Nurses Club; admission of male members to a nurses' social club would, at that time, have created a major scandal.

The establishment of physiotherapy was greatly facilitated by the 1914–18 war, when large numbers of war-wounded servicemen, especially amputees, greatly increased the experience of orthopaedic surgeons. Many more patients survived disabling injuries and the surgeons looked to the masseuses for rehabilitation work. This increased reliance by the medical profession on trained masseuses, who had extended their range of techniques and treatments to provide a wider range of services, resulted in greater public recognition of the profession.

Recognition was symbolised in 1920 by the granting of the Royal Charter by King George V. This had been preceded in 1916 by the Queen having become Patron of the Society. On the granting of the Royal Charter, the Society changed its name to the Chartered Society of Massage and Medical Gymnastics, and in 1920 men were admitted to membership for the first time.

Between 1920 and 1939, the Chartered Society of Massage and Medical Gymnastics continued to develop as a national organisation. A structure of Boards and local Branches was established throughout the country.

The Second World War created an increased demand for physiotherapy services and the Armed Forces set up their own physiotherapy schools. A group of male medical gymnasts set up an organisation, the Society of Remedial Gymnasts.

The founding of the NHS in 1948 allowed the Chartered Society of Physiotherapy, as it had been known since 1942, to further develop as a profession.

Training schools were absorbed into the new NHS, which provided financial security.

In the newly formed NHS, the Chartered Society continued as the qualifying association and professional body, and further developed a centralised and efficient bureaucracy. The tradition of medical patronage remained strong for some years. The decision-making body within the Society, its Council, appointed doctors as chairmen until 1972 when the first physiotherapist since the granting of the Royal Charter was elected Chairman of Council. Since that time independent policy and decision making has been decided by the profession; the process of slowly evolving autonomy of decision making accorded with the idea of the development of professionalisation on a continuum: movement of occupational groups through a variety of intermediate changes 'culminating in approximation to an "ideal" type of profession'.[17]

The CSP has evolved into a decision-making body with its own ethical code of practice. It participates in the control of education for the membership, and takes action against those members who breach its code of ethics and against unqualified people who 'hold out' to use the title 'Chartered Physiotherapist'. The establishment of the physiotherapy professional association did not give rise to interoccupational conflict in the early days. The medical profession retained a firm control over the new Society, the founders having actively sought the patronage of eminent medical men. The ethical code of practice of the profession in the early days forbade the treatment of patients, other than by direct referral from a doctor. Originally, physiotherapists carried out doctors' instructions much in the same way as a pharmacist would dispense a prescription. During the Society's early decades, the willingness of members to be directed by doctors served to reinforce this practice. The term 'semi-professions' was coined by Etzioni[18] to identify those would-be professions which exhibited some of the characteristics of the 'ideal' professions. This is an elaboration of the trait method of definition, which comprises a list of attributes which are said to represent the

Table 3.1 Elements in the continuum of professionalisation

Traits and characteristics	AHPs
1 Formation of an association	National organisation set up
2 Ethical Code of Practice and Standards of Conduct	Ethical code introduced
	Rules of Professional Conduct
	Organisation takes sanction against members who breach ethical code
3 Qualifying examinations and tests of competence	Certificates of Competence awarded
	3 and 4 year degree courses
	Move towards all graduate profession
	Opportunity for higher degree study
4 Public, community sanction/ recognition	Royal patronage, for example, CSP Royal Charter, Royal College of Speech and Language Therapists, Princess Royal Patron of BAOT
	1960 – Professions Supplementary to Medicine Act – inauguration of CPSM
	2001 HPC
	2005 protection of titles through HPC
5 Discrete body of knowledge and areas of practice	Degree courses in AHP areas of practice
	Royal Charters enshrine core areas of practice
6 Specialised service	Each AHP demonstrates different core areas of practice – HPC protection of title
7 Training schools, systematic theory and specialist body of knowledge	Many universities in UK providing BSc and MSc courses of study in different AHP areas of practice, for example, BSc in Orthoptics or Speech and Language Therapy
	Increasing evidence-based literature
	Increasing research base
	Creation of professorial chairs
	Wide range of clinical interest groups
8 Full-time practice	Full-time service provision in NHS and outside it including, for example, independent sector, social services, private practice
9 Support of the law for practice	1960 – Professions Supplementary to Medicines Act
	2001 – Health Professions Council in place
	HPC responsibility for registration of AHP practitioners and compilation and holding of registers
	HPC power of sanction
10 Autonomy	Well-developed clinical and managerial autonomy
11 Autonomy of decision making	Governing councils of professional bodies
12 Restricted entry	Full professional membership through education and examination

common core of professional occupations. Etzioni suggested that semi-professions were deficient as professions because their training was shorter, their mandate to control their work was less fully granted, their right to privileged communication was less established, there was less of a specialised body of knowledge and less individual autonomy because there was more supervision. Measured against the criteria laid down by Carr-Saunders and Wilson,[3] Friedson,[2] Etzioni[18] and others (a discrete body of knowledge, length of training, formation of an association, ethical codes, community sanction and so on), physiotherapy, as an occupational group in common with the other AHPs, moved along the continuum of professionalisation (*see* Table 3.1).

AHPs work in specific areas of practice and have their own distinct history, characteristics, roles, and relationships with other health professions and agencies. The important issue is that AHPs have many characteristics which have a significant influence on the way in which the service is managed and provided.

AHPs have well-developed professional associations with selective entry and ethical codes which place constraint upon their members and they form a distinctive culture within the Health Service having knowledge, competencies and skill bases peculiar to the grouping, and undisputed expertise. There is well-developed clinical and managerial autonomy, and acceptance of the clinical roles by the public.

The rise of competence and decline of the profession?

Increasingly healthcare systems worldwide are developing their workforces and capacity through the use of highly skilled and competent practitioners rather than depending on workforce development based on the traditional profession-centred approach. The emphasis today is increasingly on the patient's journey through the health and social care system, with services provided by multidisciplinary teams, in vertical integration models not interrupted by organisational boundaries or professional barriers which militate against streamlined working. This may increasingly involve alternative patterns of employment in which staff are employed in multidisciplinary networks centred around specific clinical clusters such as cancer networks, children's trusts or elderly care services rather than uniprofessional structures. This process, however, is by no means complete. Whilst most people would regard George Bernard Shaw's aphorism that 'All professions are conspiracies against the laity'[19] as cynical and inappropriate to the modern NHS, there can be little doubt that the role and power of the profession have evolved in the context of a rapidly changing NHS from the early days when the so-called 'ideal professions' might have been accused of behaving in a similar manner to exclusive gentlemen's clubs of the 19th and early 20th centuries. In place of the little challenged power of the dominant 'ideal' and 'would-be' professions of yesterday, services today are increasingly structured around bodies of knowledge, skilled competent practitioners from a variety of backgrounds, flexibility in working arrangements, expert cultures and networks breaking down professional roles and boundaries, clustering patients and service users into care or specialty groupings. In parallel with these changes organisational and management structures are likely to evolve to meet the altered configuration of service provision.

There are many factors influencing the development of new models of service provision and weakening of professional dominance – among these are important changes in professional regulation (*see* Chapter 9) in which there is greatly enhanced transparency and accountability to and involvement of the public and Parliament and decreased professional input to the regulatory process with a requirement to ensure and monitor continuing professional development of all staff. Changes in regulation resulted from serious clinical failures which had resulted in public inquiries and extensive media probing and attention, causing the public's confidence in the NHS to be shaken. Bristol Paediatric Cardiac Surgery,[20] Cervical Screening at Kent and Canterbury,[21] the Shipman[22] and Alderhey[23] scandals – resulting in formal inquiries – are examples of such service failures.

Improved communication and availability of knowledge with the advent of the World Wide Web have greatly enhanced opportunities for patients to obtain more detailed information than ever before and question or challenge advice, opening the possibility for a wider range of choice in clinical intervention, together with the introduction of expert patient programmes (EPP) and patient and public involvement (PPI).

Political imperatives are strong triggers for change with, for example, the implementation of 'Choose and Book', practice-based commissioning (PBR) and service modernisation, all aimed at creating a patient-led NHS.

> Its focus is on creating a step-change in the way services are commissioned by front line staff, to reflect patient choices. Effective commissioning is a pre-requisite for making these choices real.[24]

The implementation of Agenda for Change,[25] *Meeting the Challenge*[26] and many other government initiatives, with their emphases on opening up opportunities for staff to progress their careers through developing new and more challenging competencies, taking advantage of the 'skills escalator' and development of skill mix within the workforce, are strong influences in breaking down professional barriers. This includes new, extended and specialist clinical roles through, for example, the development of consultant AHP and nursing posts, extended and advanced practitioner roles and clinical specialist posts. A further example of this is the development of the paramedic role to provide emergency care as first contact in the patient's home, a role often previously undertaken by general practitioners. Many of these new roles challenge traditional professional boundaries through the development of robust competencies and capabilities enabling postholders and would-be postholders to work across previously established professional lines of demarcation.

> Ultimately the government has imagined a healthcare service designed around the patient, provided by teams of healthcare workers, who could develop some flexibility in the scope of what they do, to suit the healthcare environment.[27]

A further important factor in the weakening of professional autonomy and consequent changes in patterns of service provision over recent years has been the transfer of education and training provision for AHPs, nurses and many others into the higher education sector. Previously the professional bodies were responsible for prescribing curricula of study, examining candidates for entry to the professions and state registers and ensuring the quality of education provision. Today, many courses have substantial shared, multidisciplinary elements and the professional bodies have a much smaller role in the approval of courses and quality assurance, all of which increases the potential for cross-professional boundary working and development of new and extended roles.

AHP management: the future?

The 'trait' theory of professionalisation has been explored indicating in part why the professions were managed for many years on a unidisciplinary basis. However, developing government policy and radical changes taking place in the politics, structure, organisation, regulation and management of the NHS indicate weakening of professional autonomy, authority and power in tandem with strengthening public and patient influence, regulatory transparency and independence, multidisciplinary and team working, vertical integration and matrix management.[28]

Clearly it will always be important for the AHPs to have professional management and leadership at the appropriate level to ensure high-quality service provision, staff management, strategic and operational management. However, within the multidisciplinary, vertically integrated NHS it is likely that AHPs will require an increasingly matrix management style system (*see* Chapter 6) which means:

> . . . simply that in addition to the 'islands' there will now be a clear bridge linking team talent, funding and management.[29]

The key to unlocking the widest possible range of opportunities for the AHPs to participate fully in influencing strategy and policy development, and their ability to impact on management and service provision at all levels, is dependent on the professions themselves placing emphasis on being 'allied to one another' so that they are no longer regarded as supplementary, or 'allied to medicine'. There is a critical need for the AHPs to have a single voice in order to exert influence at international, national, regional and local levels. The challenge for AHPs is to make this a reality.

References

1 DHSS. *Working for Patients*. London: HMSO; 1989.
2 Friedson E. *Profession of Medicine*. New York: Dodd, Mead and Company; 1970.
3 Carr-Saunders AM, Wilson PA. *The Professions*. Oxford: The Clarendon Press; 1933.
4 Greenwood E. Attributes of a profession. *Social Work*. 1957; **2**: 45–55.
5 Wilensky HL. The professionalisation of everyone. *Am J Sociology*. 1964; **70**(2): 137–58.
6 Johnson TJ. *Professions and Power*. London: MacMillan; 1972.
7 Ministry of Health. *Memorandum sent by Ministry of Health to Regional Health Boards, Hospital Management Committees and Boards of Governors of Teaching Hospitals*. RHB(49)114, HMC(49)43. London: HMSO; 1949.
8 Ministry of Health. *Report of the Committees on Medical Auxiliaries – the Cope Report*. Cmd.8188. London: HMSO; 1951.
9 Larkin G. *Occupational Monopoly and Modern Medicine*. London: Tavistock Publications; 1983.

10 *Council for Professions Supplementary to Medicine Act 1960*. London: HMSO; 1960.

11 DHSS. *Rehabilitation: report of a Sub-Committee of the Standing Medical Advisory Committeee – Tunbridge Report*. London: HMSO; 1972.

12 DHSS. *Statement by the Committee on the Remedial Professions*. London: HMSO; 1972.

13 DHSS. *The Remedial Professions – a Report by a Working Party Set Up in March 1973 by the Secretary of State for Social Services – McMillan Report*. London: HMSO; 1973.

14 DHSS. *Health Services Development – Relationship between the Medical and Remedial Professions*. HC(77)33. London: HMSO; 1977.

15 Macdonald EM, MacCaul G, Mirrey L, Morrison EM, editors. *Occupational Therapy in Rehabilitation*. London: Baillière Tindall; 1972.

16 Wickstead JH. *The Growth of a Profession*. London: Edward Arnold and Company; 1948.

17 Goode WJ. The theoretical limits of professionalisation. In: Etsioni A, editor. *The Semi-Professions and their Organisation*. New York: The Free Press; 1969.

18 Etzioni A. *The Semi-Professions and their Organisation: teachers, nurses, social workers*. London: Collier MacMillan; 1979.

19 Shaw GB. *The Doctor's Dilemma*. Act 1; 1911.

20 Kennedy I. *Learning from Bristol: The Report of the Public Inquiry into Children's Heart Surgery at the Bristol Royal Infirmary 1984–1995; Cm5207-1*. Norwich: The Stationery Office; 2001.

21 Department of Health. *Cervical Screening Action Team – The Report*. London: NHSE; 1998.

22 Smith J. *The Six Reports of the Shipman Inquiry*. London: HMSO; 2005.

23 Redfern M. *The Royal Liverpool Children's Inquiry: Report*. London: HMSO; 2001.

24 Department of Health. *Commissioning a Patient-led NHS*. Gateway ref no. 5312; 2005. www.dh.gsi.gov.uk.

25 Department of Health. *NHS Knowledge and Skills Framework and Development Review Guidance*. London: HMSO; 2004.

26 Department of Health. *Meeting the Challenge*. London: HMSO; 2000.

27 CSP. *Physiotherapy Competence and Capability Resource Pack*. London: CSP; 2005.

28 Mueller J, Neads P. Allied Health Organisational structure: massaging the organisation to facilitate outcomes. *New Zealand Journal of Physiotherapy*. 2005; **33**(2): 48–54.

29 Lautenbacher CC. *Matrix Management*. www.ppi.noaa.gov/matrix.htm.

Chapter 4

Allied Health Professions management and organisation: what structure?

Fiona Jenkins and Robert Jones

Introduction

Changes in healthcare are driven by several factors: financial, political, economic and social. Consumer changes, with increasing life expectancy, the growth of long-term illnesses, widespread access to health information and increasing demand for both quality and quantity of healthcare, have required health strategists to re-evaluate the organisation and structure of healthcare services in Britain and other western economies. In response to the increasingly competitive and demanding health environment, AHP managers have frequently been required to consider what might be the 'best' organisational structures for their services in several different healthcare systems.[1–6] This has been a recurrent challenge for British AHP managers during the numerous NHS management reviews, reorganisations and reforms (*see* Chapter 2), the purpose of which has been to manage effective clinical service delivery and improve clinical outcomes within resource constraints.

The importance of organisational structures cannot be ignored. They establish the context for many aspects of healthcare: commissioning, patient flows, cross-organisational boundary working, information management, communication processes, clinical governance and the management of risk. Management structures should be defined after the functions of a service are determined. Organisational structure directly influences the provision of patient care, affecting both staffing and service issues.

The way in which AHP services are organised and managed has a significant influence on patient services and staff. The management structure of an organisation should be determined by service need – for health services, structure should be determined by patient need. There have been significant changes in NHS resource management and services have been subject to perpetual changing organisational structures.[7] AHP services have undergone restructuring as a consequence of NHS reorganisations (*see* Chapter 2). The 1997 DoH-commissioned report *Providing Therapists' Expertise in the New NHS: developing a strategic framework for good patient care*[8] noted that therapists, like most other professional groups in the NHS, had been reorganised several times in the recent past, with resulting structures and management arrangements not being in place sufficiently long enough to be fully evaluated. The report commented on the effects of organisation and role conflict, stating that:

> Therapists often find themselves at the 'heart of the problem' in that they provide specialist services within very complex multi agency environments to people who often require different types of specialist advice and treatment, whose need is likely to change over time.

Structural changes have caused concerns for AHP services.[3] These have related to AHP service fragmentation into small teams managed by directorates, divisions or general managers, thus destroying the work of many years building services. The individual issues included fears that staff would not get the professional support needed and professional standards would drop. Øvretveit[2] proposed that many concerns regarding the impact of organisational changes on therapy services had been overlooked. These included difficulties with recruiting and retaining staff, lack of career progression and the head of service being accountable for professional standards without authority.

Heysall et al[9] reported that the move towards managed competition and the introduction of relatively decentralised management units based largely on medical specialty groupings has often been perceived by AHPs as a need to 'make them fit' with a desire for neat organisational boxes on organisational charts. Underlying the difficulty of incorporating AHPs into decentralised structures is the failure to realise that the concept of specialty is not necessarily identical for medicine and AHPs. Many AHP services follow patients across organisational boundaries, which does not fit the organisational and management model of either primary or acute trusts.

Management arrangements for AHPs are not uniform across the NHS. In some places a single head of service manages each of the professions as individual entities. In others they are managed in a variety of different groupings, for example in directorate structures or in combined AHP groups, either within one trust or across several trusts. The management role is sometimes divided between management and professional functions. These roles are sometimes separated and may be undertaken by different individuals not necessarily from the same professional backgrounds.

Despite their recognised contribution to patient care in the NHS,[8] research into AHP management structures in Britain has been limited.[2,3,10–13] Jones[3,10,11] surveyed Physiotherapy Managers in the 1980s and again in the 1990s to gather information relating to their roles and responsibilities. Øvretveit[2] proposed a concept of three tiers of structure for therapy services in the early 1990s, describing 11 different models of management at that time. Berry also researched this subject in the 1990s[12] and Jenkins in 2005.[13] The AHPs have lacked influence in comparison with medical and nursing colleagues in the larger policy process of structural reforms at national, regional and local levels. Thus, the potential for strategic influence has been fragmented and diluted. This lack of strategic presence has impacted on the success of local engagement by AHPs in influencing the management arrangements for their professional groups within trusts and at the Strategic Health Authorities (SHAs).

The strategy for AHPs, *Meeting the Challenge* (2000),[14] suggested that the AHPs require strong management and leadership to deliver the requirements of the NHS Plan (2000).[15] The NHS Plan encouraged the wider involvement of the AHPs in providing high-level clinical and managerial leadership. Additionally there was a requirement for NHS employers to ensure that AHP skills were fully utilised, including representation on NHS Trust Boards. Organisational structures for AHP services appear to have 'swung' between full devolution to localities and clinical directorates and centralisation to AHP directorates and individual departments, without full consideration for the impact of these decisions on patient care and the many factors affecting clinical governance.

The research

This chapter reports on research undertaken by Jenkins,[13] reviewing the roles, responsibilities and duties of AHP managers in England in 2004. This builds on the previous research undertaken by Jones.[3,10,11] Three questionnaire surveys were undertaken, which included AHP managers, AHP advisors and SHA AHP Officers. The questionnaires were used to obtain data on the organisational management arrangements and structures in place at that time. The survey included an overview of the spectrum of management models in operation and the impact of management arrangements on strategy, planning, service provision, operational management, patient care, resource use and human resource management within the AHPs. The views of the respondents about the possible advantages, disadvantages and impact of their management arrangements were sought. Their opinions about representation arrangements and input to SHAs and Trusts at strategic and senior management levels were also obtained.

The questionnaires were sent to:

- the most senior AHP manager or advisor in a representative sample (two Acute Trusts, two PCTs and one 'other' type of Trust) of NHS Trusts in each of the 28 SHA areas (140 questionnaires)
- the officer with responsibility for AHPs in each SHA in England (28 questionnaires).

There was a 77% response rate indicating a high level of interest in management arrangements for AHP services. The findings are reported in three sections, relating to the three different questionnaires that were used:

1 AHP managers
2 AHP advisors
3 SHA AHP officers.

A further section presents the respondents' perceived advantages and disadvantages of current management and representational arrangements.

AHP managers' responses

An AHP manager was defined as an AHP holding management responsibilities for one or more AHP services across their entire Trust; 83% of Trust respondents fulfilled these criteria. The remaining 17% held professional advisory roles only, not undertaking full management duties, or only managing part of a service within their Trust (these responses are reported under 'AHP advisors' responses').

The AHP managers responded to several questions about their posts.

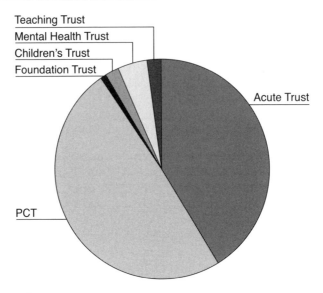

Figure 4.1 Type of trust

Type of trust

The majority of respondents were employed by PCTs, with Acute Trusts being the second largest group as shown in Figure 4.1. The other Trust types were few in number. A total of 12% of Trusts indicated that they did not employ any AHPs within their organisation. These responses were all from PCTs, indicating that they would have had their AHP services provided by other organisations such as Acute Trusts or neighbouring PCTs.

All Acute Trusts employed an AHP manager, whereas PCTs demonstrated some sharing of AHP management posts. PCT management structures were less well established due to the recent development of primary care organisations and would be more likely to be restructured during future evolution of primary care services.

Title and profession of AHP managers

The titles of the most senior AHP managers were most commonly Head of Therapies and Head of Physiotherapy. Physiotherapists held the majority of AHP Manager posts – both uniprofessional managers and Head of Therapies posts (48%). Occupational Therapists were the second largest profession represented in this role (26%). The larger AHP professions held the major proportion of senior AHP Manager posts in Trusts.

Length of time in post: weekly hours worked

Most AHP managers worked full time. Some managers had been recently appointed, with others having been in post for more than 11 years. The majority had held their current posts for between two and five years. There were also recent appointments, indicating that these posts were considered attractive as a career path for AHPs, particularly physiotherapists and occupational therapists.

Table 4.1 Number of trusts with AHP management arrangements covering more than one trust

Number of trusts	2	3	4	5	6	7	8	9	10	11
AHP managers managing services in more than one trust	12	12	6	3	2	2	1	0	0	1

Job title of postholders' manager

The majority of AHP managers reported to a director-level post. Accountability to two higher level officers at the same time – dual accountability – was not uncommon (*see* Chapter 1) e.g. responsible to a General Manager and either Director of Nursing or Medical Director.

Where AHP managers report to a director-level post, there is the advantage of being able to influence Board-level discussions and decisions more readily than if the accountability is through a less senior manager.

Of the 92 Trusts with AHP managers, there were 39 respondents (42%) who identified that they managed AHP services in more than one Trust. The number of multiple Trusts managed ranged from two to 11. All different types of Health Trusts had shared management arrangements. PCTs had the greatest number of these shared posts, perhaps indicating that PCTs were either too small to have effective AHP management arrangements, or that PCTs recognised the benefits of having management arrangements that crossed organisational boundaries.

A total of 42% of Trusts had management arrangements which could facilitate vertical integration of services, ensuring continuity of healthcare for patients.

Whole time equivalent (WTE) staff managed

There was a wide variation in the number and range of WTE staff employed by Trusts (*see* Figure 4.2). Physiotherapists were the largest group, with between 0 and 140 WTE staff employed. Some Trusts 'hosted' services on behalf of other organisations, which would account for some of the nil employed figures. Occupational therapists (OTs) were the second largest and speech and language therapists the third largest professional group. Assistants were employed by

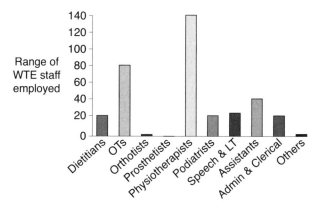

Figure 4.2 Whole time equivalent (WTE) staff managed

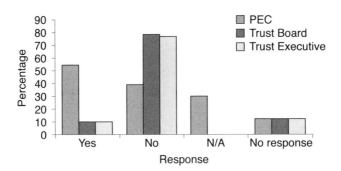

Figure 4.3 AHP managers with a seat on Primary Care Executive Committees (PEC), Trust Board and Executive Board

several professional groups. There was only one orthotist and no prosthetist directly employed by Trusts who participated in the survey. This would indicate that the vast majority of orthotic and prosthetic services were provided by orthotic companies.

AHP managers with a seat on Primary Care Executive Committees (PEC), Trust Board and Executive Board

Only a few AHP managers had seats on Trust Board and executive committees (*see* Figure 4.3). The position most likely to be held was on the Primary Care Executive Committee (PEC), although only managers from PCTs would have been eligible to apply for these positions along with other PCT-based AHP clinical staff.

Lack of AHP representation on senior committees represented a lost opportunity for organisations in harnessing the full skills of these senior staff.

Postholders representing service at Trust Board

A Trust Board comprises: Trust Chairman, Trust Directors, CEO and non-executive Directors, the Board being responsible for ensuring the Trust meets its statutory requirements. There was a range of professions representing AHPs at Trust Board level. Only 18% of these were AHPs themselves.

This indicated that only small numbers of AHPs were working at the most senior levels of management in the Trusts.

Postholders representing AHPs at Executive Board level

A Trust Executive committee reports to its Board. This committee generally has clinical as well as managerial representation, as this tier of management is intended to be the 'clinical conscience' of the Trust, ensuring that clinicians are included in the business of the Trust. Clinicians should include staff from a range of clinical professions. There were 22% (20) of AHP managers representing their own services on Trust executive levels. The other 78% (72) of representatives for AHPs were Directors, with 30% (28) of these being nurses. It is significant in terms of AHPs' ability to influence service planning that such a low percentage of AHPs represented their own services at this level and that more nurses than AHPs represent AHP services at Executive Board level. Trusts were not utilising the skills of all their Senior Managers at Executive level and not harnessing all the expertise that AHPs could contribute.

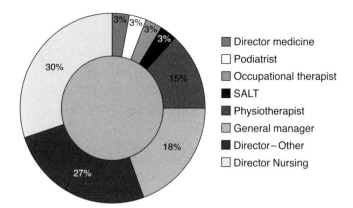

Figure 4.4 Postholders representing AHPs at Executive Board level

AHP managers' seats on senior management committees

Senior Trust management committees set strategy and direction for the Trust as well as monitor performance; 58% of AHP managers had a seat on a Clinical Governance committee, with 23% holding a seat on another senior management committee, such as commissioning and operations committees. The limited representation of AHPs on senior management committees was consistent with their lack of representation on Board and executive committees. Trusts were largely missing out on input of AHPs at senior committee level. This again would adversely affect the ability of AHPs to contribute to strategy, planning and policy.

Roles in addition to AHP manager role

AHP managers often held roles in addition to their professional managerial function. AHP services covered a wide breadth of clinical specialisms; the manager's knowledge and skills could be used in many ways to support Trust business. In all, 46% of AHP managers had roles in addition to their AHP management role; PEC representative was the most common. However, the

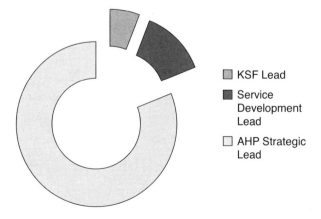

Figure 4.5 Roles in addition to AHP manager role

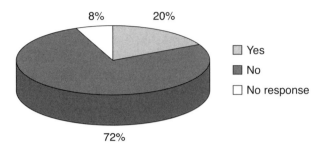

8%   20%

☐ Yes
■ No
☐ No response

72%

Figure 4.6 AHP managers who undertake regular clinical work

role titles were diverse, including a range of strategic leadership functions for the organisations. AHP managers had potential and some opportunity to extend their roles into other areas of Trust managerial work.

AHP managers who undertake regular clinical work

All the AHP managers came from an AHP professional background, having started careers as clinical staff and then progressed through career promotions, into a senior managerial role (*see* Figure 4.6). A full 80% of AHP managers no longer undertook regular clinical work. The role of an AHP Manager was shown to take significant working time to undertake all its components. Those who no longer undertook clinical work were working in a strategic capacity that did not require a regular clinical workload.

AHP manager satisfaction with representation at senior management level

There was a low level of satisfaction with representation of AHP services at senior levels within Trusts; 77% of AHP managers felt that there was room for improvement in representation arrangements. This figure correlated with the low percentage of AHP Managers (<22%) holding seats at Board and Executive Board levels. AHP managers felt disenfranchised by management structures suggesting that representation on key committees could be seen as an indicator to satisfaction with service management arrangements for AHPs.

The SHA is the link between the Department of Health (DH) strategy and monitoring with local service delivery by Trusts (*see* Table 4.2). The SHA is the focus of two-way communication, both gathering and disseminating information to AHP service managers. There was a low level of satisfaction with the effectiveness of mechanisms for AHP input to SHAs; 55% of AHP managers reported that there was a mechanism for AHP input to their SHA. However, 66% indicated that they did not have effective AHP representation at the SHA.

Table 4.2 SHAs with a mechanism for AHP input. Is the mechanism for AHP input to SHAs effective?

AHP input	Yes	No	Don't know	Did not answer
Is there AHP input to SHA?	55%	32%	nil	13%
Effective AHP representation at SHA?	34%	51%	2%	13%

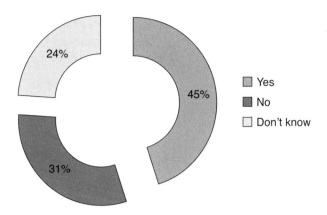

Figure 4.7 SHAs with an AHP officer

The lack of effective representation frustrated AHP managers in their ability to be engaged at strategic level, not only within their Trusts, but also at SHA level. AHP expertise was not being harnessed sufficiently and the links with the SHA where AHP skills could be deployed were considered less than satisfactory.

SHAs with an AHP officer

Only 45% of AHP managers reported that there was an officer at the SHA with responsibility for liaising with AHPs. Significantly, 24% did not know whether there was an officer or not. This indicates that almost a quarter of AHP managers had no communication from the SHA to indicate whether there was an officer. This was in contrast to their medical and nursing colleagues who have dedicated roles in all SHAs and who have established networks with Trusts.

Profession of the SHA AHP officer

Of the 111 AHP Managers respondents, 41 (37%) did not know the profession of their SHA AHP Officer (*see* Figure 4.8). This indicated a lack of knowledge about the SHA AHP Officer and poor levels of communication.

In all, 10% of SHA officers with a remit for AHPs were nurses, which may be regarded as less than satisfactory by the AHPs, with organisations missing out on AHP input. The other 22% did not have an officer, which would disadvantage the

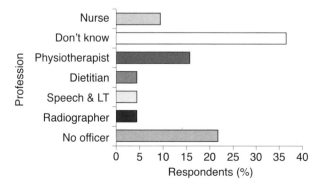

Figure 4.8 Profession of the SHA AHP officer

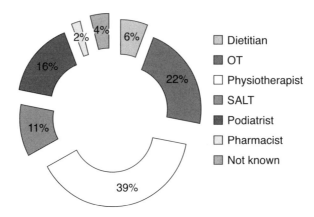

Figure 4.9 Profession of AHP PEC representatives

AHP services and organisations in these areas. Poor networks and communication between the SHA and AHP managers affected the frequency and quality of information flows between Trusts and SHAs. In areas without a SHA AHP lead, the health community was not making the best use of valuable AHP intelligence.

Effectiveness of AHP representation within SHAs

Two thirds of respondents thought that the arrangements for representing AHPs within their SHA were ineffective, which represented their desire for better engagement and networking at strategic levels.

Profession of AHP PEC representatives

Five professions held PEC representative roles for AHPs. The majority of posts were held by physiotherapists. A pharmacist also undertook this role, even though pharmacists are not AHPs (*see* Figure 4.9).

The PEC is the only strategic committee in Trusts that has a mandatory requirement for AHP membership. Eligibility to apply for the role is only open for staff undertaking work in PCTs. The PEC representative could be an AHP manager, advisor or one undertaking clinical work only. Although there was an AHP PEC representative, unless this post was held by an AHP Manager, the Trust would not be engaging the AHP senior manager in the strategic business of the Trust.

Of all the AHP managers, PCTs reported the highest percentage of effective communication with the PEC representatives (*see* Table 4.3). This was not

Table 4.3 Mechanism for two-way communication between AHP PEC representatives and managers

Communication	Yes	No	No response
Mechanism with Acute Trust AHP managers	40%	25%	35%
Mechanism with PCT AHP managers	50%	10%	40%
Mechanism with 'Other' type of Trust managers	32%	23%	45%
Is the communication effective?	40%	41%	19%

surprising as the PEC representatives were based in PCTs and some who completed the questionnaire were also PEC representatives themselves. The Acute Trust managers had the least effective communication with PEC representatives, which demonstrated difficulties in cross-boundary working. Sixty percent of managers were dissatisfied with communication effectiveness, indicating poor communication between Acute Trusts and PCTs which would impact on continuity of patient care and a wide range of issues affecting clinical governance.

There was a high degree of consistency in the work that AHP managers performed, with 71% or more undertaking 23 different roles. The exceptions were involvement with the transformational NHS IT development Connecting for Health[16] (49%), and pre-registration education commissioning (70%) (*see* Table 4.4).

Table 4.4 Roles, responsibilities and duties of AHP managers

Do you have responsibility for:	*% of 'yes' answers*
Strategic development of the service(s) you manage?	87
Managerial input to Local Delivery Plan?	82
Performance management of your service(s)?	85
Developing policies for the service(s) you manage?	86
Managing the budget for your service(s)?	84
Data collection for your service(s)?	84
Data analysis for the management of your service(s)?	78
Involvement with Connecting for Health (IT)?	49
Drawing up Service Level Agreements?	70
Managing Service level Agreements?	72
Implementation of 'Meeting the Challenge'?	78
Patient and Public Involvement in your service(s)?	80
Workforce planning for your service(s)?	83
Participation in the process of education commissioning via the WDC?	70
Staff recruitment processes?	85
Appraisal/IPR/Personal Development Plans?	87
Implementation of disciplinary procedures?	87
Implementing 'Improving Working Lives'?	84
Monitoring HPC registration/fitness to practise?	81
Health and Safety monitoring and reporting?	83
Risk management within service(s)?	83
Complaints management?	83
Development of guidelines for your service(s)?	78
Implementation of National Service Frameworks?	79
Ensuring evidence-based practice?	85
Research and development within your service(s)?	73

Table 4.5 Frequency of contact by AHP manager with their networks

AHP managers' contacts	Nil	Annual	Quarterly	Monthly	Weekly	Did not answer
SHA AHP lead	42%	12%	23%	8%	1%	14%
SHA AHP group/forum	38%	10%	34%	3%	1%	14%
Regional AHP group	39%	8%	30%	7%	1%	15%
SHA/regional uniprofessional group	32%	14%	32%	9%	1%	12%
PCT AHP PEC representatives	23%	5%	18%	24%	18%	12%

AHP managers undertook a wide range of duties that included both operational and strategic management responsibilities. It was surprising that involvement in IT was low given the importance of AHP involvement during the development of this significant service improvement programme for the NHS. IT systems provide managers with information to enable them to effectively perform their roles. Lack of input from AHP managers during the design and development phases must be a cause for concern. If AHP services are to be effectively managed, meaningful data is needed. The collection of this data requires clinical and managerial input – which appeared to be lacking, impacting adversely on the future management of AHPs.

Comparison with previous research undertaken by Jones,[3,10,11] commented on in Chapter 1, shows that AHP managers' roles, responsibilities and duties are relatively unchanged since the early 1990s despite several Health Service reorganisations. The greatest changes have been the development of additional roles for AHP managers, the development of primary care services and increasingly complex organisational management structures.

AHP managers had differing frequencies of contact with their networks. Less than half of the respondents had any contact with the SHA AHP Officer, or had an AHP group for the SHA area. There were varying degrees of contact between AHP groups and uniprofessional groups. Even at local level there was no contact for nearly a quarter of AHP managers with their local PEC representatives.

These groups provide varying types of support: information exchange, peer support, consultation of professional AHP policies, training and development as well as advice and support. It was apparent that AHP managers needed to have a range of networks to perform effectively in their roles to enable them to be well briefed, to influence upwards and to perform effectively at local level. Although the concept of a Health Region had disappeared following an earlier NHS reorganisation, many AHP managers still met in larger geographical groupings, both uniprofessionally and as AHP groups. This demonstrated that SHA groupings alone did not meet the needs of AHP managers in fulfilling their strategic development and professional needs.

AHP advisors' responses

A total of 17% (19) of respondents held professional advisory roles only, not undertaking full management duties – an AHP advisor. All of these respondents held uniprofessional AHP roles, being advisors for their own professional group only.

Part management and advisor role

The advisors were asked whether they managed services in part of their Trust only; seven responded 'yes'.

Advisor responsibilities across more than one Trust

Only two of the 19 AHP advisors had roles that extended beyond one Trust. Advisory roles therefore generally operated in less complicated organisational structures than the AHP managers.

Managers of professional group across trust

In Trusts where AHP services were managed by a non-AHP there were several different arrangements for the management of AHP services (*see* Figure 4.10). In 11 organisations the AHP advisors undertook some management duties but did not manage the whole service; this may have been for management of their own AHP staff group, or for other AHP groups. Eight organisations with AHP advisors employed general managers to undertake all the AHP staff management, with the advisors working in a non-managerial capacity.

AHP advisors were asked to rate their level of satisfaction with their current management arrangements, on an analogue scale of 0–4, where 0 indicated no satisfaction, and 4 full satisfaction (*see* Table 4.6).

AHP advisors gave a range of opinions regarding the operational management of their own profession. There were more advisors who were completely dissatisfied with the management arrangements than were completely satisfied. It was interesting to note that all the AHP advisors held uniprofessional posts; if they had been in larger AHP groupings their level of dissatisfaction may possibly have not been so high. The same pattern of dissatisfaction was apparent for representation of their profession at Trust Executive level, although some of these

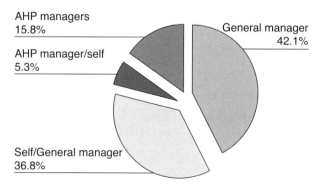

Figure 4.10 Managers of professional group across trust

Table 4.6 Level of satisfaction with management arrangements for AHP services

Management activity	Rating				
	0	*1*	*2*	*3*	*4*
Operational management of profession	16%	26%	11%	37%	10%
Representation of profession on Trust Executive	21%	21%	5%	37%	16%
Representation of profession on Trust Board	16%	21%	10%	37%	16%
Communication links for profession with SHA	16%	21%	0	47%	16%

staff held PEC seats and would be likely to be satisfied with this arrangement, if they were the postholder themselves.

The majority of advisors had some degree of satisfaction with representation of their professional group at Board level. All advisors expressed a view regarding their levels of satisfaction with links for their profession with the SHA. Twelve were dissatisfied with these arrangements and only three completely satisfied. This comment concurs with the results expressed by the AHP managers, where it was shown that 10% of the SHA AHP Officers were nurses and 59% either had no AHP Officer or did not know the profession of the officer. These arrangements were perceived to be unsatisfactory by both the AHP advisors and managers and must be reviewed in the context of the reconfigured SHAs.

A total of 74% (14) of AHP advisors had a role in addition to their professional advisory role (*see* Figure 4.11). Of these, four (28%) were PEC representatives. One advisor was a Knowledge and Skills Framework Lead (KSF), which was a recent appointment linked to the changing NHS pay structure – Agenda for Change. Four (28%) of those who held an additional role did not describe the work.

AHP advisors had more capacity to undertake additional roles, as they did not undertake management roles to any great extent. However, it was noteworthy that a significant proportion of these roles was based in PCTs as PEC representatives. AHP advisory roles were more common in primary care and in 28% of appointments the AHP advisor was also the PEC representative.

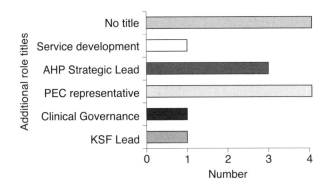

Figure 4.11 AHP advisors' additional roles

Advisors undertaking clinical work

Only three (16%) AHP advisors undertook regular clinical work. This was less than the AHP managers of whom 20% undertook at least one day a week clinical duties. As the advisors did not undertake management duties for a whole service and undertook little or no clinical work, it would be worth further investigation to determine what roles and duties they performed that took so much of their time, as they were not managing their services and not taking on significant other 'lead' roles.

SHA AHP officer responses

This questionnaire was sent to the SHA AHP officer. There was a 64% (18) response rate from the 28 SHAs in England.

Title and profession of person completing the questionnaire

The title of the SHA AHP officer was not consistently used and was not a post in every SHA (*see* Figure 4.12, with one no response to this question). Several of the respondents were evidently not AHP officers but were senior officers completing the questionnaire. In all, 67% respondents were AHPs, several were either seconded into the role or in an 'acting' position, and one respondent did not complete the question. The responses suggested that the role of AHP officer was poorly established in SHAs.

Job title of accountable officer for SHA AHP officer

Over 90% of SHA AHP officers reported to a Director or CEO post (*see* Figure 4.13 with one no response to this question). These posts were therefore largely engaged at senior levels within the SHAs and arguably in a good position to influence policy, as well as communicate with Trust AHPs. The level of management reporting for these AHP officer posts enabled the officers to be engaged at the highest level in the organisations. Unfortunately only a few SHAs had these posts in place.

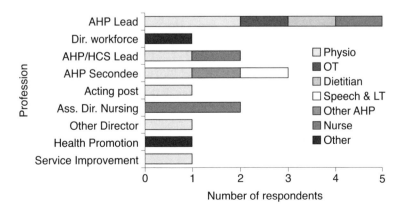

Figure 4.12 Title and profession of person completing the questionnaire

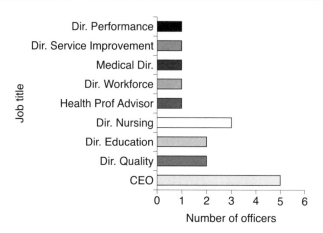

Figure 4.13 Job title of accountable officer for SHA AHP officer

Number of AHP staff employed within SHA area

Of the 10 SHAs that responded to this question, the mean number of AHPs employed was 1645 WTE, with a range from 1054 WTE to 2800 WTE. These figures included dietitians, occupational therapists, orthotists, prosthetists, physiotherapists, podiatrists and speech and language therapists. A total of 44% (8) of the respondents did not complete this question, which may have indicated the difficulty in obtaining information relating to the AHP workforce and the lack of consistency in AHP representation at this level. It would have been surprising if the number of WTE nurses and doctors was not known by SHAs.

Mechanism for obtaining AHP input

SHAs were asked if they had a mechanism for obtaining AHP input to the SHA; 94% (17) of SHAs who responded indicated that they did. This contrasted with responses from the AHP mangers, where only 45% reported an AHP officer at the SHA and only 32% of managers thought the arrangements for representing AHPs and input to the SHA were effective. There was a difference of opinion between Trust AHP mangers and SHA officers about the effectiveness of current representation mechanisms. These mechanisms were in need of improvement to ensure that Trust AHPs had robust links with the SHA. This would include having a named officer and networks for two-way communications which was lacking in some areas.

SHA AHP officer

Of the 18 respondents, 83% (15) indicated that they did have an officer with responsibility for AHPs. Ten SHAs did not respond to the questionnaire, therefore it is not known whether these organisations had an officer or not.

Reasons for not employing a SHA AHP officer

The 17% of respondents who indicated that they did not have an AHP officer at the SHA all cited 'lack of funds' as the reason for not employing an officer. Some of the AHP officer roles were shared with other roles, for example Nurse lead officer, which may also have indicated a funding problem for AHP lead officer

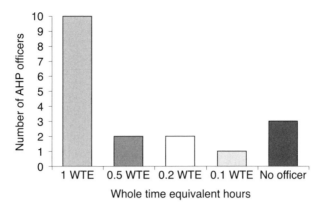

Figure 4.14 Working hours of SHA AHP officers

posts. Funding for an AHP Officer was evidently a major factor. SHAs could look at innovative ways of engaging AHPs in strategic business. Secondment of Trust AHP managers would be likely to improve the engagement of AHPs. As the AHP workforce nationally is 160 000 perhaps SHAs should put plans in place to address this issue.

Working hours of SHA AHP officers

The majority of SHA AHP officers – 10 out of the 18 – worked full time (*see* Figure 4.14). When this response was further analysed it was clear that some full-time officers had responsibilities in addition to their AHP work. The part-time officers were often seconded from Trusts for some of their time.

Profession of SHA AHP officer

There were three respondents who indicated why their officer was not an AHP. Two used a SHA AHP forum to inform the SHA of AHP matters. One amazingly responded that the role was not advertised for AHPs to apply; in this case the role was held by a nurse.

AHPs were not afforded the same opportunity to represent their services and contribute to the SHA, compared to other large groups.

Of the 18 respondents, eight had responsibilities for professions other than AHPs. The least involvement was in advising Trust AHPs on evidence-based practice and research and development, as well as undertaking strategic level performance management of AHP services and advising on AHP input to service improvement initiatives. The main duties that SHA AHP Officers undertook were (*see* Table 4.7): liaison with the DH AHP Officer, facilitating a SHA AHP forum, and developing a communication strategy with AHPs. It was interesting to note that 16 (89%) of AHP Officers at the SHAs reported that they had responsibility for facilitating a forum for communication with AHPs, whereas only 55% of AHP managers reported a mechanism for AHP input to the SHA, with 66% reporting this mechanism as being ineffective. The SHA AHP Officer roles were narrower than those of AHP managers; they concentrated on policy areas rather than operational management tasks. To fulfil these roles excellent communication networks would be vitally important to gather information from Trusts but also to help develop and steer the strategic direction of AHP services within the SHA.

Table 4.7 Roles, responsibilities and duties of SHA AHP officer

In your role do you:	% of 'yes' answers
Have responsibilities for professions other than AHPs?	56
Develop AHP policies and procedures at the SHA?	56
Input to Department of Health AHP Officer?	89
Have a liaison role with AHP professional bodies?	67
Have a liaison role with Health Professions Council?	67
Advise SHA on AHP service planning?	72
Facilitate a forum for communication with AHPs?	89
Develop a communication strategy for AHPs?	84
Advise the SHA on resource allocation to AHP services?	45
Represent AHPs on workforce planning at WDC?	67
Influence pre-registration education provision for AHPs?	78
Influence post-registration education provision for AHPs?	78
Identify leadership needs for AHPs?	78
Identify leadership development opportunities for AHPs?	83
Identify management needs for AHPs?	50
Identify management development opportunities for AHPs?	50
Advise on evidence-based practice for AHPs?	28
Input to development of IM&T (Connecting for Health) for AHPs?	44
Undertake performance management of AHP services?	22
Advise on AHP input to NSF services?	56
Actively lobby and support NHS Trusts in the development of AHP consultant posts?	78
Actively lobby and support NHS Trusts in the development of AHP extended roles?	72
Actively lobby and support NHS Trusts in the development of AHP clinical specialist roles?	61
Input to Research and Development initiatives for AHPs?	6
Initiate innovations in AHP practice?	53
Monitor innovations in AHP practice?	6
Monitor the implementation of Improving Working Lives within AHP services?	25
Collect and disseminate information about innovative AHP practice?	80
Advise on AHP input to service improvement initiatives?	80
Initiate AHP service improvement initiatives?	53
Advise on development roles for AHP assistants?	80

Table 4.8 SHA contact with trust AHPs

Contact	Nil	Annual	Quarterly	Monthly	Weekly	No Response
PCT AHP managers	0	5.6% (1)	11.1% (2)	38.9% (7)	27.8 (5)	16.7% (3)
PCT AHP advisors	11.1% (2)	5.6% (1)	22.2% (4)	33.3% (6)	11.1% (2)	16.7% (3)
Acute Trust AHP managers	0	5.6% (1)	11.1% (2)	38.9% (7)	27.8% (5)	16.7% (3)
Acute Trust AHP advisors	11.1% (2)	5.6% (1)	22.2% (4)	33.3% (6)	11.1% (2)	16.7% (3)
PCT PEC representatives	0	11.1% (2)	22.2% (4)	38.9% (7)	11.1% (2)	16.7% (3)

Without dedicated time to develop this role the task would be difficult, which may account for the dissatisfaction expressed by Trust AHP managers.

SHA AHP Officers reported monthly contact most frequently with Trust AHP managers (*see* Table 4.8). AHP managers had more frequent contact than advisors. PEC representatives also had more frequent contact with the SHA AHP Officer than AHP advisors.

The use of AHP fora should be seen as one of the tools to facilitate engagement with AHP managers, however they must be effective and inclusive and not the only way of gaining AHP engagement and inadequate to fulfil the needs of either the SHA or AHP managers. Limited communication with Trust AHP managers and advisors might reduce the two-way exchange of information.

In order to support AHP managers and advisors in Trusts it is imperative that robust links with SHAs are in place. There was inconsistent representation of AHPs at SHA level which could adversely affect AHP development. SHAs could benefit from the breadth of AHP expertise. Enhanced strategic links between Trust AHP managers and the SHAs would be likely to have a positive effect on health service development.

Advantages and disadvantages of the current management structures for AHPs

All three questionnaires asked respondents to give their views on the advantages and disadvantages of the current management arrangements for AHPs. The respondents came from different organisational structures and had differing roles; the majority of respondents were AHP managers, but views were also gathered from AHP advisors and AHP SHA officers. The responses were analysed and then themed.

Perceived advantages of current management arrangements: AHP managers

- The managers' most frequently recurring theme was the benefit of having one cohesive and integrated service that spanned both secondary and primary care with a 'critical mass' of staff being the highest rated advantage of the current management arrangements, where this was in place. Although not all AHP managers provided services that crossed organisational boundaries, those who did cited this as their top rated advantage when linked with having a 'critical mass' of staff – which was a response received from those who worked in single organisations as well as those who worked across organisations.

- The second strongest theme was the autonomy for AHPs to manage their own services, which linked with strong professional management and leadership. This was a consistent theme for both uniprofessional AHP managers and those who managed a range of AHP services.
- The third most highly rated advantage was the need for effective communication: within the employing organisation, at strategic levels and with other organisations and agencies.
- The last cluster of advantages related to good interprofessional working relationships, and a feeling of being 'valued', where the managers reported that their contribution to healthcare was positively acknowledged along with their working with colleagues from multidisciplinary teams.

From this analysis it is deduced that the managers who expressed an opinion about the advantages of their current management arrangements highly rated having a service that crossed organisational boundaries, with the ability to manage and lead the service with good communication links both within their service and the other services that they interacted with. The concept of vertical integration – ensuring that services follow patients across organisational boundaries – was supported by these managers.

Perceived advantages of current management arrangements: AHP advisors

- The strongest theme highlighted the advantage of AHP advisors having part managerial roles as well as leadership responsibilities.
- The second-rated response related to the ability to work across primary and secondary care. The AHP advisors described advantages to patient care where patient services spanned across organisational boundaries, preventing 'hand-offs' in treatment and ensuring services remain patient focused rather than organisation focused. This response was surprising because only two of the 19 AHP advisors carried responsibilities that crossed organisational boundaries.

Interestingly these perceived advantages were similar to the managers' responses. It would appear that those holding advisory posts felt that their position was strengthened if they also had some management responsibilities, even if these did not cover the whole of their organisation. Once again vertical integration was strongly supported.

Perceived advantages of the current mechanism for AHP representation to the SHA

- The most frequently recurring theme related to raising the profile of AHPs by ensuring that AHP issues were included on appropriate agendas.

- The second strongest theme highlighted the advantages of including AHP issues in strategic planning which required representation at senior levels.
- The final theme raised the issue of communication and networks to involve Trust AHPs in informing the SHA. The SHA AHP officers felt that it was important to engage Trust AHPs in informing the SHA – even though many AHPs in Trusts felt there was considerable room for improvement.

All of these advantages related to ensuring that AHP issues were included at SHA level and not lost in the nursing and medical agendas.

Perceived disadvantages of current management arrangements: AHP managers

1 The strongest theme related to what the respondents viewed as poor representation: at executive levels within the Trusts, at the SHA and by the PEC representatives.
2 The second themed disadvantage related to management restructuring and resultant service fragmentation and inability to offer an equitable service. These contained explanations describing services that had undergone restructuring often where a PCT set up its own service that had previously been provided by an Acute Trust. The inequity cited related both to numbers of staff and quality of the clinical service following service fragmentation. There was a strong view expressed that service restructuring often took place on the basis of organisational desire for service ownership, rather than being based on the needs of effectiveness and efficiency of patient care services and the need to maintain critical mass in staffing.
3 The final cluster of themes related to poor communication within organisations, between organisations and with the SHA.

The disadvantages perceived by the managers all linked to poor representation and the weaknesses associated with fragmented services, reducing their ability to offer comprehensive patient care, effective and efficient service management.

Perceived disadvantages of current management arrangements: AHP advisors

There were many more responses detailing disadvantages than advantages from the AHP advisors; these indicated their level of dissatisfaction with their current management arrangements.

1 The most significant theme related to service fragmentation resulting from the lack of a professional manager. Problems associated with this included recruitment and retention difficulties, limited career development opportunities for AHP staff, reduced sharing of expertise by specialist staff and loss of professional identity.
2 The second strongest theme cited was the difficulty in AHPs being able to influence senior management. Linked with this was difficulty in engaging with strategy, and the increased number of general managers to communicate with, together with poor communication links and loss of budget.

It is interesting to note that both managers and advisors saw crucial strengths of having non-fragmented services and a 'critical mass' of staff. Many of the advisors would have previously worked in professional management structures and would have been able to compare their current arrangements with former experience.

Perceived disadvantages of the current mechanism for AHP representation to the SHA

One strong theme emerged. This was the limited time that the SHA AHP officer role was allocated, either due to the postholder having other responsibilities, or being a part-time role, or the fact that the post was for a time-limited period without any certainty that it would continue.

This response indicated that much more could be achieved by the SHA AHP officer if additional time and commitment to make roles substantive were given. Ten SHAs did not respond to the questionnaire possibly because they did not have an AHP officer – which would make this theme even more significant. The SHA AHP officer role needed development in all SHAs.

Conclusion

Management structures are important in delivering quality healthcare. Mintzberg[17] (*see* Chapter 1) commented that Alfred Chandler in 1962 first pointed out that management structure should follow organisational strategy; he further developed this concept, proposing that:

> Effective organizational change is really the relationship between structure, strategy, systems, style, skills, staff and . . . superordinate goals.

The structure adopted by an organisation has an impact on the five 'recognised' dimensions of delivering a quality service.[18]

1 Patient satisfaction.
2 Information and emotional support.
3 Amenities and convenience.
4 Decision-making efficiency.
5 Outcomes.

There are many possible models of management for AHP services. The requirement for effective and efficient management of AHP services is of paramount importance for patient care. Review of management structures and the continued development of management models are required to enable AHP services meet service needs in the 21st-century NHS.

Management arrangements for the AHPs have changed significantly during the last 30 years. One of the most influential changes was the move away from District Heads of individual AHP services. The fragmentation of provider services to include PCTs has created many more organisations, breaking down the old District structures in which AHPs were managed. PCTs have a range of different management models for their AHP staff. Some do not manage AHPs within their organisation – instead having a 'hosted' arrangement for AHP services, most frequently provided by Acute Trusts for the larger professions and PCTs for the smaller professions. Other PCTs do manage their own services; this is likely to change again during future NHS reorganisation, with the introduction of contestability.[19] Across all types of health Trusts there has been a gradual move away from uniprofessionally managed AHP services towards AHP management units – with one overall AHP manager, supported by uniprofessional managers at lower levels. The development of Foundation Trusts may once again change management arrangements. It is possible that AHP services could be managed in Foundation Trusts with some staff providing community-based AHP services.[20] PCT reconfiguration will change the provider status of primary care organisations and introduce the concept of contestability into primary care services, which is likely to include AHP services.

For services that work across traditional models of care delivery matrix management may be effective in providing more than one line of management and accountability, providing an alternative solution for services that do not 'fit' traditional hierarchical structures of management, though some AHP services that have tried this model advise against it.[6] At the same time AHPs need to influence the debate relating to their management arrangements. The model for the early 21st century should encompass interdisciplinary and interagency working, without losing the professional identity of the AHPs. Grouping AHPs together would pool AHP expertise and promote closer working of the professions, minimising 'silo' working, while providing a structure that could offer effective professional management.

AHPs need to be able to participate to enable them to be fully engaged in healthcare commissioning and the development of strategic capability. To support this, the role of the SHA AHP officer needs to be strengthened in the areas where this is deficient. There would be advantages to SHAs and Trusts in employing an AHP officer who would ensure that AHPs participate in the mainstream of health agendas at strategic levels. The posts, we would suggest, need to be fully funded and given sufficient time to enable the officers to establish effective networks with Trust AHPs – supporting them, representing them and engaging them – ensuring input from this diverse group, offering a wide range of expertise and experience.

Fragmentation of AHP services is a cause for concern for AHP managers as it adversely affects their ability to provide effective patient care and development of staff, therefore management structures are of the highest importance. The evidence of our research and that of others indicates that in order to have an effective and efficient AHP service, there must be several factors in place (*see* Box 4.1).

Box 4.1 Factors required for an effective and efficient AHP service

- A 'critical mass' of staff, with a range of expertise to be able to deliver comprehensive patient care and staff development in all specialties.
- A service that facilitates cross-organisational working and integrated care pathways.
- Access to AHP consultants and specialists who can develop clinical services and more junior staff expertise and provide a high standard of clinical care.
- Provision of equality of access for service users across the area.
- Inclusion of all core areas of the professional service, ensuring the provision of comprehensive staff CPD, education and training, staff rotations and student placements.

- Cross-service facilitation of support for assistant workforce.
- Optimum use of IM&T systems; uniform data collection interpretation, analysis and performance management.
- Service that enables the manager to have authority with accountability and responsibility rather than responsibility for providing professional advice only.
- Structure that links AHP services into senior committees within the Trust, with postholder accountability to a Director or CEO level post or hold director-level posts themselves.
- Service that is in a position to make full contribution to the objectives of the employing organisation.
- Uniformity of clinical governance management and procedures.
- Effective and efficient uses of all resources to achieve economies of scale and prevention of wasteful duplication.
- Structure that facilitates cross-boundary team working
- Flexibility to deploy staff to meet variable demand for specialist knowledge and skills.
- The ability to deploy staff into less 'popular' areas.
- The ability to provide cover quickly for staff sickness or other absence.
- Mechanisms to prevent isolation of staff members working in small teams
- Co-ordination of response to government priorities and policies including NICE and NSFs in the development, provision and monitoring of services.
- Co-ordination of input to commissioners.
- Uniformity of implementation of Payment by Results and the 'Choice' agenda.
- Reconfigured AHP services designed for the benefit of patient care rather than organisation 'whim'.

There are several possible structures which could fulfil these requirements. The challenge to senior officers and AHP managers is to improve service delivery and clinical outcomes for service users and ensure that the full potential and aspirations of the AHPs are fully harnessed. We have designed and developed an assessment tool for the evaluation of possible management structures and models of service provision. This assessment tool is presented in Chapter 5.

References

1 Mueller J, Neads P. Allied Health Organisational structure: massaging the organisation to facilitate outcomes. *New Zealand Journal of Physiotherapy*. 2005; **33**(2): 48–54.
2 Øvretveit J. *Therapy Services: organisation, management and autonomy*. Reading: Harwood Academic Publishers; 1992.
3 Jones R. *Management in Physiotherapy*. Oxford: Radcliffe Medical Press; 1991.
4 Lopopolo R. The effects of hospital restructuring on the role of physical therapists in the acute care setting. *Physical Therapy*. 1997; **77**(9): 918–32.
5 Boyce R. Hospital restructuring – the implications for allied health professions. *Australian Health Review*. 1991: **14**(92): 147–54.

6 Robinson M, Compton J. Decentralised management structures – the physiotherapy experience at John Hunter Hospital. *Australian Journal of Physiotherapy*. 1996; **42**: 317–20.
7 Packwood T, Keen J, Buxton M. *Hospitals in Transition: the resource management experiment*. Milton Keynes: Open University Press; 1991.
8 Department of Health. *Providing Therapists' Expertise in the New NHS: developing a strategic framework for good patient care*. Part 1. Brighton: Practices made Perfect; 1997.
9 Heysell R, Gainter JR, Kues IW, Jones AA, Lipstein SH. Decentralised management in a teaching hospital. *New England Journal of Medicine*. 1984; **310**: 1477–80.
10 Jones R. *Physiotherapy and its Management in the National Health Service Districts of England and Wales*. MPhil thesis. University of Kent; 1989.
11 Jones R. *An Investigation into the Development of a Computerised Information System for NHS Physiotherapy Services in England – An Action Research Study*. PhD thesis. University of Kent; 2000.
12 Berry M. *Management of the Therapy Professions in the National Health Service of the 1990s*. MBA thesis. University of Kent; 1994.
13 Jenkins F. *Management Arrangements for the Allied Health Professions within the National Health Service in England – A Research Study*. MA dissertation. Exeter University; 2005.
14 Department of Health. *Meeting the Challenge: a strategy for the allied health professions*. London: HMSO; 2000.
15 Department of Health. *The NHS Plan: a plan for investment, a plan for reform*. London: HMSO; 2000.
16 Connecting for Health; 2006. www.connectingforhealth.org.
17 Mintzberg, H, Quinn J, Voyer J. *The Strategy Process*. New Jersey: Prentice Hall; 1995.
18 Chilingerian J. Evaluating quality outcomes against best practice: a new frontier. In: Kimberley J, Minvielle E, editors. *The Quality Imperative*. Michigan: Imperial College Press; 2000.
19 Department of Health. *Creating a Patient-Led NHS: delivering the NHS Improvement Plan*. London: HMSO; 2005.
20 Britnell M. *Foundation Trusts – The Future and Beyond*. Proceedings of the IHM Conference, 2005 Manchester, UK.

Chapter 5

Introducing our assessment *Tool* for evaluating AHP management structures

Robert Jones and Fiona Jenkins

Introduction

The first four chapters of this book have demonstrated the many complexities of the NHS and that AHPs are essential service providers in primary, secondary and tertiary care. Management arrangements for the AHPs often lack consistency and clarity as they do not comfortably 'fit' organisational structures within trusts. In this chapter we present our assessment *Tool* (Table 5.2) for use in evaluating AHP management and organisational structures in the context of quality, effective, efficient and economical service provision. We believe that the proposed *Tool* is unique in that it can be used to evaluate a wide range of management functions of AHP services.

   The *Tool* has been constructed using evidence-based information from our combined research spanning two decades, which has provided a valuable and rich source of data on AHP managers' roles, responsibilities and duties, together with the views of postholders regarding the management and organisational structures in which they work. Our research has also included comprehensive literature reviews and investigation of organisational models internationally. The *Tool* has been developed primarily to assess AHP structures in England and the termin-ology used reflects the English NHS although it is designed to be transferable to a range of health systems worldwide; it has been reviewed by AHP colleagues in the UK and Ireland.

   The *Tool* assesses AHP management structures under 10 management *Domains* which were identified from our research. The 10 *Domains* are:

1 strategic management
2 clinical governance
3 human resource management
4 clinical/professional requirements
5 operational/service management
6 resource management
7 information management
8 education
9 commissioning
10 service improvement/modernisation.

The *Domains* are not listed in any particular priority order.

Application of the *Tool*

The *Tool* may be used in two ways. Firstly, the current AHP service is assessed using the scoring sheet. Each management *Domain* has several sub-domains or *Elements* which are scored individually using a 'traffic light' scoring mechanism. When all the *Elements* of the *Domain* have been traffic light scored, comments and conclusions are recorded. All 10 *Domains* are assessed in this way.

On completion of the scoring the results are analysed, enabling AHP managers to determine strengths and weaknesses of the current management and organisational arrangements, how structure impacts on this and importantly, how the existing management arrangements facilitate or impede the AHP services in providing high-quality, responsive patient care. This enables managers to determine which *Domains* of the service:

- function as near as possible to optimal levels (green traffic lights)
- function less satisfactorily (amber traffic lights)
- function unsatisfactorily (red traffic lights).

If there is an initiative within an organisation to review or change management structures, the AHP manager can use the *Tool* to score the 10 *Domains* and individual *Elements* to assess the likely impact on the service organisation and stakeholders. A comparison between the existing and proposed management structures would then be possible, enabling conclusions to be drawn and constructive dialogue to take place with senior trust managers and commissioners about the likely advantages and disadvantages of the proposed new arrangements.

Scoring system: assessment *Tool* for AHP management models

We have designed the *Tool* to assess strengths and weakness of different management models. It can be used to assess management arrangements already in place and proposals for new arrangements. The two management models (existing system and proposed new system) may then be compared.

The assessment *Tool* is constructed in tabular form using a separate box for each *Domain* (*see* Table 5.1, which illustrates a completed example assessment template for one *Domain*). Each *Domain* is numbered: for example, *Domain* 1 – Strategic Management, *Domain* 2 – Clinical Governance and so on. The *Elements* within each *Domain* are also numbered, with space for comments to be recorded if desired. A Green, Amber or Red score is allocated as appropriate and totalled at the end of each *Domain*. Following this there are text boxes for comments and conclusions about the *Domain*.

The assessment *Tool* is appropriate for evaluating both individual AHP services – unidisciplinary – and clusters of AHP services where these are managed as one large grouping. There are 10 management *Domains*, under which the *Elements* are listed. Not all *Elements* will apply to all services, and therefore these may be left unmarked. Some *Elements* apply to more than one *Domain*, for example, workforce planning which appears in more than one *Domain*.

Example

Domain 1 comprises 10 *Elements*. The traffic light scoring system is completed where:

- Red = No, unable to fulfil this function, unsatisfactory (<25%)
- Amber = Only partially able to fulfil this function
- Green = Yes, able to fulfil this function, satisfactory (>80%).

Comments are made in the element boxes, traffic light scores are totalled, then comments and an overall conclusion about the satisfactoriness or otherwise of the *Domain* are entered in the box at the end of the *Domain*.

We recommend that a separate assessment proforma is used to evaluate each possible or proposed management model.

Conclusion

Our overarching objective in developing this assessment *Tool* has been to ensure – as far as possible – that AHP management arrangements, structures and service organisation are focused on infrastructures that facilitate and support provision of the best possible outcomes for our patients, the service providers themselves and the organisations in which they work.

Change is constant in the NHS and it is essential that we contribute proactively to the process in order to improve services without compromising the legitimate goals of those providing the services, ensuring as best we can that any changes proposed are in the best interests of patient care, are successful and good value for money. There is no simple 'right' or 'one way' of configuring AHP services; however, it is intended that the assessment *Tool* will be helpful to those AHP managers and others to evaluate their current services or proposed restructuring and changes.

So often we hear of restructuring which takes place without proper consideration of the likely advantages and disadvantages, or put forward on the basis of 'politics' or 'ownership agendas' of particular organisations or managers. Sometimes, this takes place without proper consideration of how services might be structured to provide optimum high-quality clinical outcomes, appropriate care pathways, patient flows, development for staff, economies of scale, 'critical mass', elimination of duplication, excellent communication and networking and many others. The assessment *Tool* incorporates a 'big picture' overview, it is evidence based, informed by research and detailed studies of the available literature and examination of a wide range of models – some in place, and some theoretical.

There are approximately 170 000 registrants in the professions within the remit of the Health Professions Council in the UK and a large number of support staff in a wide variety of roles (*see* Chapter 1). This represents a very significant percentage of healthcare provision and use of resources. This workforce undertakes many millions of healthcare interventions and patient contacts every year. It is essential, therefore, that decisions about management arrangements, structures and organisation of these services are evaluated using a methodical approach. Our assessment *Tool* may be used to contribute to this process.

Table 5.1 Completed example template of assessment *Tool*

	Red	*Amber*	*Green*
1 Strategic management *Domain*			
Mark and comment on each element answering this question: Do the management arrangements enable effective:			
1.1 Contribution to Local Development Process for the whole service *Comments: Yes, fully engaged in LDP making recommendations for whole service.*			✓
1.2 Medium and long-term planning and service development for whole service (strategic plan for whole service for 1–3 years) *Comments: Have a plan for 2 years ahead, not 3 years.*		✓	
1.3 Contribution to the SHA workforce plan for the professional group(s) *Comments: No, not involved in input to workforce plan for my service, HR do the SHA return without my input.*	✓		
1.4 Medium- to long-term workforce planning for the whole service (for 1–3 years) *Comments: Yes I have a workforce plan developed within the service.*			✓
1.5 Non-fragmented service through effective strategic management of whole service. *Comments: Provide both acute and community services, staff managed as one group.*			✓
1.6 Clear lines of accountability for the whole service(s) (both management and professional accountability) *Comments: All staff have one management and professional line of accountability.*			✓
1.7 Management authority for the whole service(s) (full and equitable management authority) *Comments: Limited management authority in PCT, locality managers hold staffing and training budgets in several areas, which limits management authority.*		✓	
1.8 Management responsibility for the whole service(s) (full and equitable management responsibility) *Comments: Full management responsibility for Acute Trust staff, but not for all PCT staff.*		✓	
1.9 Initiation and management and monitoring of Service Level Agreements (where these are in place) *Comments: Do not have any SLAs in place but should have as provide services in other Trusts.*	✓		
1.10 Strategic development and partnership working with other organisations such as social services and education *Comments: Yes, have well-established senior level strategic mechanisms.*			✓
1.11 Initiation and management and monitoring of external contracts (where these are in place) *Comments: Yes, have contracts with care homes which I initiated and monitor.*			✓
1.12 Implementation of government policies and initiatives across the entire service(s) *Comments: Have authority to do this in only part of the service*		✓	
1.13 Comprehensive strategic overview for the profession(s), to be fully engaged at strategic level *Comments: Head of service not engaged at strategic level, only input is from band 7 clinician*	✓		
Traffic light totals	3	4	6

Overall domain conclusion:
Mostly positive, however, room to improve strategic workforce planning, develop SLAs and engage head of service.
PCT-based staff have less access to training funds as these are held by the locality managers and less flexibility with staff management as staff budgets held by PCT.

Table 5.2 Assessment of management structures: the assessment tool

Assessment criteria	Red	Amber	Green
1 Strategic management domain			
Mark and comment on each element answering this question: Do the management arrangements enable:			
1.1 Effective contribution to Local Development Planning process for whole service *Comments:*			
1.2 Medium and long-term planning and service development for whole service (strategic plan for whole service for 1–3 years) *Comments:*			
1.3 Contribution to the SHA workforce plan for the professional group(s) *Comments:*			
1.4 Medium- to long-term workforce planning for whole service (for 1–3 years) *Comments:*			
1.5 Non-fragmentation of the service through effective strategic management of whole service *Comments:*			
1.6 Clear lines of accountability for the whole service(s) (both management and professional accountability) *Comments:*			
1.7 Effective management authority for the whole service(s) (full and equitable management authority) *Comments:*			
1.8 Effective management responsibility for the whole service(s) (full and equitable management responsibility) *Comments:*			
1.9 Initiation and management and monitoring of Service Level Agreements (where these are in place) *Comments:*			
1.10 Strategic development and partnership working with other organisations such as social services and education *Comments:*			
1.11 Initiation and management and monitoring of external contracts (where these are in place) *Comments:*			
1.12 Implementation of government policies and initiatives across the whole service(s) *Comments:*			

Table 5.2 (*cont.*)

Assessment criteria	Red	Amber	Green
1.13 Strategic overview for the profession(s) to be comprehensive *Comments:*			
Traffic light totals			
Overall domain conclusion:			
2 Clinical governance domain			
Mark and comment on each element answering this question: Do the management arrangements enable:			
2.1 The provision of effective patient-centred services – including cross-boundary working to deliver care pathways and the involvement of service users in planning and service evaluation *Comments:*			
2.2 Effective implementation of evidence-based practice equally across whole service(s) *Comments:*			
2.3 Consistent management of research and development activity across whole service(s) *Comments:*			
2.4 Consistent management of clinical audit across whole service(s) *Comments:*			
2.5 Effective management of service risk across whole service(s) *Comments:*			
2.6 Effective management of health and safety across whole service(s) *Comments:*			
2.7 Management of equitable staff education and training across whole service(s) *Comments:*			
2.8 Management of efficient, equitable staffing and staff management across the whole service(s) *Comments:*			
2.9 Effective communication across whole service(s) *Comments:*			
2.10 Rapid and equitable management of and response to complaints across whole service(s) *Comments:*			
Traffic light totals			
Overall domain conclusion:			

Table 5.2 (*cont.*)

Assessment criteria	Red	Amber	Green
3 Human resource management			
Mark and comment on each element answering this question: Do the management arrangements enable:			
3.1 Effective staff recruitment to all grades and all specialties throughout the service(s) *Comments:*			
3.2 Career progression opportunities and succession planning across the entire service(s) *Comments:*			
3.3 Flexibility of staff deployment across the service(s) to cover absence, sickness, leave, etc. *Comments:*			
3.4 Flexible working arrangements such as provision of 7-day working *Comments:*			
3.5 Uniform application of grievance and disciplinary procedures across entire service(s) *Comments:*			
3.6 Consistent application of HR policies and procedures for all staff across entire service(s) *Comments:*			
3.7 Equitable and consistent application of Agenda for Change across the entire service(s) *Comments:*			
3.8 Equitable implementation of Improving Working Lives across entire service(s) *Comments:*			
3.9 Appropriate high level professional responsibility and authority to recruit and dismiss staff across the organisation *Comments:*			
3.10 Nationally required regulatory procedures (HPC) to be implemented and monitored across the whole service(s) *Comments:*			
3.11 Workforce planning for whole service(s) including appropriate skill mix and input to workforce commissioning procedures *Comments:*			
Traffic light totals			
Overall domain conclusion:			

Table 5.2 (*cont.*)

Assessment criteria	Red	Amber	Green
4 Clinical professional requirements			
Mark and comment on each element answering this question: Do the management arrangements enable:			
4.1 Appropriate high level clinical and professional leadership and consultancy across whole service(s) *Comments:*			
4.2 'Critical mass' of staff – a broad range of grades and specialisms to be in place across whole service(s) *Comments:*			
4.3 Effective non-fragmented service provision and good communication across organisations *Comments:*			
4.4 Professionally relevant and consistent development and implementation of Knowledge and Skills Framework profiles across service(s) *Comments:*			
4.5 Professionally relevant and consistent Personal Development Plans and CPD in place across entire service(s) *Comments:*			
4.6 A range of appropriate post-registration education to meet staff needs, with expertise in all clinical specialties across service *Comments:*			
4.7 Comprehensive in-service training and education to meet needs of all staff *Comments:*			
4.8 Effective management development and relevant professional mentoring across entire service(s) *Comments:*			
4.9 The management of career progression and succession planning on an equitable basis throughout the entire service(s) *Comments:*			
4.10 Effective leadership development across entire service(s) *Comments:*			
4.11 Appropriate professional supervision and support to be in place for all staff across service(s) *Comments:*			
4.12 Clinical supervision systems in place for staff *Comments:*			

Table **5.2** (*cont.*)

Assessment criteria	Red	Amber	Green
4.13 Appropriate supervision and support for newly qualified staff including staff rotations across specialties in all core areas across whole service(s) *Comments:*			
4.14 Undergraduate (student) clinical placements across all core areas *Comments:*			
4.15 Undergraduate clinical placements across specialist areas *Comments:*			
4.16 Effective implementation of evidence-based practice across entire service(s) *Comments:*			
4.17 Implementation, consistent use and monitoring of appropriate validated outcome measures across the entire service *Comments:*			
4.18 Design and implementation of protocols, procedures and guidelines (managerial and clinical) for the whole service *Comments:*			
4.19 Consistent implementation of national guidelines and policies across the entire service(s) *Comments:*			
4.20 Effective clinical and managerial engagement of appropriate staff in national, regional and local professional fora *Comments:*			
4.21 High-quality record-keeping systems, in line with legal and professional standards, throughout the entire service(s) *Comments:*			
Traffic light totals			
Overall domain conclusion:			
5 Operational/service management			
Mark and comment on each element answering this question: Do the management arrangements enable:			
5.1 Effective and efficient use of staff resources – use of time, skills and expertise in all areas across service(s) *Comments:*			
5.2 Effective day-to-day management for clinical staff in all areas of service(s) *Comments:*			

Table 5.2 (*cont.*)

Assessment criteria	Red	Amber	Green
5.3 Appropriate staff deployment in all areas across service(s) – to ensure right skills in the right place at the right time *Comments:*			
5.4 The elimination of unnecessary duplication of service provision, expertise and resource use *Comments:*			
5.5 Effective day-to-day management of clinical practice in all areas of service(s) *Comments:*			
5.6 Effective performance management and monitoring of clinical standards across whole service(s) *Comments:*			
5.7 Effective day-to-day management of clinical pathways and vertical integration across all areas of service(s) *Comments:*			
5.8 Continuity for service users between acute hospital and primary care services *Comments:*			
5.9 Effective networking across services/organisations to facilitate non-fragmented patient care *Comments:*			
5.10 Effective collaborative working between the service and other agencies such as social, education, voluntary and independent sector *Comments:*			
5.11 Ensure effective interdisciplinary working across organisation(s) *Comments:*			
Traffic light totals			
Overall domain conclusion:			
6 Management of resources			
Mark and comment on each element answering this question: Do the management arrangements enable:			
6.1 High-level professional input, accountability, responsibility and authority for budget management across entire service(s) *Comments:*			
6.2 High-level professional input to the budget-setting process for the entire service(s) *Comments:*			

Table 5.2 (*cont.*)

Assessment criteria	Red	Amber	Green
6.3 Active participation in financial planning and monitoring processes throughout the year for whole service(s) *Comments:*			
6.4 Achievement of economies of scale – economic use of resources (human and financial) throughout the entire service(s) *Comments:*			
6.5 Optimum use of facilities and equipment across entire service(s) *Comments:*			
6.6 Income generation projects including innovative use of NHS facilities across entire service(s) *Comments:*			
6.7 The most senior AHP manager input to the Payment by Results process to ensure consistent application across entire service(s) *Comments:*			
6.8 The most senior AHP manager input to the Practice-Based Commissioning process to ensure consistent application across entire service(s) *Comments:*			
6.9 Equitable management of AHP charitable trust funds across entire service(s) where these exist *Comments:*			
6.10 Involvement in capital project planning and management relevant to entire service(s) *Comments:*			
6.11 Effective mechanisms for procurement and shock control for entire service(s) *Comments:*			
6.12 Effective input to relevant tendering procedures to be in place *Comments:*			
Traffic light totals			
Overall domain conclusion:			
7 Information management			
Mark and comment on each element answering this question: Do the management arrangements enable:			
7.1 Effective management of clinical and managerial information throughout service(s) *Comments:*			
7.2 Uniformity of IM&T across service(s) *Comments:*			

Table 5.2 (*cont.*)

Assessment criteria	Red	Amber	Green
7.3 Proactive input in the development of uniform IM&T across the service(s) including implementation of Connecting for Health *Comments:*			
7.4 Consistent interpretation of information across entire service(s). *Comments:*			
7.5 Management of timely, accurate and relevant information across entire service(s) *Comments:*			
7.6 Consistent data analysis of activity and referral patterns across entire service(s) *Comments:*			
7.7 The application of uniform data sets and coding across the entire service(s) *Comments:*			
7.8 The provision of uniform quality information for patients across the entire service(s) *Comments:*			
7.9 Uniform record keeping across service(s) *Comments:*			
7.10 Uniform availability of timely and accurate staffing establishment information for entire service(s) *Comments:*			
7.11 Uniform availability of timely and accurate budget information for entire service(s) *Comments:*			
7.12 Uniform collection and analysis of data on activity and throughput across entire service(s) *Comments:*			
Traffic light totals			
Overall domain conclusion:			
8 Education and training			
Mark and comment on each element answering this question: Do the management arrangements enable:			
8.1 High-level professional input to the SHA in pre-registration education contract setting and monitoring for whole service(s) *Comments:*			
8.2 High-level professional input to post-registration education demand forecasting for entire service(s) *Comments:*			

Table **5.2** (*cont.*)

Assessment criteria	*Red*	*Amber*	*Green*
8.3 High-level professional input to pre-registration education demand forecasting based on service needs for entire service(s) *Comments:*			
8.4 Budget management for whole service postgraduate education and training to ensure equity and appropriate use of funding across service(s) *Comments:*			
8.5 The initiation and management of R&D projects across the entire service(s) *Comments:*			
8.6 Implementation of appropriate education and training programmes for support staff across entire service(s) *Comments:*			
8.7 Higher education institutions to have a clearly identified point of contact for the management of undergraduate placements for the entire service(s) *Comments:*			
8.8 Higher education institutions to have a clearly identified professional senior manager point of contact for input to course evaluation and development *Comments:*			
Traffic light totals			
Overall domain conclusion:			
9 Commissioning			
Mark and comment on each element answering this question: Do the management arrangements enable:			
9.1 Effective professional senior manager input to the commissioning process for the entire service(s) *Comments:*			
9.2 Effective involvement of service users in evaluation and development of service(s) *Comments:*			
9.3 Management of consistent Service Level Agreements across the entire service(s) *Comments:*			
9.4 Management of professionally relevant service specifications across the entire service(s) *Comments:*			
9.5 Management of professionally relevant service contracts with non-NHS purchasers, e.g. hospices or voluntary organisations *Comments:*			

Table 5.2 (*cont.*)

Assessment criteria	Red	Amber	Green
9.6 Active senior professional management engagement in Practice-Based Commissioning for entire service(s) *Comments:*			
9.7 Active senior professional management engagement in 'Choice' agenda for entire service(s) *Comments:*			
9.8 Active senior professional management engagement in Payment By Results procedures including costing tariff determination and activity for entire service(s) *Comments:*			
Traffic light totals			
Overall domain conclusion:			
10 Service improvement and modernisation			
Mark and comment on each element answering this question: Do the management arrangements enable:			
10.1 Management, leadership and implemention of innovative service improvements and modernisation across entire service(s) *Comments:*			
10.2 Development of consultant AHP posts *Comments:*			
10.3 Development of extended scope AHP posts *Comments:*			
10.4 Development of clinical specialist and advanced practitioner AHP posts *Comments:*			
10.5 Introduction of new ways of working across entire service(s), e.g. 7 day a week working *Comments:*			
10.6 Active engagement in multidisciplinary service developments, e.g. stroke service redesign for entire health community *Comments:*			
10.7 Skill mix review and service re-profiling across entire service(s) as appropriate *Comments:*			
10.8 Appropriate professional senior management input to the development of new types of posts and generic roles *Comments:*			

Table 5.2 (*cont.*)

Assessment criteria	*Red*	*Amber*	*Green*
10.9 Inclusion of staff of all grades to input to service improvement and innovation *Comments:*			
10.10 Patient/service user engagement in service improvement *Comments:*			
10.11 The introduction of expert patient programmes as appropriate throughout the entire service(s) *Comments:*			
10.12 Involvement of voluntary and public sector organisations in service improvement initiatives across entire service(s) *Comments:*			
Traffic light totals			
Overall domain conclusion:			

It is the intention of the authors to produce the assessment tool in CD format.

Chapter 6

Using organisation as a strategic resource to build identity and influence

Rosalie Boyce

Editors' note

Rosalie's chapter sets out an overview of AHP organisational structures and management arrangements in Australia. The editors strongly suggest that this powerfully challenges the traditional unidisciplinary approach to AHP structures and points the way to possible developments for AHPs in the UK and elsewhere at both local and national levels.

Introduction

The AHPs in Australia have been able to access greater managerial and political influence since the emergence of an 'allied health' movement in the late 1980s. The purpose of this chapter is to explain how the renaissance in allied health influence has occurred and to demonstrate how organisation can be used as a shared strategic resource by the professions to accomplish better outcomes than they could obtain from working separately.

Healthcare systems are complex entities. Smaller health professions with few resources at their disposal for engaging with large government bureaucracies face significant challenges. However, within that system complexity are pockets of ambiguity and opportunity that can be leveraged to produce the possibility of change. The specifics of national policy contexts will determine to some extent where the potential for generating change is most likely to lie and whether a bottom-up or top-down strategy of change can prevail. Within the cauldron of complexity that permeates healthcare systems how can smaller marginalised professions harness their resources to gain greater influence in policy and decision-making forums? How can AHPs make their voice, and the voice of the patients they serve, heard in the crowded market place of national and local level reforms that consistently sweep through the health system?

The Australian story has shifted from one of uneven change with early pockets of opportunism and enthusiasm coexisting with resistance and traditionalism in the late 1980s, to a situation of explicit recognition by the professions of the need to work together within the rubric of 'allied health' by the mid-1990s.[1,2] By the turn of the millennium clear markers of allied health infrastructure (leadership, organisational structures, artefacts and events) were evident. A new 'allied health' identity founded on the notion of 'allied to each other' rather than the more traditional 'allied to medicine' was also increasingly apparent.[3] Analysis of the changes that have occurred within the allied health rubric since the late 1980s suggests that public sector health agencies, particularly hospitals, have been the locus of innovation and the springboard to higher order change.[4,5]

The crucial change that occurred within Australian public hospitals in the 1990s that impacted on the patterning of interprofessional relations between allied health professions was organisational restructuring. The establishment of clinical directorate type sub-units and the internal decentralisation of financial management to patient care units typically headed by doctors was the single most important stimulus for change.[6] Restructuring, which was primarily aimed at medicine and nursing, raised the question of 'who should manage allied health?' for the first time. It is the events that unfolded from this question that hold the key to the cultural identity and evolving institutional power of allied health in Australia today.

Before examining the evolution of the allied health movement it is necessary to provide some contextual detail about the Australian healthcare system as an aid to understanding the conditions which both facilitated and limited the potential for change. This is followed by examining the nature of the allied health workforce in Australia so that international comparative analysis can be undertaken.

The chapter then proceeds by reviewing the specific organisational models that emerged for allied health and their utility at organisational and health system levels. New forms of institutional organisation (and the Director of Allied Health positions that have accompanied them) have been the major form of infrastructure to amplify the influence of allied health in Australia. Although we have identified organisational restructuring as a key event in the genesis of change, it was the development of the cultural identity of 'allied health' that accounts for the sustainability of change and the growth in higher order changes beyond organisational boundaries. The final sections of the chapter examine how cultural change was sustained and review the evidence of allied health infrastructure that consolidates and reinforces the identity of 'allied health'.

Healthcare 'down under': system and policy context

The Australian healthcare system is complex due to the geographical distances involved in the provision of health services, the burden of federal-state relations in the organisation and funding of healthcare and the mixed nature of public and private sector services.[7] Australia is a vast continent with a small dispersed population of approximately 20 million people concentrated around coastal regions. There are distinct and inequitable problems, with a growing disparity between the services available to, and the health profile of, citizens living in rural and remote areas compared to their urban counterparts. The health profile of indigenous Australians continues to parallel those of third world nations whilst non-indigenous people have amongst the best health status and longevity of the developed world.

The organisation and funding of the Australian healthcare system are divided between the federal government and the six states and two territories. Governments fund almost 70% of health expenditure with patient-funded contributions and private health insurers making up the bulk of the remainder. Almost half of all funding for public hospitals comes from the federal government but it is the states and territories that are responsible for regulating and operating the hospitals. The federal government also funds the Medicare (universal health insurance) system, which primarily provides rebates on fees incurred by visits to general practitioners and medical specialists. Australian AHPs do not have access to the Medicare system except for some special purpose-funded programmes. There is a vibrant private sector for AHPs and clients have access to rebates from private health insurance funds. Practitioners have independent practice rights and have enjoyed 30 years as first-contact practitioners.[8,9]

The Australian allied health workforce

Defining the composition of the allied health workforce is problematic but necessary. The Australian Bureau of Statistics gathers data on occupations for the national census (last performed in 2001) and has a category called 'Allied Health Worker' that consists of 12 occupational classifications (*see* Table 6.1).[10] Dissatisfaction with the Bureau's classification system precipitated an extensive national study in 2004 by SARRAH (Services for Rural & Remote Allied Health), a leading national allied health association. The SARRAH study sought to establish a definition of 'clinical allied health professions' from a 'common

Table 6.1 Membership of allied health workforce

Australian Bureau of Statistics (Census)*#	SARRAH National Study
Audiology	Audiology
Clinical psychology	Clinical psychology
Dietetics	Dietetics
Occupational therapy	Occupational therapy
Optometry	Optometry
Orthoptics	Orthoptics
Orthotics	Orthotics & prosthetics
Physiotherapy	Physiotherapy
Podiatry	Podiatry
Speech pathology	Speech pathology
Therapy aide	Pharmacy
	Radiography
	Social work

Source: Assembled from *Health and Community Services Labour Force 2001*,[10] Lowe and O'Kane[11]

* Also included a category called Health Professional (not elsewhere classified) – 2512 persons in the 2001 census.

Separate classifications sections for medical imaging workers, complementary therapies, other health workers (15 subclassifications including medical scientist, ambulance officer, indigenous health worker, anatomist or physiologist) and social work.

Note: dental, medical and nursing are considered as non-allied health in both databases.

Table 6.2 Relative growth of health professions 1996–2001

Classification	Growth
Allied health workers	+ 26.6%
Medical imaging workers	+ 25.0%
Medical workers	+ 12.6%
Nursing workers	+ 5.4%
All health occupations	+ 11.4%
Population growth	+ 6.0%

Source: Assembled from *Health and Community Services Labour Force 2001*[13]

usage perspective' following an extensive survey of key stakeholders in the healthcare system.[11] Table 6.1 shows the 13 professions that were 'generally agreed' as AHPs from the SARRAH study. A further 35 were 'variously included' depending on the context.

The largest occupation from the ABS allied health database was physiotherapy, with just over 10 000 persons in the category. The relative size of the national allied health workforce compared to nursing (registered nurse categories) and medicine can be quantified using the ABS data for each of the 13 professions in the SARRAH categories. The national allied health workforce is approximately the same as the medical workforce (~50 000) and close to one third of the registered nurse workforce. Growth rates in the allied health category (26.6%) have outstripped all other health professions and national population growth in the inter-census years of 1996–2001 (*see* Table 6.2). Further analysis of 10-year trends shows that the relative growth for allied health was stronger in the 1991–1996 period than the 1996–2001 period. Despite significant growth rates of the constituent professions in the allied health collective, eight of the 12 health professions on the national skills shortage register in 2004 were AHPs.[12]

Organisational restructuring and the development of 'allied health'

The 1990s heralded a period of sweeping change in the internal organisation of Australian hospitals around clinical directorates and patient-focused care models.[14,15] The organisational arrangements at Johns Hopkins Hospital in the USA and Guys Hospital in London were particularly influential on the decentralisation of financial and management responsibilities to internal clinical business units typically headed by medical clinicians.[16] The National Health Strategy, a leading thinktank guiding the change agenda in Australia, released an issues paper in 1993 which endorsed internal decentralisation and clinical unit models.[17] They advocated a shift away from profession-based organisational structures. However, their recommendations did not explicitly mention the AHPs. Prior to the restructuring of hospitals in the 1990s there was generally only one way of organising the AHPs in Australia: professional departments reporting to an overarching medical manager position (classic medical model). As the restructuring movement took hold two more general models emerged for allied health (division of allied health and the unit dispersement model).[1,18]

The *classic medical model* involved the head of each AHP reporting to a medical director or deputy. The medical director occupied a position on the executive of the hospital and represented medicine and the AHPs. The executive typically consisted of the CEO, the medical director, the nursing director and a finance/general services manager. During the 1990s hospitals were typically stand alone entities. Area and district models emerged more widely as part of restructuring in the 1990s.

The *division of allied health model* was similar to the concept of therapy directorates in the UK but was typically a larger entity in Australia covering up to 14 different professions in some hospitals. The key change was that the Director of Allied Health was required to have a background in one of the AHPs and in many cases a stand alone division reporting to the CEO was established. The separation of allied health from medicine organisationally (not clinically) and the ability to speak with a united voice through a single position were identified as powerful catalysts to enhanced organisational status. Further, the organisational arrangements set in place clear expectations that the 'tribalism' of individual allied health disciplines would have to be suppressed in order for the new division of allied health to be effective as a managerial entity.

The *unit dispersement model* is a form of programme management in which the positions of each profession are assigned to one of several clinical directorates or units. Profession management was no longer evident in this model although there was typically a nominal advisory professional leadership position for each allied health discipline. Management of the professions was dispersed throughout the organisation's clinical unit structure, usually under medical leadership. No cohesive capacity for a whole-of-organisation voice for either the disciplines or collective allied health was possible in the unit dispersement model because of the fragmentation of services throughout the organisation.

The response to the new models by AHPs was not uniform. The division of allied health was received cautiously in settings where tribalism was more pronounced. In some health agencies the professions enthusiastically welcomed or demanded the model and executive level representation. The professions and unions uniformly rejected the unit dispersement (programme management) approach and invoked industrial bans at the leadership site attempting to establish the first unit dispersement model for allied health. Opposition to programme management models was usually based on the loss of profession management and leadership and the inability to move professional resources to areas of need because of their grid-locking within particular clinical units.[4,18]

Evaluating allied health organisational models

Øvretveit's analysis[19] of professional power and the state in the United Kingdom was amongst the first to propose that local management approaches and organisational structure were unrecognised, but significant, sites of power for the allied health professions. In particular, he proposed 'profession management autonomy' as an important concept through which the impact of different organisational designs for the allied health professions could be evaluated. Øvretveit's work is a significant collection which makes the explicit link between institutional organisational design and workplace influence.[20–23]

The author's research on allied health management and organisation built on the important foundational work of Øvretveit and developments in the UK in particular. The goal was to address the lack of rigorous research assessing the utility of the different organisational models through a series of comparative longitudinal case studies using the classic medical model as the reference model.[24] Each of the three structural models discussed above was evaluated for the degree to which *profession management autonomy* was enhanced or diminished. Medical, nursing and management staff from clinical and executive levels in the organisation were included in the data collection so that the effect of the structural arrangements on the relationship with medicine and hospital managers in particular could also be assessed.

The concept of 'structural utility' was utilised to unbundle the competing claims about the different models and to provide a balance between profession-centred and organisation-centred perspectives. This was accomplished by assessing the alternative models in terms of the production of managerially valued processes and outcomes such that the structural model for allied health was defined, or not defined, as a source of 'organisational benefit'. For example, the division of allied health model was positively perceived for the greater ease of achieving collective change within a previously disparate set of disciplines.

Typical responses from executive level non-allied health management staff showed they valued the division of allied health approach because:

> Having a single clearly defined point (Director of Allied Health) enables (the organisation) to effectively manage both the risk and development aspects of professional matters. It also provides a clear point of contact for discussion on relevant policy and planning matters pertaining to that discipline.

Senior AHPs working in the *classic medical model* reported frustration at not being able to obtain a division of allied health model:

> We would be crazy if we did not stick together. Divided we fall, no, divided we will always be able to provide patient care, but we will not be able to impact on policy that will impact on patient care.

Medical clinicians leading clinical directorates in the *unit dispersement model* noted the lack of influence of allied health priorities:

> I do not think the advocacy for allied health has been strong enough by [leaders of the clinical units] because they have got a priority list which more often than not has allied health down the bottom.

The data supported and extended Øvretveit's original proposition about the importance of organisational structure and profession management autonomy to the organisational power and influence of the AHPs. The case studies demonstrated how structure and organisation can be appropriated as a device to advance the local workplace interests of the AHPs. The cases also demonstrated how structural organisation can act as a barrier to the achievement of those objectives.

The research on comparative models concluded that organisational designs such as the *allied health division model* were associated with greater profession management autonomy and organisational influence.[24] There was consistent evidence that an unambiguous allied health director position located in the top management strata of the hospital played a crucial role in communicating the importance of allied health priorities. The model appeared to offer greater opportunities for influence at the organisational level through the visibility of the Director of Allied Health role and its organisationally endorsed legitimacy of the 'voice' of allied health.

In contrast the *unit dispersement model* was more likely to be associated with a low level of profession management autonomy and organisational influence in the executive-level or strategic managerial domain.[24] Structural impediments associated with the fragmentation of professionals through the organisation limited their capacity to speak with a united voice at a discipline level or at a collective allied health level. The evidence suggested that the *unit dispersement model* offered advantages for influence by the allied health professions in the clinical domain and the managerial domain at the sub-unit level but not at the whole organisation level.

A key question arising from the research conclusions was: can structural features of the new models be integrated so that benefits accrue at both the organisational level and the clinical operational level? What type of organisational design could deliver such outcomes? In the following section this question is addressed.

Integrated decentralisation: the allied health internal matrix

The organisational design 'integrated decentralisation' was first proposed in Australia in 1996 as a cross-over design building on the benefits of the *division of allied health* model and the programme management-based *unit dispersement* approach.[25] The model, shown in Figure 6.1,[24] was synthesised to accommodate the interests of general management and the professions in preserving a whole, organisation focus (profession management autonomy) and the organisation's and clinicians' needs for a structural approach which was compatible with clinical directorate development and devolved budgeting frameworks. Thus the model was both 'integrated', that is, the profession members remain structurally consolidated preserving economies of scale and expertise, but they are also 'decentralised' to mirror the needs of the clinical sub-unit organisation and financing system.

As shown in Figure 6.1, the internal matrix consists of allied health departments and allied health teams. The allied health department is the traditional profession-managed entity, for example, a department of physiotherapy. The allied health team is designed to closely map the clinical directorate structure of the organisation, for example, a women's health programme. The allied health teams are assembled from the requisite professionals available from the allied health departments. In start-up models, the department heads also act as the formal co-ordinators of the teams. These roles perform important boundary spanning work in the organisation and in building the allied health culture in the teams. These dual roles are the point at which flexibility meets complexity in the model. The successful implementation and functionality of the model may

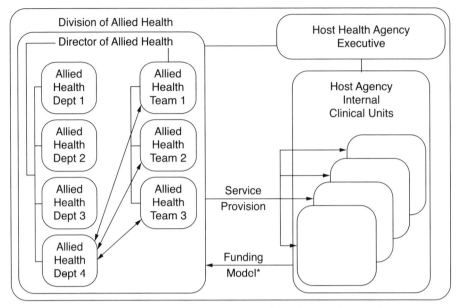

*Allocated budgets or zero-based budget model to fund packages of care

Boyce RA (1996) Researching the organisation of allied health professions: sorting fact from fantasy.
Proceedings of the 2nd National Health Services Conference, 14-15 November, Sydney, Australia.

Figure 6.1 Integrated decentralisation: a model for allied health services

require pre-existing experience with collective 'allied health' structures and a
high degree of interprofessional trust. The internal complexity of the *integrated
decentralisation* model is an overhead but it delivers flexibility dividends. Unlike
the *unit dispersement* model, professional resources can be moved between the
allied health teams to respond to unexpected service demands or staff absence
because they are not 'owned' or gridlocked by the clinical directorates. Integrated
decentralisation can operate with any internal funding system including service
agreements or internal trading. Additionally it can operate in stand alone
hospitals or complex geographical or interagency arrangements. Figure 6.1
shows an integrated decentralisation model as it would operate in a single agency.

The central organising principle of integrated decentralisation was to form a
matrix model for allied health services but to do it within the division of allied
health rather than at the level of the organisation. The key idea in the new model
was the recognition of two distinct governance arenas. The governance requirements for managing professionals and the governance principles for delivering
clinical services are different for the AHPs. The rationale has been explained as:

> The two arms of the internal matrix deal with different, but equally
> important, domains of activity in complex organisations such as public
> hospitals. The professional [departmental] structure leads service
> management and development of an organisational and clinical
> nature, whilst the 'allied health teams' dimension is involved in
> service delivery. Another way of thinking of this is that one arm
> performs strategic level work of a developmental and managerial

nature whilst the other arm has primarily an operational focus. The close integration of the two arms suggests that developmental initiatives could be efficiently operationalised into the service delivery domain.[4]

A small body of literature is available that has reported early experiences with models based on the integrated decentralisaton principle.[4,5,26] A national review of the organisational structure of allied health services in Australian public hospitals with more than 100 beds (n=107, 94% participation rate, 35 936 hospital beds) was conducted in 1999. The results showed that in the decade from the late 1980s when the classic medical model was virtually universal the division of allied health model had moved to rival it in dominance.[4] For example, the *classic medical* model had declined to 56 of the 107 sites, whilst the division of allied health model had risen to 37 sites with a further nine in a matrix variant. The *unit dispersement* model was *in situ* in six sites. The other trend in the data was that the division of allied health was the model of choice for the larger hospitals as it was *in situ* in 45% of the total beds in the sample. Growth in the division of allied health model has continued, particularly in sites implementing district or area-based health services involving several campuses. At the time of the national survey five sites had implemented or were planning to implement a variant of integrated decentralisation.

Leadership and allied health organisation

The emergence of distinct 'allied health' organisational forms legitimised by public sector health agencies, and therefore by government, provided a vehicle for the development of a cohort of new leaders. The task for these leaders was difficult in the early 1990s because of the lack of role models and on-going resistance in some sites from medical and nursing colleagues and allied health professionals. AHPs did not uniformly welcome models such as the division of allied health which sought to impose new accountability frameworks on service and financial activities. A further area of resistance was the concern that the individual profession identity would be submerged, genericised or diminished in such 'allied health' models.

A key point in understanding the contextual development of 'allied health' in Australia is that the leaders that emerged in the workplace restructuring exercises drove the changes that today appear as a rich allied health infrastructure. For example, there was no formal 'allied health' policy advisor *in situ* in federal, state or territory health department bureaucracies until much later in the mid-1990s. Western Australia will appoint their first Chief Health Professions Officer for allied health and health sciences in 2006. There has never been such a position in the federal health department. Additionally, there was no corollary changes observed in the university system that educates the AHPs: the individual disciplines remain intact as the dominant force. Small signs of change have emerged in the higher education sector with the first Professor of Allied Health title appearing in 2004.

A historical analysis of the emergence of the new 'allied health' in Australia supports the critical role played by attention to issues of organisation.[24] Øvretveit's extensive work showed how issues of workplace organisation impinged on influence and power in the United Kingdom. Similarly Hugman's research commented on the comparative position of the remedial therapies with nursing and social work in Britain.[27] Hugman drew a link between the 'semi-marginalised' status of the British remedial therapies and their neglect of the importance of organisational issues:

> It appears probable that the structural location of the remedial therapies is reflected in the inattention to organisational and structural issues in the writings of remedial therapists, and the relative ignoring of remedial therapists in academic studies of organisation, in comparison either to nursing or to social work.

From organisation to identity through cultural change

The early development in allied health influence was contained within distinct organisational settings following the organisational restructuring movement. By the mid-1900s there was clear evidence of the reach of allied health influence extending outside individual organisational settings in Australia. As early as 1992 there were calls by a cohort of hospital-based Directors of Allied Health for a new national allied health management organisation. As we shall see later in the chapter, it took a further 12 years for that aspiration to be fully achieved.

As was alluded to earlier, our further research identified cultural change as an important feature in sustaining the developments in allied health identity.[3] Professional identities such as physiotherapist, occupational therapist and dietitian were firmly established and the historical tyranny of tribalism amongst the professions ensured that encroachment by adjacent professions was dealt with defensively. How then did professionals in allied health disciplines and especially the leadership profession-manager segment of the professional bodies deal with the emerging new identity of allied health? Could an allied health identity be embraced without damaging the integrity of the discipline-based identity?

Longitudinal case studies of several high-functioning and low-functioning allied health groups in public sector hospitals were undertaken to explore and compare how the allied health collectives operated across professional boundaries to 'speak with one voice' and to examine how they perceived their identity.[5,24,28] From these studies, particularly the intensive PhD research, it was concluded that the 'new' allied health operated primarily in the management domain, not in the clinical domain, where the integrity of the individual discipline was highly prized.

Further study of the highest functioning division of allied health in the late 1990s showed they had adopted a quasi-corporate boardroom model of management in which the head of each discipline and the director were considered 'shareholders' in an asset called 'allied health'.[5,28] A culture of supported risk taking, explicit cross-professional leadership development and entrepreneurialism was evident. The quasi-shareholders were focused on asset growth and a somewhat unique external orientation open to exploiting opportunities that reached beyond the boundaries of their workplace organisation to international opportunities.[29] There are some parallels between the business culture and entrepreneurship observed here and the concept of 'business autonomy' developed by Øvretveit and his study of the British therapy professions in the 1990s.[22,23] In contrast, low-functioning allied health collectives relied on a 'stakeholder' orientation vested in protecting their asset (the discipline) from managerial or clinical encroachment.

The notion of the allied health professions speaking 'with one voice' was highly attractive to government. Change could be rolled out more efficiently if the individual professions were more cohesively organised at every level of inter-action with decision making and policy. On the other hand, the allied health disciplines had learnt within their organisations that they could get greater access to information, resources and status opportunities if they stopped divisive competition in favour of co-operation. Could the lessons learnt locally be applied regionally and nationally?

Regional and national initiatives in allied health organisation and influence

The 1990s were a period of rapid change in the Australian healthcare system. Casemix funding, clinical budgeting, evidence-based practice, internal market reforms, outsourcing, purchaser–provider models, best practice and clinical governance are just a few examples of the raft of policy initiatives that abounded. The leadership of high-functioning allied health collectives in public hospitals responded quickly to these opportunities. The first national allied health con-ference was staged in 1992 and 300 professionals from 19 disciplines partook of a managerially oriented conference programme in which no clinical or discipline-oriented papers or workshops were delivered. An outcome of the conference was the call for a national Allied Heath association. A national allied health manage-ment group consisting of influential Directors of Allied Health was formed to progress the association but it failed to reach implementation largely, but not exclusively, due to resistance from the individual profession associations.[3]

The efforts of the professions, unions and the growing body of allied health leaders secured funding from the federal government to support the activities of the National allied health Casemix Committee (NAHCC) and the National Allied Health Best Practice Consortium (NAHBPC) in the early and mid-1990s. Regional and state-based unfunded allied health councils and alliances emerged. The regional bodies typically consisted of a loose federation of allied health workplaces and directors whilst the state-based councils or alliances were structured around a federation of the state branches of the professional associations. Interestingly, there was no formal relationship between these state-based councils and alliances with each other or with the Health Professions Council of Australia (HPCA). The HPCA, formerly the Allied Health Professions Council of Australia (AHPCA), was structured as a federation of the national allied health profession associations. Despite attempts to expand its ambit of influence the 30 year old Council was largely marginalised from policy debate or influence on operational issues at the institutional and national level. Gardner and McCoppin's 1995 review of the influence of non-medical professions in Australia concluded that despite the Council being the obvious forum for influence, it had 'never realised its potential as a powerful, peak organisation in allied health'.[30]

Special issue allied health consortiums of a national character also appeared by the mid-1990s, for example, the NAHBPC mentioned earlier and the National Allied Health Benchmarking Consortium (NAHBC). Perhaps the most important national initiative was the work by AHPs to create SARRAH (Services for Rural and Remote Allied Health). SARRAH, now 10 years old and enjoying substantial federal government funding, was created from the dissatisfaction of rural and remote allied health directors and professionals with the urban-centric focus of the professional associations.

By the mid-1990s organisational models and the language of 'allied health' were becoming increasingly embedded in the Australian health system. For policy makers 'allied health' has assumed the status of a comfortable and efficient umbrella term for including the multiple health professions outside medicine and nursing. It became commonplace to hear politicians talk about the providers in the health system as 'doctors, nursing and allied health'. Political efforts by allied health increased in the mid- to late 1990s and principal allied health advisor positions were created in the bureaucracy of several state health departments. In 2004 the first joint health service/university professorial level appointment with the words 'allied health' in the title was announced, with a second following in 2006. A Research Centre for Allied Health Evidence also appeared about this time. By 2005 six biennial national allied health conferences had been held and the World Congress of Allied Health secured for Perth in 2008.

The increasing intensity of 'allied health' responses to government and institutional policy initiatives continued to reinforce the development of a unique sense of 'allied health'. The body of research work on the development of allied health in Australia suggested that the traditional notions of an allied health identity as 'allied to medicine' was shifting to one of 'allied to each other'. The PhD research discussed earlier concluded that 'under a set of certain conditions an 'allied health' subculture could emerge as a 'profession community' in its own right, augmenting the traditional exclusive individual discipline-based orientation. An intermediate phase, known as a 'community of professions', was also identified in some settings in which there was emergent collectivity and recognition of common interests. In the latter circumstance of a community of professions, 'allied health' would be constructed as the aggregate of the individual professions. Conversely, where allied health professionals are identified as a distinct subculture or profession community, 'allied health' is explained as greater than the sum of the individual parts, such that it can be described as the synergy that emerges from the collective routines and subculture development of the profession community.[18]

Future vision: a National Allied Health Alliance

Taking all the developments together it is clear that a diverse and diffuse allied health infrastructure has emerged in the last 15 years in Australia. Encouraged but not steered by government, it is primarily the outcome of the vision of the leadership cohort (urban and rural) that assembled after the first National Allied Health Conference in 1992. The one big-ticket item that remained unachieved was the call from professionals involved in workplace allied health management roles for a national organisation. The call for such an organisation was fuelled in part by the desire of the management group for formal recognition and in part because the rural and remote allied health group SARRAH had shown how effective a formal organisation was in leveraging influence. The call for a national allied health organisation was a call for a distinctly different entity to the federation of professions model such as the HPCA. The national allied health organisation concept was vested in the 'profession community' ethos discussed earlier, not a summative 'community of professions' model of which the HPCA was an example. The call for the association was made after each of the five national allied health conferences. After the fifth conference in 2003 a small group was charged by the conference with developing a model to take to a National Summit in 2004 with a view to launching it at the sixth national conference in 2005. The national association model had evolved from one for managers in 1992 to an inclusive national peak representative body by 2003.

On each prior occasion the call for a national body was based on a preference for the HPCA to alter its governance structure to accommodate the 'new' allied health. On each occasion the proposals failed to advance. In 2004 a National Allied Health Summit was organised by the post-2003 conference group progressing the new association concept. Fifty leading AHPs from a diverse range of settings (Directors of Allied Health from health agencies, government advisors, university educators and researchers, professional associations) gathered to once again try to progress the call for a new national peak body approach. The mood from the Summit was clear: a national peak allied health body would be launched in 2005 and the professional associations were welcome as full partners if they would participate in the process of renewal. The Summit participants voted 51:1 in support of a new body building on the strengths of existing entities. In February 2005 the new peak organisation, Allied Health Professions Australia (AHPA), was launched at the sixth National Allied Health Conference. The alliance draws together allied health interests from all sectors.

- Health.
- Higher education.
- Community services.
- Private and public sectors.
- Urban and rural.

The governance model is complex and evolving but it is focused on each sector of interest formalising its own organisation and linking into an overarching group that provides a member to the board of the AHPA. The creation of the alliance turned the 15-year vision into a reality.

Conclusions

The nature of 'allied health' is specific to each national milieu. A critical moment of opportunity in the development of allied health in Australia occurred as a result of organisational restructuring in health agencies in the late 1980s. New models of organisation for allied health were created which provided direct representation on executive-level decision-making forums for the first time without the filtering influence of medical supervision. Subsequently, these models, and the new professional identities and leadership competencies that emerged as a result of them, were leveraged to create further opportunities for influence at the state and national health system levels. The culmination of this change agenda was the formation in 2005 of a national allied health alliance drawing together allied health interests from all sectors into one organisation – Allied Health Professions Australia (AHPA).

The organisational models in which AHPs find themselves are important determinants of their influence within local, state and national health services.

Without contextually appropriate organisational models the AHP voice cannot be heard, nor incorporated within higher level decision-making forums. Underpinning the success of the new organisational models was the recognition by AHPs that significant influence could only be achieved by reducing the tyranny of tribalism and joining with other professions under the umbrella of 'allied health' to create a new identity. That identity has involved a shift from a self-concept of 'allied to medicine' to one of 'allied to each other and the communities we serve'.

The celebratory speech launching the AHPA in 2005 looked back on the 15-year journey and stated it was:

> Quite simply a tale of leadership and I see it as a reflection of allied health's coming of age reflecting a lot of accumulated experience and wisdom in the politics of health . . . By trusting each other enough and taking courage to achieve the right vision of becoming one body and one voice for Allied Health . . .

References

1 Boyce RA. Hospital restructuring – the implications for allied health professions. *Australian Health Review 1991;* **14**(2): 147–54.

2 Boyce RA. Internal market reforms of health care systems and the allied health professions: an international perspective. *International Journal of Health Planning and Management.* 1993; **8**: 201–17.

3 Boyce RA. Health sector reform and professional power, autonomy and culture: the case of the Australian allied health professions. In: Hugman R, Peelo M, Soothill K, editors. *Concepts of Care: developments in health and social welfare.* London: Arnold; 1997.

4 Boyce RA. Organisational governance systems in allied health services: a decade of change. *Australian Health Review. 2001;* **24**(1): 22–36.

5 Rowe PA, Boyce RA, Boyle MV *et al.* A comparative analysis of entrepreneurial approaches within public healthcare organisations. *Australian Journal of Public Administration.* 2004; **63**(2): 16–30.

6 Degeling P, Kennedy J, Hill M. Mediating the cultural boundaries between medicine, nursing and management – the central challenge in hospital reform. *Health Services Management Research.* 2001; **14**: 36–48.

7 Duckett S. *The Australian Health Care System.* 2nd ed. Oxford: Oxford University Press; 2004.

8 Galley P. Physiotherapists as first-contact practitioners – new challenges and responsibilities in Australia. *Physiotherapy* 1977; **63**: 246–8.

9 Wong WP, Galley P, Sheehan M. Changes in medical referrals to an outpatient physiotherapy department. *Physiotherapy* 1994; **40**(1): 9–14.

10 Australian Institute of Health and Welfare. *Health and Community Services Labour Force 2001, National Health Labour Force Series no. 27.* Canberra: Australian Institute of Health and Welfare. Report No.: AIHW Cat. no HWL 27 and ABS Cat. No 8936.0; 2003.

11 Lowe S, O'Kane A. *National Allied Health Workforce Report.* Canberra: National Rural & Remote Allied Health Advisory Service (NRRAHAS)/Services for Rural and Remote Allied Health (SARRAH); 2004.

12 Australian Health Ministers' Conference. Sydney: National Health Workforce Strategic Framework; 2004.

13 Australian Institute of Health and Welfare. *Health and Community Services Labour Force 2001, National Health Labour Force Series no. 27.* Canberra: Australian Institute of Health and Welfare. Report No.: AIHW Cat. no HWL 27 and ABS Cat. No 8936.0. 2003.

14 Braithwaite J. Organizational change, patient-focused care: an Australian perspective. *Health Services Management Research*. 1995; **8**(3): 172–85.
15 Braithwaite J, Westbrook M. Rethinking clinical organisational structures: an attitude survey of doctors, nurses and allied health staff in clinical directorates. *Journal of Health Services Research and Policy*. 2005; **10**(1): 10–17.
16 Boyce RA. *The Organisational Design of Hospitals – A Critical Review. A Report on the 1992 Australian College of Health Service Executives Overseas Study Award*. North Ryde, NSW: Australian College of Health Service Executives; 1993.
17 National Health Strategy Unit. *Health That Works: reform and best practice in the Australian health industry*. Melbourne: National Health Strategy Unit; 1993.
18 Boyce RA. The allied health professions in transition. In: Clinton M, editor. *Management in the Australian Health Care Industry*. 3rd ed. Frenchs Forest, NSW: Pearson Education Australia; 2004.
19 Øvretveit JA. *Professional Power and the State: a study of five professions in state welfare agencies in the UK*. PhD dissertation. Brunel University, United Kingdom; 1988.
20 Øvretveit JA. Future organisation of therapy services. *Health Service Management*. 1991; **87**: 78–80.
21 Øvretveit JA. *Therapy Services: organisation, management and autonomy*. Reading: Harwood Academic Publishers; 1992.
22 Øvretveit JA. Issues in contracting occupational therapy services. *British Journal of Occupational Therapy*. 1994; **57**(8): 315–18.
23 Øvretveit JA. Changes in profession-management, autonomy and accountability in physiotherapy. *Physiotherapy*. 1994; **80**: 605–8.
24 Boyce RA. *The Organisation of Allied Health Professions in Australian General Hospitals*. PhD dissertation, Queensland University of Technology, Brisbane; 1996.
25 Boyce RA. Researching the organisation of allied health professions: sorting fact from fiction. Proceedings of the 2nd National Allied Health Conference, 15–16 November 1996; Sydney, Australia.
26 Law D, Boyce RA. Beyond organisational design: moving from structure to service enhancement. *Australian Health Review*. 2003; **26**(1): 161–71.
27 Hugman R. *Power in Caring Professions*. Basingstoke: Macmillan; 1991.
28 Rowe PA, Boyce RA, Boyle MV. Case study methodology: modes of organising at two health services organizations. *Contemporary Nurse*. 2002; **13**(1): 83–93.
29 Boyce RA, Shepherd N. Entrepreneurship as a dimension of professional culture. Proceedings of the Annual Conference of the Australian Sociological Association, 6–8 December; Adelaide, Australia; 2000.
30 Gardner H, McCoppin B. Struggle for survival by health therapists, nurses and medical scientists. In: Gardner H, McCoppin B, editors. *The Politics of Health: the Australian experience*. Melbourne: Churchill Livingstone; 1995.

Chapter 7

Leadership in the Allied Health Professions

Christina Pond

Introduction

Traditionally leadership in the NHS has been perceived as hierarchical, defined by position and job title, but leadership to deliver a redesigned health service is no longer about an individual's position or authority in an organisational structure, but is instead a way of thinking and a way of behaving regardless of position or seniority.

With the agenda for modernisation, leadership in the NHS is now about effecting change and enabling others to think and behave differently in order to bring about positive improvements in the experience of patients and service users, through redesigning the current systems of care that are offered.

Leadership activity may occur anywhere on a continuum from small actions that are hardly noticed except by those immediately involved, to significant acts which affect many people; however, an action may be no less an act of leadership for its being applied on a small scale. This understanding is central to the concept of developing leadership at all levels in the NHS and in clinicians and non-clinicians alike, the challenge is in encouraging each individual to recognise when and where they can make a leadership contribution.

Equally important in this is the understanding that the efficacy and impact of that leadership contribution exist within the relationships between people working together in a system, so that we move beyond the emphasis on leaders as individuals to the concept of leadership as a social process characterised by relevant and influential action where such action is not necessarily associated with formal structures or positions of authority.

This chapter offers a brief overview of leadership theory, considers the current context for leadership in the NHS, examines the nature of current and future leadership roles and describes the work that was undertaken by the former NHS Leadership Centre to support the development of AHP/HCS leadership at all levels in the service.

The leadership concept: a brief history

As leadership is essentially a personal process, a relationship between the leaders and those they work with, there are differing views on what constitutes effective leadership and how it can best be developed and promoted. Over the years, theories of leadership have each in their time become fashionable, shaping our thinking and determining how we attempt to select and grow our leaders.

Thinking and theorising about leadership have their roots in the work of Socrates and Xenophon. Socrates taught that professional or technical competence should be a prerequisite for holding a leadership position.

This reflects the importance of the authority of knowledge, one of the three main forms of authority, the others being the authority of position or rank and the authority of personality.

Xenophon, however, demonstrated that the authority of knowledge alone was not sufficient to be acknowledged as a leader and that personal qualities also play a part. In describing this, Xenophon implied that some degree of leadership potential had to be present in the first place.

Thus began an ongoing debate on whether leaders are born or made and the attempt to answer this question or argue for a particular position in the debate can be clearly seen in the leadership research and theories of this century.

Modern studies of leadership began with trait theories in the 1920s, which argued that successful leaders possessed certain inherent qualities, which were present and natural to them and could be identified. The trait theory approach to leadership, in essence, is based on the study of successful leaders, and the attempt to identify a pattern of individual characteristics and traits associated with successful leadership, i.e. a personality-based approach.

Researchers often demonstrated differences of opinion in what these qualities were. However, the concept of the existence of predetermined leadership qualities being inherent, as exemplified in this approach, often resulted in an emphasis on selection for leadership rather than development for leadership.

Subsequent theories focused to a much greater degree on the behaviours and styles of leaders with attempts to identify a 'best' style. In the 1950s and 1960s, much of the leadership research and thinking focused on the impact and effectiveness of sets of leadership behaviours which were categorised into styles or types and deployed to suit particular situations. This approach was underpinned by a belief that there was a 'best' type but evidence demonstrated that there were occasions when success was still achieved despite the application of less desirable styles of leadership behaviours.

The limitation therefore of these situational theories led to the application of contingency theory to leadership. Hersey and Blanchard[1] drawing on the earlier work of Fiedler postulated that it was not the leadership style *per se* which led to effective leadership but the ability of the leader to adapt their style to the needs of the followers. Much research has subsequently explored the relationship between leaders and those they lead.

The idea of balancing the needs of the followers with the situation or task in hand was further developed by John Adair[2] in his functional model in which he defines three variables which bring together the characteristics of the leader with the needs of the other members of the team and the situation or context in which they are working.

Stogdill and Bass[3] developed a model of leadership which identified different sets of behaviours and characteristics required in situations of organisational change and organisational stability. They labelled these as 'transformational' and 'transactional' leadership respectively. This work has been influential in building an understanding of leadership in a changing environment.

Transactional leadership was seen as encouraging performance by making rewards contingent on delivery and only intervening actively when performance did not meet expectations. In contrast, transformational leadership was driven by a genuine concern for the individual needs of followers with regard to achievement and an emphasis on inspiring, encouraging and supporting others.

Transformational leadership then is characterised by ability to:

- inspire and align others in a common purpose
- encourage others to challenge the status quo
- release creativity and support innovation
- a genuine concern for an individual's feeling, aspirations and development.

Alimo-Metcalfe and colleagues,[4] researching leadership in the UK public sector, have proposed modifications to this transformational leadership model to align it with the culture of British organisations such as the NHS.

They describe this new model as being:

> not based on heroism but on enabling others to lead themselves, not about being an extraordinary person but being an ordinary and humble one – or at least very open, accessible and transparent.

They go on to describe the model as having a constant theme of team working and 'consistently echoing the ability to see the world through the eyes of others'.

This theme of leaders working with and through others is developed by a number of writers. Badaracco[5] refers to staff working behind the scenes as 'quiet leaders' claiming that 'quiet leadership (driven by people behind the scenes) is practical, effective and sustainable'. This idea of 'quiet' or 'behind the scenes leadership' is also evidenced in the work of Jim Collins[6] who, in a study of successful leaders, identified the two common characteristics of the most successful as humility – being self-effacing and with an absence of arrogance – and will – persistence in the pursuit of goals and implementation of required actions which he summed up as 'quiet leadership dedicated to building the company rather than individual glory'.

These leadership qualities are also central in the concept of the leader as servant, which can be traced back to Taoist philosophy. Servant leadership emphasises mutual service in society, reinforcing the concept of leadership as a function not a position or rank and describes the leader as the person who supports or facilitates the endeavours of others, leading from 'behind'.

Greenleaf[7] describes servant leaders as having three key skills, which are:

- listening deeply
- building creative consensus
- honouring the paradox.

In essence, servant leaders are able to work with difference and tolerate ambiguity and complexity in a way that allows them to work in partnership with others, on an equal footing, whilst still being able to operate in formal structures and hierarchies.

Current theories, only some of which are represented here, of what constitute effective leadership are abundant and, though the terminology may differ, share a common core which stresses the importance of personal qualities and behaviours in conjunction with the application of specific skills demanded by the context for leadership to be effective.

However, any understanding of effective leadership and how we develop it must be informed by an appreciation of the importance of emotional intelligence.

Leadership and emotional intelligence

The concept of emotional intelligence and its relationship to effective leadership has contributed considerably to the theory and practice of leadership and leadership development. Characteristics such as self-awareness, emotional resilience, interpersonal sensitivity, conscientiousness and integrity have been identified as some of the key components in effective leadership.

Daniel Goleman's[8] work on Emotional Intelligence has been taken up by many people. Fundamentally, his theory states that:

> Leadership certainly involves conventional intelligence (IQ); without it a leader will always struggle. However, the most recent research on what makes for outstanding leaders demonstrates without a doubt that they also have a high EQ (emotional intelligence). One study compared average senior managers with star performers. Nearly 90% of the difference was due to EQ factors. In addition, EQ correlated with 'hard edged' performance factors.

Goleman identifies five aspects of emotional intelligence.

- Self-awareness: 'knowing thyself', having a deep understanding of yourself.
- Self-regulation: being able to control your impulses; to know how you feel about something but to be able not to act it out semiconsciously or unconsciously.
- Motivation: self-motivation to achieve, from an inner sense of commitment and engagement with the work/task/people.
- Empathy: ability to put yourself in the shoes of the other person, being sensitive and thoughtful about the feelings of others.
- Social skills: friendliness with a purpose; social grace, confidence and interest in others.

Goleman describes Emotional Intelligence as our potential for learning the practical skills (competencies) based on the five aspects. Emotional competencies show how much of that potential we have translated into on-the-job skills.

The ability to understand and motivate others, an essential quality of leadership, begins with the ability to know and manage oneself. Self-awareness is an essential underpinning of effective leadership behaviours and many of our current diagnostic tools for assessing leadership style are designed to identify the individual's strengths and weaknesses in these areas and their impact on others.

Emotional Intelligence, whilst having a genetic component, can be learned and developed and also increases with age, but developing one's EI takes time and commitment and will not happen without a genuine desire to change and concerted effort on the part of the individual.

Emotional Intelligence is located in the neurotransmitters of the brain's limbic system which govern feelings, impulses and drives. Research shows that the limbic system learns best through motivation, extended practice and feedback; any development opportunity for Emotional Intelligence, therefore, needs to apply these methods of learning to the situation.

Leaders and followers

Our understanding of leadership needs also to explore the nature of the leadership process.

Effective leadership does not exist in a vacuum, but as a function of the relationship between people working together in a system. As such it is a social process with leadership characterised by relevant and influential action where such action is not necessarily associated with formal structures or positions of authority.

Considerable research has been conducted into the relationship between leaders and those they lead. 'Followership' is frequently discussed as the other side of the coin to leadership, the label of follower often suggesting a subordinate or passive relationship, but we know that the dynamic nature of the leadership process is determined by the active contribution of all parties.

Bennis[9] suggests that the capacities of effective leaders are very similar to the qualities of effective followers, and talks about 'leaders of leaders' rather than leaders of followers.

Heifetz[10] describes the most interesting leadership as operating:

> without anyone experiencing anything remotely similar to the experience of following.

Such leadership instead mobilises people to become active participants and partners.

Goffee and Jones[11] have identified three emotional responses that are necessary for the leadership relationship to be effective, suggesting that these responses need to be satisfied if individuals are to be prepared to work with and for the person in the leadership role.

- **Significance:** This relates to the human drive to be valued and is evidenced in leadership behaviours that demonstrate that the personal contribution of individuals, however small, makes a difference and is valued, what Warren Bennis describes as the 'power of appreciation', the leaders who says thank you and well done.
- **Community:** A sense of community occurs when individuals feel a unity of purpose around work, a shared drive to deliver on objectives, the co-creation of a vision. Effective leaders are able to engender this feeling of community.
- **Engagement:** For individuals to feel excitement and challenge in their work, leaders need to 'engage the heart' of those individuals and motivate them in a way that liberates their creativity and contribution.

John Adair[12] states that:

> Leadership comes into its own when people are free and equal, leaders create not followers but partners in a common enterprise.

The concept, then, of individuals as partners in the leadership relationship, with each making their contribution to the process, resonates strongly with current models of effective leadership described earlier.

This concept also leads us to recognise the importance of the team as well as the individual, and the need to understand how the leadership role may be shared amongst team members, each taking the responsibility of leadership at different times, dependent upon the task and context. In this way, leadership responsibility becomes distributed and strengthened.

Leadership and management

In seeking to understand what constitutes effective leadership it is important to understand how leadership differs from management since the concepts of leadership and management are frequently confused and often misunderstood.

This is not to say that leaders do not need management skills, and managers may need to be effective leaders, but there are fundamental differences. We commonly refer to 'leaders' in organisations when we are actually describing those in positions of managerial authority. Many individuals may be skilled at gaining authority but this is not synonymous with leadership. One can consider management to form the basis for institutionally varied, but broadly consistent professional practices: management is the systematic, contractual execution of formally determined organisational rules, whilst leadership takes place in the space left undefined by managerial constraints, but confusion often arises because the same people do both.

Leadership action is usually non-routine and can be thought of as occurring on a spectrum that ranges from small actions, which may be hardly noticed except by those involved, to significant actions requiring considerable skill and courage and affecting many people. Such action is not necessarily associated with positional authority, and may not always be in strict accordance with organisational rules or processes. What is particularly important to note is that an action may be no less an act of leadership for its being applied on a small scale and we can judge such action through the tests of effectiveness in furthering goals and appropriateness in context.

Kotter[13] describes management as being about coping with complexity whilst leadership, by contrast, is about coping with change. These two different functions, coping with complexity and coping with change, define the key activities of leadership and management. He describes the different ways in which managers and leaders function in order to do this, with managers planning, organising structure and resources, controlling and problem solving in contrast to leaders who set a direction, align and facilitate, motivate and inspire.

Importantly these are distinctive but complementary systems of action. Leadership complements management but does not replace it. As the rate of change increases, however, and this is certainly true in the health service, leadership becomes a growing part of managerial work, resulting in a single individual being called upon to perform both roles and develop the skills of both.

This is often a difficult tension to manage particularly in achieving the balance between control of outcome through process and achievement of outcome through motivation and inspiration. This dilemma is perhaps best resolved in the degree to which control can be handed over or delegated within the system.

Each system of action involves deciding what needs to be done and accomplishing this through others, by creating networks of people and relationships that can achieve this. Hence the skills set common to both leaders and managers includes the ability to coach and develop others, to create an enabling climate and finally to provide a role model for others of the desired organisational values and behaviours.

Similarly, Adair[12] observes that the nature of management has shifted perceptibly and irreversibly in the direction of leadership and that managing change needs to be done effectively at both strategic and operational levels. Common therefore to the role of leader and manager is the skill to manage relationships, recognising both mutual dependence and connectivity. Developing and maintaining successful relationships will be characterised by mutual expectations, a flow of information, reliability and honesty.

It is apparent then that management and leadership roles are both becoming increasingly more complex and, whilst still distinct one from another, are at the same time finding areas of commonality in the skills set required to discharge both roles. Whilst leaders continue to encourage and enable change the role of managers is to promote and encourage consistency and stability. In Kotter's[13] terms, only organisations that 'embrace both sides of the contradiction can thrive in turbulent times'.

Leadership development

There is considerable debate about whether or not leadership can be taught. What is apparent, however, is that individuals and teams can be supported to identify, understand and develop their leadership skills, to learn to lead more effectively. Learning rather than teaching also implies the more active involvement of the individual in a process, which gives rise to behavioural change, and allows for a variety of different learning styles to be accommodated. Development of leadership ability is an ongoing process and, as with other skills, needs to be identified, planned, practised and supported.

Development starts with a robust diagnosis of what needs to be developed and an understanding of the types of development available to support that learning, which may not be through taught programmes but through a variety of other methods such as participation in action learning sets, work-based learning, shadowing or mentoring.

A variety of diagnostic tools are available to allow individuals both to self-assess their leadership abilities and to involve others in that assessment through 360° appraisal mechanisms which are valuable in offering insight into the way behaviour is perceived by others. In response to the development agenda, the NHS Leadership Centre developed a framework that provides a common language and a consistent approach for bringing behavioural qualities into play in all aspects of leadership development.

The framework supports the development of leaders in further developing capacity to:

• ensure that patients and carers are at the very heart of the health service and the wider health and social care context

Figure 7.1 The model

- manage the balance between strategy and delivery and achieve the transformation of services
- communicate the vision and take people in the service with them.

The model (*see* Figure 7.1) defines the standards for leadership, which provide benchmarks against which leaders can assess themselves and their teams and identify the means for developing greater and more effective capacity.

The NHS Leadership Qualities Framework describes the key characteristics, attitudes and behaviours to which leaders in the NHS should aspire.

It has been tested within the NHS and validated in the context of *The NHS Plan* and *Shifting the Balance of Power*.

There are 15 qualities within the framework arranged in three clusters.

Personal qualities

Personal qualities and values are at the core of the framework. The scale and complexity of the change agenda facing leaders in the NHS mean that they need to draw deeply upon their personal qualities to see them through the demands of the job.

Setting direction

Outstanding leaders set a vision for the future, drawing on their understanding of the organisation(s) in which they work, and their political awareness of the health and social care context. This, combined with action orientation and intellectual flexibility, allows them to move between the big picture nationally and local operational detail. Coupled with a drive for results, this orientation towards seizing the future is key in inspiring and motivating others to work with them.

Delivering the service

High-performing leaders work across the organisation as well as the wider health and social care community to make things happen, to deliver service results. They use a range of styles that challenge traditional, organisational and professional boundaries and ways of working, and emphasise empowerment and partnership. Empowering others and collaborative working are essential in leaders who place the needs of patients and carers at the heart of delivery.

The framework is supported by a 360° assessment tool in this series (see *Developing the Allied Health Professional*, Chapter 8). This is derived from the qualities and can be used by both individuals and organisations to establish capacity and capability.

The framework can also be used for:

- personal development
- board development
- leadership profiling for recruitment and selection
- career mapping
- succession planning
- connecting leadership capability and performance management.

The framework is now also being used to describe learning outcomes for a range of national and local leadership development opportunities.

Further information on the model can be accessed via the website at www.NHSLeadershipQualities.nhs.uk.

Once assessed, leadership skills can be developed through a range of different mechanisms, individually or in teams. Development need not only be through exposure to programmes but also through accessing other opportunities, which allow individuals to practise their leadership skills, reflect on their impact and share their learning and experiences.

Leadership in the NHS

Leadership responsibility needs to be exercised at three key levels within the NHS – individual, team and system – and whilst at each level the skills demanded may vary, the central core of leadership values and behaviours must nevertheless remain constant and will inform the application of those skills at any given time.

The essential personal qualities of integrity, honesty and a genuine care and concern for others are the 'bedrock' of effective leadership behaviour and are, one could argue, the elements of leadership that have to be already present in order to underpin the leadership skills set that can then be developed; that is to say that leaders are both 'born' and 'made'.

The argument for effective leadership behaviour being a mix of inherent qualities and acquired skills is supported by much of the recent leadership theory and effective leadership is very aptly described by Goffee and Jones[11] as 'being yourself with skill'. Central to the process of leadership development, however, is the degree of individual self-awareness which can in itself be developed and matures over time.

In today's NHS the skills set demanded of leaders has become increasingly more complex.

In recent years, we have seen considerable structural change coupled with national approaches to improving standards and redefined relationships with patients and the public, all of which are resulting in a major cultural shift and a fundamental change in the way the system operates.

Increasingly we require leadership that can function across inter- and intra-organisational boundaries and build alignment and networks to effect change. Such skills include not just effective strategic influencing, negotiation and high degrees of political astuteness but also an ability to work collaboratively and build partnerships with those who provide and those who use the services.

Effective leadership must challenge, and demonstrate itself to be open to challenge in order to:

- ensure that patients and carers are at the heart of the health service and the wider health and social care context
- manage the balance between strategy and delivery and achieve the trans-formation of services
- co-create and communicate a vision that provides a shared and owned direction of change.

Leading for improvement

What then is the role of leadership in supporting the challenging agenda for service improvement and redesign in the NHS?

Partnership and ambition are the key ingredients of service transformation and have characterised the approach that successful health and social care commu-nities have adopted in achieving transformational change.

Leaders and partnership

Increasingly leaders are required to lead across whole systems where the oper-ating methodology is one of partnership working. We have seen the emergence of many such examples in healthcare both explicitly through structural reformation such as care trusts and children's trusts and implicitly through a recognition that care systems can only be improved by adopting a collaborative methodology.

However, the current, and indeed growing, complexity of the environment in which leaders are required to operate does not necessarily give clarity to the meaning of partnership working or what constitutes success.

Building partnerships

Partnerships or partnership working can be defined as a context where two or more organisations or organisational members work together as a way of achieving better outcomes.

A number of benefits can accrue from successful partnership working.

- Faster results can be achieved through maximising synergy.
- Partnerships can adapt readily to changing circumstance.
- Risk can be shared or spread.

- Gains can potentially be made in the overall efficiency and effectiveness of the system supported by the partnership model to improve the 'bottom line' or, in health terms, the patient outcome.
- Organisations may bond in areas of mutual interest.

Ultimately, the added benefit of partnership is that the total value is, or can be, greater than the sum of the parts. Building successful partnerships requires a number of elements to come together beginning with a recognition by all members of the value of partnership working in terms of both process and outcome. It is essential for the partnership to identify a shared vision and to create shared areas of activity by creating opportunities for staff to work together. Members of the partnership and particularly those leading in this context will essentially have to model collaborative behaviour. Already, then, in establishing and building the partnership we see the classic leadership skills of co-creating a vision and role modelling desired behaviours coming to the fore.

The concept of challenge is also central to successful partnership such that all participants need to challenge assumptions and existing working models if they do not contribute to the agreed outcomes for the partnership. Developing a collaborative mind set requires in the first instance an understanding, not just of the benefits and perceived disbenefits of partnership working but also a genuine appreciation of what each member of the partnership may be 'giving up' to work in this way. The agreement of objectives and process and the decision-making framework and clarity around parameters for monitoring and evaluation are essential elements in the infrastructure of successful partnerships.

Communities who were engaged in the former Modernisation Agency's Pursuing Perfection programme have achieved system level transformations that have been shown to be dependent on both those with positional authority transforming themselves and the way they work and on leadership being distributed throughout the system such that everyone is empowered to effect change and lead improvement through partnership working.

The experiences of the Pursuing Perfection sites have demonstrated a number of behaviours, which underpin the creation of leaders at every level of the system, and crucially leadership that transcends traditional boundaries to construct effective partnerships for change.

These include:

1 the awareness to transform oneself and act as a role model for others
2 an understanding of cultural patterns and systems which impact on change
3 a desire to build capability through development and learning
4 an ability to work across boundaries and build collaboration
5 the understanding to connect desired change with values and beliefs
6 a willingness to nurture change agents to create a critical mass and energy for change.

Effective leadership for partnership working requires the leader(s) not just to demonstrate ownership and support for the aims of the partnership but also an ability to take a wider view of where the partnership sits within the wider organisational system.

This will ensure that the partnership itself does not create new barriers or a sense of exclusivity.

Different partnerships may be created for different issues and the leader(s) need to offer clarity about both the composition and lifespan of the partnership.

AHPs as leaders

It is increasingly apparent that AHP and HCS professionals, who are often involved throughout many stages of the care pathway, are ideally and uniquely placed, therefore, to challenge and change the structural barriers that may exist and impact negatively on the patient's experience of care.

These professions often work at the patient/carer interface, retaining clinical involvement at senior levels whilst also fulfilling management responsibilities and are therefore well placed to ensure a patient focus'.

Such roles often combine elements of both operational and strategic leadership.

In addition, AHP and HCS staff by the very nature of their work operate in teams and within multiprofessional and multiagency settings, and can and do operate effectively across boundaries. Staff in these professions therefore have the potential to make a leadership contribution at all three levels: individual, team and system.

The AHP and HCS leadership focus was initiated by the launch of two key publications – *Meeting the Challenge: a strategy for Allied Health Professions*, launched in November 2000, and *Making the Change: a strategy for the professions in healthcare science* launched in February 2001. These strategies clearly acknowledged leadership development as a high priority.

In response to this the former Leadership Centre, over a four-year period, supported a number of initiatives to build leadership capacity and capability within the AHP/HCS population. These programmes offered a variety of development activities to many levels of Allied Health Professions and healthcare sciences in the health service. Examples of some of these approaches are described below.

AHP and HCS consultant development

A Leadership Development Programme was developed for these ground-breaking new posts. The first event took place in March 2003 and the programme was completed in March 2005. As a result of the programme, a consultant network was created which continued the learning and supported new consultants as they came into post.

Middle manager bespoke leadership development

Two successful conferences were held in December 2002 and January 2003. The main focus of these events was to gain an insight into the current policy context, leadership skills development, innovative thinking and self-awareness interactive workshops.

PCT clinical PEC member development

Following a successful one-day event held in November 2002 and the national PEC members and PEC chairs survey results, 30 events were organised around the country to enable clinical PEC members to define and start to implement their own development, using reflection and networking opportunities.

Director-level programmes

Sixty-four directors successfully attended a director-level programme. A further one-day workshop was held in 2003. At least eleven of the delegates subsequently achieved a director post within the NHS.

Leading strategic change

This programme, focusing on developing leaders who could build on clinical initiatives to modernise the NHS, was accessed by a number of AHPs.

Targeting leaders in clinical roles, the programme built knowledge, patient focus and skills and demonstrated how these could be applied in practice.

Leading an empowered organisation (LEO)

A total of 12 613 AHP and HCS attended a three-day LEO programme between August 2001 and March 2004. Sixty-eight AHP and HCS LEO facilitators were trained to deliver the programmes. A large number of organisations purchased organisational licences to continue to run LEO locally.

Editor's note

Even though more than 12 500 AHPs and HCSs attended the LEO course the outcomes and quality of this programme were not evaluated at national level – surprising given the level of investment in LEO training.

Leaders for the future

Our understanding of leadership has then moved away from the 'great man' (or woman) theories to a more sophisticated interpretation of the leadership process within teams and across whole systems.

This resulted in demand for leadership skills that could increasingly deal with the complexities generated by these situations – Greenleaf's[7] concept of 'honoring the paradox' or working with and valuing difference.

Senge[14] and Kotter [13] comment that in today's organisations, leadership should be vested in many people and not just at the top of an organisation or as part of the formal organisational hierarchy, since change cannot occur if only driven from the top. Shortell[15] similarly emphasises the importance of developing leaders at all levels in the healthcare system.

These concepts resonate strongly with the type of successful leadership that can be seen emerging in the NHS and across other parts of the public sector.

For leadership to have an impact and support the degree of fundamental change required to achieve service improvement we need to be developing leadership at all levels, distributing responsibility and clear accountability throughout the system.

Supporting and sustaining the relationships that allow this to happen is undoubtedly more complex and calls for a shift in the behaviours of those in leadership roles.

Based on an understanding of current theory and emerging practice, three models describe particularly well how we might now conceive of what is required of leadership in the NHS.

Leaders as partners

Effective leaders will see other people as partners or colleagues. The concept of the leader as an equal partner suggests that the leader is one who functions from within the group or team, not from outside it in some hierarchical sense.

This requires leadership behaviours that not only role model the way to do things but also show a willingness to distribute leadership in a way that enables others and encourages them to make the best contribution that they can to the process; leadership that, in essence, hands over both the freedom to act but also the responsibility for that action, whilst maintaining support and accountability. Within the NHS, partnership implies a new relationship not only with colleagues and stakeholders but most importantly with the patient themselves.

Leaders as mentors

The leader as coach or mentor reinforces the concept of those in leadership roles having a responsibility to act as role model for behaviour, to nurture aspiration and create inspiration through what they say and what they do. The leader in this role takes a keen interest in the development of those they work with and acts in a way that encourages that potential, coaching and supporting, and demonstrating, in transformational terms, a genuine care and concern. The successful development of a distributed leadership system, with leadership emerging at all levels, requires leaders to take on a more active coaching and mentoring role within their organisation or team.

Leaders as 'tempered radicals'

Meyerson[16] discusses the impact of staff not usually thought of as leaders in the traditional sense. She describes these individuals as 'tempered radicals' who:

> exercise a form of leadership within organisations that is more localised, more diffuse, more modest and less visible than traditional forms – yet no less significant.

This concept sits well with our recognition of the need to develop leaders at all levels of the healthcare system regardless of position or authority. We know that it is often those staff at the front line of care who can do most to affect the patient experience and who are therefore ideally placed to model and lead change.

Meyerson describes some of the personal characteristics of leaders and influencers working quietly behind the scenes.

- Sees things differently from the norm, pushing conventional expectations.
- Aims to use difference as an impetus for positive change.

- Challenges prevailing wisdom or assumptions.
- Through their perspective provokes learning and adaptation.
- Encourages others to learn.
- Doesn't see themselves as a leader.

Meyerson concludes that tempered radicals inspire change through their ability to inspire people; in staying focused and committed, their efforts make a difference because they accumulate into meaningful change and their efforts matter not only to themselves but also to other people and the organisation in which they work.

Conclusion

Leadership cannot be taught through academic study alone or learned purely through experience. It is the combination of knowledge, experience and reflection which develops future action. Leadership is learnt primarily through doing it, the cycle of trial and error, and learning from both success and failure.

In conclusion, then, effective leadership is a blend of personal qualities and specific skills and it is perhaps helpful to finish with a very practical checklist of actions that you can take to increase the effectiveness of your leadership behaviour.

- **Find your supporters/friends** in order to build a receptive local culture and a critical mass for change. A successful leader should engage with colleagues and key stakeholders to build support and trust. This is particularly important during periods of change or uncertainty. Identifying who your supporters are and how that support translates into action is vital for leaders seeking to undertake change.
- **Don't be afraid to ask the 'killer' question** and challenge existing models. Just because something is done a certain way does not mean that it is being done in the best way. Seek advice from those who have knowledge in areas where you are lacking, invite challenge, but do not be afraid to challenge others. A 'fresh set of eyes' can bring clarity to a situation or identify improvements that might otherwise remain hidden by assumptions or ingrained working practices.
- **Keep it simple**. It is important that an organisation has a shared direction of travel that everyone understands. It is equally important that those involved in delivering the change have ownership and feel involved in the creation of the vision for change (co-creation). Your role as a leader may be to support the development of a vision for the entire organisation or it could be to translate a national or organisation-wide vision to the local level, making it relevant to your workplace.
- **Show your appreciation** by valuing people. Any organisation is only as good as its staff. Showing appreciation to staff for a job well done can motivate and help build morale and corporacy. Think about creative ways of recognising the efforts of staff and celebrating achievement. Saying thank you and praising appropriately can have a huge impact.
- **Admit mistakes** – and be honest with yourself and others when you have got it wrong or simply don't know. Personal integrity and openness are important characteristics of any leader. Good corporate governance and social responsi-

bility are now the rule rather than the exception and leaders are expected to exemplify these behaviours.

- **Remember the benefit of 'team' and do not try to go it alone** – you need to encourage the creative input of all team members. A good leader should have the confidence to draw upon all available resources, including the wide range of skills and abilities of others around them, and by delegating and sharing, you enable and develop their skills. Good communications can play an important role in building a sense of team within an organisation and can help encourage meaningful dialogue between different parts of an organisation.
- **Really listen** – this is about listening without judgement, understanding the subtext of what people are saying and paying as much attention to the non-verbal signals as to the verbal presentation. The importance of good listening skills should not be underrated. People often 'hear' what they want to hear rather than what is actually being said. Take time to listen to other people's points of view, put yourself in their position and think about what they are really trying to tell you. Building empathy underpins effective working relationships.
- **Be what you want others to be** – as a leader, you will be a role model for other people in your organisation and you need to ensure that what you do and what you say is congruent and reflects the values and behaviours that you expect of others. People can be quick to judge leaders who fall below the level of expectation that they set for their staff or colleagues. Make sure you are setting the right example.
- **Never stop learning** – develop yourself and others. For a very few people, leadership comes naturally; for the vast majority leadership skills need to be developed. In today's ever-changing workplace it is important to not only develop your leadership skills but to also work on the skills and knowledge vital to your profession. As a leader you need to create the environment in which both you and those you work with can continue to learn and where personal development and growth are demonstrably valued.
- **Know yourself** – effective leadership begins with self-knowledge. You need to understand your own emotional responses and be aware of the impact that people and situations have for you. You need to be able to manage these emotions appropriately in your interactions with others to build healthy and constructive working relationships. The skills of self-awareness and self-regulation, components of your emotional intelligence, like other leadership skills, can be developed.

With the agenda for modernisation, leadership in the NHS is now about effecting change and enabling others to think and behave differently in order to bring about positive improvements in the experience of patients and service users, through redesigning the current systems of care that are offered. Those working in and with the NHS, whatever their role, need to see themselves as these agents of change who can make a very real difference.

To succeed in delivering a redesigned and reformed system of health and social care we need to think of leadership as the right and responsibility of all, an inclusive concept that embraces every individual who sees what could be different, asks themselves and others why it is not so and sets out to do something about it.

References

1 Hersey P, Blanchard K. *Management of Organisational Behaviour*. Harlow: Prentice Hall; 1969.
2 Adair J. *Effective Leadership*. London: Pan Books; 1976.
3 Stogdill R, Bass M. *Stogdill's Handbook of Leadership: a survey of theory and research*. New York: Free Press, London: Collier Macmillan; 1981.
4 Alimo-Metcalfe B. *Effective Leadership*. London: Local Government Management Board; 1998.
5 Baradacco J. We don't need another hero. *Harvard Business Review*. 2001; **79**(8): 121–6.
6 Collins J. *Good to Great*. New York: Harper Collins; 2001.
7 Greenleaf R. *Servant Leadership: a journey into the nature of legitimate power and greatness*. Mahway: Paulist Press; 1977.
8 Goleman D. What makes a leader? *Harvard Business Review*. 1998; **Nov/Dec**: 94–102.
9 Bennis W. *Old Dogs, New Tricks*. London: Kogan Page; 1999.
10 Heifetz R. *Leadership without Easy Answers*. Cambridge, MA: Harvard University Press; 1994.
11 Goffee R, Jones G. Why should anyone be led by you? *Harvard Business Review*. 2000; **Sept/Oct**: 62–71.
12 Adair J. *Inspiring Leadership*. London: Thorogood; 2002.
13 Kotter J. *Leading Change*. Boston: Harvard Business School Press; 1998.
14 Senge P. *The Dance of Change*. London: Nicholas Brealey; 1999.
15 Shortell S. Developing individual leaders is not enough. *Journal of Health Service Research and Policy*. 2002; 7(4): 193–4.
16 Meyerson D. *Tempered Radicals*. Boston: Harvard Business School Publishing; 2003.

DH publications

Department of Health. *The NHS Plan: a plan for investment, a plan for reform*. London: HMSO; 2000.
Department of Health. *Meeting the Challenge: a strategy for the allied health professions*. London: HMSO; 2000.
Department of Health. *Making the Change: a strategy for the professions in healthcare science*. London: Stationery Office; 2001.
NHS Modernisation Agency. *Leading For Improvement: whose job is it anyway?* London: Stationery Office; 2004.

Chapter 8

Legal issues arising in the management, leadership, and development of Allied Health Professions

Bridgit Dimond

Introduction

One of the principal responsibilities of any manager of Allied Health Professionals is to be aware of the legal context within which they manage, so that they have an understanding of the basic principles which apply, they know how to advise patients, staff and other colleagues, and most importantly they understand at what point they would need to seek expert help. The aim of this chapter is to set out the main laws which apply to the role of the manager and to provide the basic foundation of understanding upon which they can develop their more detailed knowledge.

Legal system

Laws derive from two main sources: firstly statutory provision, i.e. Acts of Parliament (known as primary legislation) and regulations (known as secondary legislation) or legislation from the European Community, and secondly the decisions in cases decided by the courts (known as the common law, or judge-made law or case law). The Assemblies of Scotland, Wales and Northern Ireland have varying law-making powers. Primary legislation often gives powers to a minister of the Crown to make further more detailed regulations. These are usually drawn up in the form of a statutory instrument which is laid before Parliament for approval or rejection before it comes into force.

Human Rights Act

This Act came into force on 2 October 2000 (in Scotland on devolution) and has three effects.

- All public authorities or organisations carrying out functions of a public nature are required to respect the European Convention of Human Rights which is set out in Schedule 1 to the Act.
- Citizens have a right to bring an action in the courts of the UK if they considered that their human rights as set out in the Schedule have been breached by a public authority.

- Judges are required to refer back to Parliament any legislation which they considered to be incompatible with the Articles set out in the European Convention of Human Rights.

One of the most significant changes brought about by this Act is that people no longer have to take their case to Strasbourg for a hearing before the European Courts of Human Rights but can avoid the additional cost and delay and bring the case in UK courts. If a judicial review is sought of a decision which is considered to be in breach of the human rights recognised in the Convention, then legal aid is available for this action.

Of specific significance to the role of the manager are the following Articles:

Article 2 – The right to life (has relevance to Not For Resuscitation policies and the withholding or withdrawing of treatment)

Article 3 – The right not to be subjected to torture or to inhuman or degrading treatment and punishment

Article 5 – The right to liberty and security of person

Article 6 – The right to fair and independent hearings

Article 8 – The right to respect for privacy, family life and correspondence

Article 9 – The right of respect for religion, belief, etc.

Article 10 – The right of freedom of expression

Article 14 – The right not to be discriminated against in the recognition of the Articles.

Managers can obtain further information about the Articles from the dedicated task force set up by the Department of Constitutional Affairs[1] (DCA). The DCA provides an update on the most recent cases where the significance of the Articles has been discussed as well as an explanation of the Articles.[2]

Health and Safety laws

The Health and Safety at Work Act 1974 places upon every employer a duty to take reasonable care of the health and safety of employees (section 2) and under section 3 the employer has a duty to safeguard the health and safety of the general public which could be affected by the employer's activities. Inevitably these duties placed upon the employer are delegated to the mangers in any health organisation. Section 7 of the Health and Safety at Work Act 1974 places a duty on employees:

(a) To take reasonable care for the health and safety of himself and of others who may be affected by his acts or omissions at work.
(b) As regards any duty or requirement imposed on his employer or other person by or under any of the relevant statutory provisions to co-operate with him in so far as is necessary to enable that duty or requirement to be performed or complied with.

The duties under the Act are supplemented by many statutory instruments which specify detailed duties to be undertaken by employers and employees. The statutory instruments include:

- Management of Health and Safety at Work Regulations 1992 (updated 1999)
- Provision and Use of Work Equipment Regulations 1992 (updated 1998)
- Manual Handling Operations Regulations 1992
- Workplace (Health, Safety and Welfare) Regulations 1992 (updated 1999)
- Personal Protective Equipment at Work Regulations 1992 (updated 1999)
- Health and Safety (Display Screen Equipment) Regulations 1992 (updated 1999)
- Lifting Operations and Lifting Equipment Regulations 1998.

These statutory duties are, for the most part, enforced through inspections, notices (prohibition and enforcement) and prosecutions by the health and safety inspectorate. A manager might have to give evidence of the steps taken to implement these statutory provisions. Whilst the burden of proving a breach of the regulations is on the prosecution to establish beyond reasonable doubt, where the duty is a reasonably practical one, then it is up to the employer to show on a balance of probabilities that it took all reasonable steps to comply with the duty. The manager would have to provide documentary evidence such as risk assessments and the action taken following a review to illustrate the reasonable steps which have been taken. Information is available from the Health and Safety Commission and Health and Safety Executive websites for employers.[3]

Breach of the main duties under the Health and Safety at Work Act 1974 does not give rise to an action for compensation in the civil courts, but breach of some of the regulations may do so. For example, the Manual Handling Regulations have given rise to many cases where compensation has been sought for back injuries.

In one manual handling case[4] (*King v Sussex Ambulance NHS Trust* 2002) the Court of Appeal held that the employers were not in breach of the directive or regulations on manual handling. King, an ambulance technician, suffered serious injuries carrying an elderly patient down the stairway of his home. He and his colleague had taken the patient down the stairway, which was narrow and steep, in a carry chair. He had been injured when forced for a brief moment to bear the full weight of the chair. The High Court judge had found in favour of the ambulance technician holding that the employers were in breach of Council Directive (90/269; Article 3(2)) and the Manual Handling Regulations, and that the employers had acted negligently by discouraging employees in circumstances such as those in this particular case from calling the fire brigade to take patients from their homes.

Sussex Ambulance NHS Trust appealed against this finding. The Court of Appeal held that the NHS trust was not liable either under the Directive or under the Manual Handling Regulations. There was nothing to suggest that calling the fire brigade would have been appropriate in the case. The evidence showed that such an option was rarely used because it had to be carefully planned, took a long time and caused distress to the patient. There might be cases where calling the fire brigade would be appropriate, but that would depend on the seriousness of the problem, the urgency of the case and the actual or likely response of the patient or his/her carers and the fire brigade. King had failed to show that giving that possibility more emphasis in training would have avoided his injuries. The ambulance service owed the same duty of care to its employees as did any other employer. However, the question of what was reasonable for it to do might have to be judged in the light of its duties to the public and the resources available to it when performing those duties. While the risks to King had not been negligible, the task that he had been carrying out was of considerable social utility.

Furthermore, Sussex Ambulance NHS Trust had limited resources so far as equipment was concerned. There was no evidence of any steps that the trust could have taken to prevent the risk and the only suggestion made was that it should have called on a third party to perform the task for it. Since calling the fire brigade was not appropriate or reasonably practicable for the purpose of the Directive and the regulations, the Sussex Ambulance NHS Trust had not shown a lack of reasonable care. Accordingly, it had not acted negligently.

Common law duties

The statutory duties are paralleled by duties in respect of health and safety owed at common law by both the employer and employee. In any contract of employment, the law will imply a duty on the employer to take reasonable care of the health and safety of the employee. This includes the duty to take reasonable care to provide competent staff, a safe system of work and safe premises, plant and equipment. Conversely the employee has a duty to co-operate with the employer in health and safety matters by obeying reasonable instructions and by taking reasonable care of himself and others.

These contractual duties are enforced through the usual remedies. Where the employer has fundamentally failed to provide reasonable care for the health and safety of an employee, the employee could assert that the employer is in breach of contract, which gives the employee a choice: the right to see the contract as ended by the breach of contract, which in effect is a constructive dismissal situation and one which, if the employer satisfies the necessary continuous service requirements, gives to the employee a right to apply for unfair dismissal or alternatively the right to see the contract as continuing but seek compensation for the breach of contract.

Where it is the employee who is at fault in failing to comply with his contractual duty, then the employer can discipline the employee – from an oral warning, first written warning to dismissal. Again the employee may have a right to apply for unfair dismissal.

The case of *King v Sussex Ambulance NHS Trust* discussed above illustrates how both common law and statutory duties under the regulations can be used in seeking compensation for harm.

Similar common law principles apply to the duty of an employer to take reasonable care to prevent an employee being subjected to unreasonable stress or violence or to being bullied. A manager who is faced by an employee who appears to be subjected to stress should take steps to interview the employee and determine what reasonable steps, if any, the employer should take to support the employee and ensure that these are taken and monitored. Records should be kept of the discussion and the resulting actions taken. Only if the employee can show that:

1   the existence of the stress was reasonably foreseeable
2   there was reasonable action which the manager could take
3   the manager failed to take that reasonable action to alleviate the stress
4   as a consequence of that failure the employee has suffered a serious mental condition

would the employee be able to recover compensation. In a recent case, the Court of Appeal has laid down the principles governing the liability of an employer for psychiatric injury caused by stress at work.[5] The onus was on the claimant to establish on a balance of probabilities that the employer had been negligent in taking reasonable steps to protect the employee from reasonably foreseeable harm from stress.

   Appropriate assessments and action should also be taken in a bullying situation or where violence is reasonably foreseeable and records of the assessment and the action taken should be kept.

Accountability and litigation

Where harm arises to a patient or colleague and an Allied Health Professional is responsible there could be several different resulting hearings.

- Where a person has died there could be criminal proceedings.
- Where compensation is being sought, then the injured person or relatives of the dead person could bring an action against the negligent health professional or, more likely, the employer of that health professional, because of the employer's vicarious liability for the negligence of an employee acting in the course of employment.
- The employer could bring disciplinary proceedings because the employee is in breach of his or her duty to use reasonable care and skill in carrying out responsibilities.
- A registered health professional could face fitness to practise proceedings before his or her registration body.

Criminal courts

The House of Lords has ruled that where the death of a patient has been caused by such gross negligence of a health professional that it amounts to a crime, a conviction for manslaughter would be appropriate.[6] The prosecution have to prove beyond reasonable doubt that the accused was guilty of gross negligence and this caused the death of the patient. In addition health professionals could face prosecution under health and safety legislation (see above).

Civil courts

Health professionals have a duty towards patients. If they are in breach of the duty of care and as a consequence cause harm, then there would be liability for the employee and the employer for that harm. At present the system for compensation is based on fault liability. The test as to whether there has been a breach of the duty of care is known as the Bolam Test. This derives from the case of *Bolam v Friern Hospital Management Committee*.[7] In this case the judge used the test of the reasonable practitioner following accepted approved practice to determine whether or not there had been negligence. If it can be established on a balance of probabilities using expert evidence that there was a failure to follow the reasonable standard of care and that this failure caused harm to the patient, then compensation may be payable. The onus is on the claimant to establish that there is a causal link between the failure of the health professional to follow the reasonable standard of care and the harm which has occurred.

In spite of the Woolf Reforms which were introduced in April 1999 to speed up the process of civil proceedings, there is continuing concern about inadequacies of the present system of obtaining compensation following medical negligence. The National Audit Office reported in May 2001 that almost £4 billion would be required to meet the costs of known and anticipated claims in the NHS.[8] A high proportion of that sum goes to lawyers. As a consequence the Government has been considering alternative schemes. A consultation paper was introduced in July 2001.[9] This was followed by a paper on 30 June 2003, *Making Amends*.[10]

Disciplinary proceedings

As discussed below there is an implied term in a contract of employment that an employee will obey the reasonable instructions of an employer and act with reasonable care and skill and failure of the employee to comply with that term could lead to disciplinary action being brought against the employee. Ultimately the employer has the right to dismiss an employee for gross misconduct or incompetence, but the employee could bring an application for unfair dismissal in an employment tribunal. New procedures require employers to follow specific procedures in relation to disciplinary and grievance actions.

Fitness to practise proceedings

The Health Professions Council (HPC) replaced the CPSM in 2001 and new fitness to practise procedures have been introduced. In 2004 the operating department practitioners became the first new health profession to achieve registered status under the HPC. At the time of writing, the response of the Government to feedback from a consultation paper of the registration of healthcare support workers is awaited and both the HPC and the NMC (Nursing and Midwifery Council) are interested in becoming the registration body for this large group of health service employees. Each profession registered with the HPC has a code of ethics and professional practice which is binding upon them and there are considerable advantages if the duty to obey the professional code were to be included as a term in the contract of employment since this would prevent possible conflicts between duties owed to the employer and duties owed under the code of ethics and professional practice. There are advantages in the manager for AHPs having access to the different codes and in ensuring the registered health professionals were aware of their duties. Serious failures to comply with the code would be reported by any employer to the HPC.

Employment law

A contract of employment would come into existence following the acceptance (usually by an applicant) of an offer (usually made by the employer) of a job. The contract may be subject to conditions precedent, e.g. the receipt of a satisfactory reference or satisfactory medical examination before the contract comes into force, or conditions subsequent, which if not complied with could end the contract. The contract itself is an abstract concept creating the relationship of an employer and employee. The sources of the terms of the contract include:

- express terms agreed at an interview or in a letter, e.g. date of commencement, job title
- express terms set out as a result of a collective bargaining agreement, e.g. Whitely Council general terms and conditions
- implied terms, i.e. terms which would be implied by case law (see above terms relating to health and safety)
- statutory provisions set by Act of Parliament or Statutory Instruments which are to be included in the contract of employment, e.g. sickness provisions; maternity benefits and rights; written statement of particulars; itemised statement of pay; payment and limitations on deductions; time off work:
  1 to take part in Trade Union activities (unpaid)
  2 if a Trade Union official, to undertake Trade Union duties and training (paid)
  3 reasonable time off to search for work in a redundancy situation (pay for at least two days)
  4 to work as member of local authority, JP, statutory tribunal, health authority or school governor (unpaid); holidays (bank holidays); patents; guarantee payments; unemployment benefit; redundancy; medical suspension payment.

Sometimes the statutory benefits may not be as beneficial to the employee as those already contained in a contract of employment and in this situation the employee has the right to opt for whichever benefit, statutory or contractual, is to his advantage and the employer can offset his provision of the contractual terms against his statutory duty.

Usually the manager would have the support of a human resource/personnel department in the implementation of contractual provisions and can access this department if there are any queries about employment issues. Some of the recent statutory provisions are considered briefly below.

Working Time Directive

A directive had been adopted by the member states of the European Community on 23 November 1996, but implementation in the UK was delayed until 1 October 1998, when the Working Time Regulations[11] came into force.[12]

The fundamental provision is that a worker's working time, including overtime, should not exceed an average of 48 hours for each seven days over a specified period of 17 weeks. Regulations also specify provisions for rest breaks and annual leave. Night work should not normally exceed an average of eight hours for each 24 hours. The employer has a duty to ensure that no night worker, whose work involves special hazards or heavy physical or mental strain, works for more than eight hours in any 24-hour period. Before assigning a worker to night work, the employer has to ensure that the worker has the opportunity of a free health assessment before he takes up the assignment. There should be a weekly rest period of not less than 24 hours in each seven-day period, or alternatively two rest periods, each of not less than 24 hours, in each 14-day period, or one rest period of not less than 48 hours in each 14-day period.

Employers are required to keep records relating to the hours of work which can be inspected by enforcement agencies. The Health and Safety Executive and local authority environmental health officers are responsible for enforcing the working time limits. Individual employees can, if internal appeals mechanisms fail, apply to the Employment Tribunal for alleged infringements of their statutory rights. The application must be made within three months of the infringement and the Advisory, Conciliation and Arbitration Service (ACAS) will provide conciliation services. The European Court of Justice has held the UK requirement of 13 weeks work before being eligible to have annual leave illegal.[13]

Part-time employees

On 1 July 2000, regulations came into force to prevent part-time workers being treated less favourably than full-time workers,[14] implementing the European Directive.[15] Paragraph 5 of these regulations gives the part-time worker:

> The right not to be treated by his employer less favourably than the employer treats a comparable full-time worker as regards the terms of his contract, or by being subjected to any other detriment by any act, or deliberate failure to act of his employer.

The right applies only if the treatment is on the ground that the worker is a part-time worker and the treatment is not justified on objective grounds. The part-time worker has to compare himself with full-time workers working for the same employer. The right also applies to workers who become part-time or, having been full-time, return part-time after absence, to be treated not less favourably than they were before going part-time. It does not give an employee the right to insist on having part-time work.

The regulations (para 6) also entitle a worker, who considers that he has been treated in a manner that infringes this right, to request from his employer a written statement giving particulars of the reasons for the treatment. The worker must be provided with a statement within 21 days of his request. Failure to provide a statement at all or only in an evasive or equivocal way will enable the tribunal to draw any inference that it considers just and equitable to draw, including an inference that the employer has infringed the right in question. The regulations also protect the part-time worker from unfair dismissal and give a right not to be subjected to any detriment (para 7).

Any worker who considers that his rights have been infringed can present a complaint to an employment tribunal within three months of the day of less favourable treatment or detriment taking place. This is subject to the right of the tribunal to consider out-of-time cases, if in all the circumstances it is just and equitable to do so.

Discrimination legislation

Employers are subject to several statutes covering discrimination on grounds of sex, race, and disability and these have been expanded by regulations which came into force in December 2003 as a result of employment directives from the European Community. The Employment Equality (Religion or Belief) Regulations[16] and the Employment Equality (Sexual Orientation) Regulations[17] protect employees and applicants and those in vocational training against discrimination, victimisation or harassment on the grounds of religion or belief or sexual orientation. At the time of writing plans are in hand to set up in 2006 a new Commission for Equality and Human Rights (CEHR) which will replace the Equal Opportunities Commission, the Disability Rights Commission and the Commission for Racial Equality. Further information is available on the present law and cases and future developments from the respective websites.[18]

Patients' rights

In addition to the rights set out in the European Convention of Human Rights (discussed above), patients have the rights to:

* a reasonable standard of care (discussed above)
* give or withhold consent
* be given information
* have their confidentiality respected
* access their personal health records
* complain.

Consent

An adult who is mentally competent has the right in law to consent to any touching of his/her person. If he/she is touched without consent or other lawful justification, then the person has the right of action in the civil courts of suing for trespass to the person – battery where the person is actually touched, assault where he fears that he/she will be touched. The fact that consent has been given will normally prevent a successful action for trespass. However, the fact of consent may not prevent an action for negligence arising on the ground that there was a breach of the duty of care to inform the patient (see below).

The Department of Health has provided a reference guide on consent to examination and treatment[19] and also practical assistance in the implementation of the legal principles together with forms recommended for use.[20]

A person over 18 is presumed to have the capacity to give consent. However, this presumption can be rebutted. Capacity is determined by the following test laid down by the Court of Appeal in the case of *Re MB*.[21]

A person lacks the capacity (to give a valid consent) if some impairment or disturbance of mental functioning renders the person unable to make a decision whether to consent to or to refuse treatment. That inability to make a decision will occur when:

(a) The patient is unable to comprehend and retain the information which is material to the decision, especially as to the likely consequences of having or not having the treatment in question
(b) The patient is unable to use the information and weigh it in the balance as part of the process of arriving at the decision.

This test was applied by the Family Division of the High Court in the case of Miss B,[22] where a woman who had been paralysed refused to be placed on a ventilator and when that refusal was ignored applied to the court for the ventilator to be switched off. Once it had been determined by two psychiatrists that she was mentally capable she was able to refuse ventilation and the judge awarded her a nominal sum for the trespass to the person which had been committed when she was ventilated against her will. She died about two weeks after the court declaration.

Once it is determined that the patient has the necessary mental capacity relevant to the decision which has to be made, then he or she can refuse to give consent for a good reason, a bad reason or no reason at all (*Re MB*).[23]

Mental incapacity

Where an adult lacks the capacity to make decisions, then actions can be taken in his best interests in accordance with the Bolam Test for reasonable practice, out of necessity. This is the principle established by the House of Lords in the case of *Re F*.[24] Statutory provision is likely to replace the common law principles of acting out of necessity when the Mental Capacity Bill currently being debated in Parliament is enacted and brought into force. The current time table for implementation is April 2007.

Children and young persons

Young persons of 16 and 17 years have a statutory right to give consent to medical, surgical and dental treatment (including diagnostic procedures and anaesthetics) under the Family Law Reform Act 1969. However, if they refuse treatment which is considered to be life-saving and necessary in their best interests, their refusal can be overruled. In the case of *Re W*[25] a 16-year-old girl under local authority care suffered from anorexia nervosa. She refused to move to a specialist hospital. The Court of Appeal held that the Family Law Reform Act 1969 section 8 did not prevent consent being given by parents or the court. Whilst she had a right to give consent under the Act, she could not refuse treatment that was necessary to save her life.

Children under 16 years and those young persons under 18 (on issues not covered by the Family Law Reform Act 1969, e.g. consent to research or tissue donation) also have the right to give consent at common law under the principle recognised by the House of Lords in the Gillick case.[26] Provided that they have the necessary competence they can give consent, without parental involvement.

To be given information

The duty of care owed by health professionals to the patient requires information about significant risks of substantial harm to be given to the patient. Even if the patient has given consent to treatment and therefore could not succeed in an action for a trespass to the person, the patient may succeed in an action for breach of the duty of care to inform him or her if information about harm which could arise has not been given to him or her and that harm arises. In a recent case the House of Lords[27] has stated that the defendant owed a duty to the claimant to inform her of the risks inherent in the proposed surgery, including that of paralysis, so that she could make her own decision. The fact that the claimant could not state that she would have declined the operation once and for all if she had been warned did not mean that she could not succeed in her action for compensation for breach of the duty of care to inform.

Confidentiality

Every health professional owes a duty to respect the confidentiality of information obtained from and about the patient. This duty arises from statutory provisions such as the Data Protection Act 1998, the duty of trust arising between patient and health professional, an implied duty in the contract of employment and also in the code of ethics and professional conduct which all Allied Health Professionals are required to observe. However, there are exceptions to this duty and these exceptions include the following.

- Disclosure with the consent of the patient.
- Disclosure in the best interests of the patient (e.g. the exchange of information between members of the multidisciplinary team caring for the patient).
- Disclosure in accordance with statutory provisions (e.g. Police and Criminal Evidence Act 1984; notification of statutory diseases; Prevention of Terrorism Acts).
- Disclosure as a result of the order of the court.
- Disclosure in the public interest (this would include situations where serious harm may be caused to the patient or other persons such as child protection cases).

The Department of Health has provided a Code of Practice on Confidentiality.[28]

Caldicott

A committee chaired by Dame Fiona Caldicott was appointed by the Department of Health to consider the issue of confidentiality across the NHS. It reported in December 1997 and included in its recommendations the need to raise awareness of confidentiality requirements, and specifically recommended the establishment of a network of Caldicott Guardians of patient information throughout the NHS. Each NHS trust and primary care trust should have a board member with specific responsibilities for confidentiality. If a manager has concerns about the duty of confidentiality and any exceptions to that duty, the Caldicott Guardian should be a useful source of advice and guidance.

Data protection provisions

The Data Protection Act 1998 applies to both computerised and manually held records. Further information on the working of the Act is provided by the Information Commissioner who has responsibility for the implementation of both the Data Protection Act 1998 and the Freedom of Information Act 2000.[29]

Freedom of Information

This Act, which was fully implemented in January 2005, gives a general right of access to information held by public authorities, but this right is subject to significant exceptions. The main exemptions from the duty are set out in Part 2 of the Act. Some of the exemptions are subject to a public interest test and include the following.

- Information intended for future publication.
- National security.
- Defence.
- International relations.
- Relations within the UK.
- The economy.
- Investigations and proceedings conducted by public authorities.
- Law enforcement.
- Audit functions.
- Formulation of government policy.
- Personal information.
- Legal professional privilege.

For the above situations a public interest test applies. This means that a public authority must consider whether the public interest in withholding the exempt information outweighs the public interest in releasing it.

Others are absolute exemptions and these include the following.

- Information accessible to the applicant by other means.
- Information supplied by or relating to bodies dealing with security matters.
- Court records.
- Parliamentary privilege.
- Prejudice to effective conduct of public affairs.
- Personal information where the applicant is the subject of the information.
- Information provided in confidence.
- Prohibitions on disclosure where a disclosure is prohibited by an enactment or would constitute contempt of court.

For the above information, there is no requirement of a public interest test.

Personal information where the applicant is the subject of the information is absolutely exempt from the Freedom of Information Act. Section 40 states that:

Any information to which a request for information relates is exempt information if it constitutes personal data of which the applicant is the data subject.

If a data subject wants access to personal information, then the route for that application is the Data Protection Act 1998, and in general the Freedom of Information Act 2000 tries to prevent an overlap between the two Acts.

Under section 14 a request which is vexatious or where the public authority has already complied with the request does not have to be complied with.

Access to personal health records

Patients have a qualified right of access to their health records under Statutory Instruments issued under the Data Protection Act. Access can be withheld to any part of the record.

1 Where the access would be likely to cause serious harm to the physical or mental health or condition of the data subject or any other person (which may include a health professional).
2 Where the request for access is made by another person on behalf of the data subject, such as a parent for a child, access can be refused if the data subject had provided the information in the expectation that it would not be disclosed.
3 If giving access would reveal the identity of another person, unless that person has given consent to the disclosure or it is reasonable to comply with the access request without that consent. This does not apply if the third party is a health professional who has been involved in the care of the patient, unless serious harm to that health professional's physical or mental health or condition is likely to be caused by giving access (i.e. it comes within the first exception).

Right to complain

In July 2004 new Regulations[30] on the complaints procedure came into force so that all NHS trusts and primary care trusts must ensure that they follow the new procedures. The initial investigation must comply with the time limits set out in the Regulations. If the complainant is not satisfied with the outcome from the initial investigation, he or she can apply to the Healthcare Commission (once known as the Commission for Healthcare Audit and Inspection) which has the power to investigate the complaint. A complainant who is still aggrieved after the investigation by the Healthcare Commission can apply to the Ombudsman (Health Service Commissioner).

Record keeping

It follows from what has been said that the importance of record keeping cannot be overestimated and the manager has a significant role to play in ensuring that the standards are regularly audited and that action is taken as the result of any monitoring. The prime purpose of patient record keeping is the care of the patient: to ensure that each member of the health team is aware of the care and treatment which have been given or which have still to be provided in order to ensure that the patient receives all reasonable care. There should be clear safe systems of record keeping, storage and transport of records in the community in place and the manager might find assistance from the Medical Records Officer of the NHS trust or primary care trust. It is hoped that if good standards of record keeping are maintained and regularly audited, then in the event of a health professional having to appear before any court, tribunal or other hearing, the records will provide a clear comprehensive unambiguous account of the actions taken.

In addition to an audit of patient records, the manager has also responsibility to ensure that the records relating to health and safety assessments and action, records relating to employee issues and many other records should be completed and kept safely.

Conclusions

The above is only a brief summary of the many areas of law with which the manager of AHPs needs to be acquainted. As a health service professional the manager would be personally accountable for his or her actions but liable for any delegation provided that the delegation was reasonable and satisfied the Bolam Test and was appropriately supervised. (In practice, of course, the employer would be vicariously liable for the actions of the health professional.) However, as a manager, with responsibilities to establish safe systems of working practice, to carry out health and safety risk assessments and set in place the necessary improvements to reduce the risk of harm, the manager could be liable for 24 hours, seven days a week, 52 weeks a year, even when on holiday and off-duty. Again, in practice the employer would probably be held vicariously liable for the manager, but the manager could face disciplinary proceedings, fitness to practise proceedings and also, if there has been an offence under health and safety legislation, prosecution in the criminal courts. There are clearly heavy responsibilities upon the manager and ones for which he or she should ensure regular training and updates, to ensure that his or her competence was maintained, not just as a health professional but as a health service manager.

Questions and answers

The editors asked Bridget:

Question 1: Do AHP staff who only work in the NHS need to have their own professional liability insurance?

Answer: In theory an employee who does no work outside his or her employment would be covered by the vicarious liability of the employer in respect of harm caused to another person, so they would not personally have to pay out compensation to the victim. Since the House of Lords decision in the *Lister v Helsey Hall* case,[31] the definition of 'in the course of employment' has been widely defined, and even disobeying orders would now come under the definition. Therefore, in principle, it is unlikely that an AHP who only worked in the NHS would have to pay compensation personally. However, there are two qualifications on this. If an AHP professional did a Samaritan act outside the course of employment and caused harm, then this would not be covered and the AHP would normally look to his or her professional association which would usually provide cover for such actions.

Secondly there is a recommendation by the Department of Health, in its guidance on extended nurse prescribing,[32] that the prescriber should obtain personal professional indemnity cover for such work. There is no explanation as to why such activities by an employee would not be covered by vicarious liability, and why such personal cover is therefore necessary. AHPs should follow the advice given by their professional registration body.

Question 2: What is my obligation as a registered practitioner if I know a colleague is not working to HPC standard?

Answer: No registered practitioner can ignore dangers to patients. There is a duty of care owed to the patient which is enforceable in the civil courts, and failures by the AHP to notify appropriate persons of the danger would be evidence of lack of fitness to practise and therefore actionable by the HPC. The Report following the Bristol Enquiry into paediatric heart surgery[33] called for an honesty and openness in the relationship of patient and professional. The Department of Health suggested in its consultation paper on a new statutory scheme for obtaining compensation for clinical negligence that there should be a statutory duty of candour.[10] However, even without such a regulation, the law would require an AHP to act to protect patients. Any AHP who 'blew the whistle' would be protected from any victimisation by the Public Interest Disclosure Act 1998 if its provisions were followed.

Question 3: What is the legal position regarding fees for reports when it is agreed that an AHP report will be submitted to a solicitor?

Answer: An employee is expected under the contract of employment to return to the employer any profits made during the course of employment, unless there is an explicit agreement between employee and employer to the contrary. Thus medical staff have an agreement that they can personally keep the fees for reports which they prepare for solicitors and the courts. Non-medical staff do not appear to have the same agreement with NHS authorities. There is no reason why such a contractual term could not be negotiated between an individual employee and his or her employer. The latter would want to be satisfied that the employee still fulfilled his or her duties, and the activities of the department were not prejudiced. It would be a question of scale. The employee would of course have to submit to the Inland Revenue a return in respect of such self-employed earnings and be aware that by receiving the fees personally, they could not rely upon the vicarious liability of the employer for such activities.

References

1 www.dca.gov.uk/hract; www.humanrights.gov.uk/whatsnew.htm.
2 *Department for Constitutional Affairs Study Guide on Human Rights Act 1998*, 2nd ed; October 2002. www.dca.gov.uk/hract/studyguide/index.htm.
3 www.hse.gov.uk/; www.hsc.gov.uk.
4 *King v Sussex Ambulance NHS Trust* [2002] EWCA 953; [2002] ICR 1413.
5 *Hartmann v South Essex Mental Health and Community Care Trust. TLR* 21 January 2005 CA.
6 *R v Adomako* [1994] 2 *All ER* 79 HL; [1995] 1 *AC* 171, *TLR* July 4 1994.
7 *Bolam v Friern Barnet* HMC [1957] 1 *WLR* 582.
8 National Audit Office. *Handling Clinical Negligence Claims in England. Report by the Comptroller and Auditor General.* HC 403 Session 2000–2001. London: Stationery Office; 2001.
9 Department of Health Press Release. New Clinical Compensation Scheme for the NHS. 2001/0313. London: DH.
10 Department of Health. *Making Amends: a consultation paper setting out proposals for reforming the approach to clinical negligence in the NHS.* CMO June 2003.
11 Working Time Regulations 1998. SI 1998 No 1833.
12 NHS Executive. Working Time Regulations: Implementation in the NHS HSC 1988/ 204; DTI A Guide to the Working Time Regulations URN 1998/894.
13 *R v S.S for Trade and Industry. TLR* 28 June 2001.
14 *The Part-time Workers (Prevention of Less Favourable Treatment) Regulations 2000.* SI 1551.
15 Directive 97/81/EC. Part-time Work Directive as extended to the UK by Directive 98/ 23/EC.
16 *The Employment Equality (Religion or Belief) Regulations.* SI 2003 No 1660.
17 *The Employment Equality (Sexual Orientation) Regulations.* SI 2003 No 1661.
18 www.eoc. gov.uk/; www.cre.gov.uk/about/about.html; www.drc-gb.org.
19 Department of Health. *Reference Guide to Consent for Examination or Treatment.* London: DH; 2001. www.doh.gov.uk/consent.
20 Department of Health. *Good Practice in Consent Implementation Guide.* London: DH; 2001.
21 *Re MB* (Adult Medical Treatment) [1997] 2 *FLR* 426.
22 *Re B* (Consent to treatment: capacity) *TLR* 26 March 2002, [2002] 2 *All ER* 449.
23 *Re MB* (Adult Medical Treatment) [1997] 2 *FLR* 426.
24 *F v West Berkshire Health Authority* [1989] 2 *All ER* 545; [1990] 2 *AC* 1.
25 *In re* W (a minor) (medical treatment) 1992 4 *All ER* 627.
26 *Gillick v West Norfolk and Wisbech AHA and the DHSS.* 1985 3 *All ER* 402.
27 *Chester v Afshar. TLR* 19 October 2004 HL.
28 Department of Health. *The NHS Confidentiality Code of Practice.* London: DH; 2003. www.doh.gov.uk/ipu/confiden/protect/ (superseding HSG(96) 18 LASSL (96)5).
29 NHS Executive. Data Protection Act 1998 HSC 2000/009 and supporting information: DoH and NHS Executive, Data Protection Act 1998 Protection and Use of Patient Information. www.doh.gov.uk/dpa98.
30 *The National Health Service (Complaints) Regulations 2004.* SI 2004 No 1768.
31 *Lister and Others v Helsey Hall Ltd. TLR* 10 May 2001; [2001] *UKHL* 22; [2001] 2 *WLR* 1311.
32 Department of Health. *Extending Independent Nurse Prescribing Within the NHS in England: a guide for implementation.* London: DH; 2002.
33 Kennedy I. *Learning from Bristol: The Report of the Public Inquiry into Children's Heart Surgery at the Bristol Royal Infirmary 1984–1995; Cm5207-1.* Norwich: Stationery Office; 2001. www.bristol-inquiry.org.uk/

Further reading

Clerk JF, Lindsell WHB, Anthony M. *Clerk and Lindsell on Torts*. 18th ed. London: Sweet and Maxwell; 2000.

Cooper J, editor. *Law, Rights and Disability*. London: Jessica Kingsley; 2000.

Dimond BC. *Legal Aspects of Occupational Therapy*. 2nd ed. Oxford: Blackwell Scientific Publications; 2004.

Dimond BC. *Legal Aspects of Midwifery*. 3rd ed. Oxford: Elsevier, 2005/6.

Dimond BC. *Legal Aspects of Care in the Community*. London: Macmillan Press; 1997.

Dimond BC. *Legal Aspects of Complementary Therapy Practice*. Edinburgh: Churchill Livingston; 1998.

Dimond BC. *Legal Aspects of Physiotherapy*. Oxford: Blackwell Science; 1999.

Dimond BC. *Legal Aspects of Radiography and Radiology*. Oxford: Blackwell Science; 2003.

Dimond BC. *Legal Aspects of Consent*. Dinton, Salisbury: Quay Publications, Mark Allen Press; 2003.

Dimond BC. *Legal Aspects of Health and Safety*. Dinton, Salisbury: Quay Publications, Mark Allen Press; 2005.

Dimond BC. *Legal Aspects of Patient Confidentiality*. Dinton, Salisbury: Quay Publications, Mark Allen Press; 2002.

Dimond BC. *Legal Aspects of Pain Management*. Dinton, Salisbury: Quay Publications, Mark Allen Press; 2002.

Hockton A. *The Law on Consent to Treatment*. London: Sweet and Maxwell; 2002.

Jones MA, Morris A. *E Blackstone's Statutes on Medical Law*. 3rd ed. Oxford: Oxford University Press, Oxford; 2003.

Jones R. *Mental Health Act Manual*. 8th ed. London: Sweet and Maxwell; 2003.

Kloss D. *Occupational Health Law*. 3rd ed. Oxford: Blackwell Scientific Publications; 2000.

Pitt G. *Employment Law*. 4th ed. London: Sweet and Maxwell; 2002.

Selwyn N. *Selwyn's Law of Employment*. 12th edn. London: Butterworth; 2002.

Sims S. *Practical Approach to Civil Procedure*. 4th ed. London: Blackstone Press; 2000.

Chapter 9

Professional regulation

Norma Brook

Background

Statutory professional regulation in healthcare commenced when the General Medical Council (GMC) was established by the Medical Act of 1858. Its role was to set up and keep a register of qualified practitioners that was accessible to the public, to oversee medical education and to self-regulate the profession. Since the inception of the GMC there have been another eight regulators of healthcare professionals established. Although government has set up the legal framework for regulation in each case, the regulatory bodies are independent organisations. The funding of the regulatory bodies comes from fees paid by each registrant. Funding by government, the employer or any other organisation would imply that they should be able to be in control of the regulatory body on a day-to-day basis. That would clearly detract from the notion of professionally led regulation.

Currently, the nine regulatory bodies for healthcare professionals in the United Kingdom are the:

- General Chiropractic Council
- General Dental Council
- General Medical Council
- General Optical Council
- General Osteopathic Council
- Health Professions Council
- Nursing and Midwifery Council
- Pharmaceutical Society of NI
- Royal Pharmaceutical Society of GB.

The prime objective of professional regulation in the field of healthcare is:

> to safeguard the health and well-being of persons using or needing the services of registrants.[1]

This is achieved by establishing and keeping a register of relevant health professionals who have been recognised as qualified to practise. Another important function of a healthcare regulator is to set the standards to be met by its registrants. These include standards of professional practice, behaviour, education and training and continuing professional development (CPD). Processes must also be put in place to deal with registered professionals who do not meet those standards.

Professional regulation is a collaborative process led by health professionals. The relevant regulatory body works with many key stakeholders such as its registrants, the public, education providers, professional bodies, employers, the government, and others who have an interest in protecting the public.

The role of registrants in the regulatory process is to practise self-regulation. They should of themselves be committed to the notion of professional regulation and continually monitor their own performance against the standards set by the regulatory body and with the patient's best interest in mind. They also participate in the development of the standards along with the professional bodies and the public and play a key role in the implementation of the regulatory body's processes, including those related to fitness to practise adjudications.

The public may not use the term 'regulation' but they do expect health professionals to be educated and trained to practise competently, behave professionally and that those who do not do so are not allowed to practise. Patients, clients or carers making allegations against a professional if they have concerns about the well-being of the person being compromised is also part of the regulatory process.[2]

Working together with the education providers is essential in establishing standards for education and training and in the approval of programmes leading to registration of their qualifiers.

Close liaison and good communication with professional bodies are vital to ensure that the work of each organisation is mutually beneficial to the profession. They are consulted on all the standards as they are being set and the support of the professional body for its members in areas of common interest is encouraged. For example, the provision of services to support members in meeting the standards of continuing professional development (CPD) set by the regulatory body.

Good collaboration with employers is essential in ensuring that only registered and, thus, competent practitioners are employed by them. They are consulted on standards of practice and behaviour and encouraged to notify those employees not meeting those standards to the regulatory body. In addition, employers play a vital role in ensuring continued good practice by supporting employees in their continued CPD.

Collaboration with government, through the Department of Health and the Minister for Health, is extremely important as it controls the legislation governing the rules under which the regulatory bodies act. Additionally, changes in healthcare delivery may have some impact on regulatory standards and fitness to practise.

Regulatory body, professional body and trade unions

The functions of regulatory bodies (*see* Figure 9.1) are sometimes confused with those of professional bodies and trade unions. On the one hand, giving due regard to the human rights of its registrants and taking their views into consideration, the regulatory body, through its statutory legislation, must have the interests of the public as its prime concern. This role is achieved by establishing and maintaining a register of qualified healthcare practitioners, setting standards, approving programmes of education and training leading to entry to the register and utilising its fitness to practise procedures in dealing with those registrants against whom allegations are made. All its processes are aimed at protecting the public. The trade union, on the other hand, has the interests of its members as its

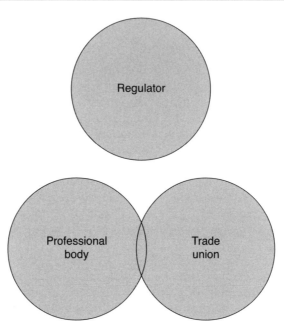

Figure 9.1 Functional separation of the regulator

main focus. It advises, supports and protects its members, particularly in matters relating to terms and conditions of employment. The professional body, which may also be a trade union and have regulatory powers, also has its members' interests and those of the profession itself as its main concerns. It is the learned society holding the profession's body of knowledge and has a major responsibility in developing the curriculum framework. It provides a wide range of services and support for its members and takes the essential leading role in the development and advancement of the profession. However, although the main focus of the professional body and that of the regulator is different, they both serve to protect the good name of the profession.

Regulation of the Allied Health Professions: Council for Professions Supplementary to Medicine

Regulation of the AHPs began in the early 1960s with the establishment of the Council for Professions Supplementary to Medicine (CPSM) through the Professions Supplementary to Medicine (PSM) Act 1960. It consisted of a Council and was allowed up to 12 statutory Boards, one for each profession that it regulated.[3] Each Board was made up of relevant professionals, doctors and lay members who had a particular expertise in the areas of knowledge and skill that underpinned that of the profession. Over approximately 40 years the number of Boards reached the Council's ceiling of 12.

The Council was composed of 36 members who were appointed to reflect a balance of interests appropriate to 1960. There was a representative member from each of the Boards, who was usually the Chairperson. In addition, there were four lay members, who included the Chairperson and two territorial members to represent the interests of Scotland and Wales, who were appointed by the Privy Council. There was also one member who was appointed by the Secretary of State for Northern Ireland. A further 13 people, who were not members of any of the registered professions, were appointed by the Department of Health. These lay members were to bring the views of patients/clients and carers, health service management and academics to Council's debates. Finally, there were nine members appointed by the Medical Royal Colleges and the General Medical Council to reflect the medical interests of the time. Two of these members were specifically Scottish.[3]

The main areas of authority of the CPSM Council were to appoint the Registrar and staff, including the Finance Officer, to support the Boards; to oversee and supervise the Boards and to act as a clearing house for issues affecting all of the Boards; to act as an appeals tribunal in disputes over registration; to make recommendations to Privy Council on approval or withdrawal of approval of courses leading to registration: to liaise with Privy Council on all matters requiring subordinate legislation and to appoint the lay members to Boards following nomination from specified external bodies. It was also the Council's responsibility to produce an Annual Report that included reports from each of the Boards.[4]

Each statutory Board had the authority to set standards for entry to the register, education and training and conduct. In order to manage these powers it established its own registration, investigating and disciplinary committees each setting the rules and regulations pertaining to its activity. In some cases a board established an education and training committee whilst others relied on the education and training activities of the relevant professional body. In later years, many of the Boards worked in partnership with the professional body of its registrants and formed Joint Validation Committees or Joint Quality Assurance Committees to undertake the role of approval of new courses for entry to the profession and to the CPSM register and to make their recommendations to the Board of CPSM and the education committee of the professional body. This joint arrangement was also used to re-approve existing courses or, where necessary, withdraw approval.

Because the Boards were independent of each other, the rules, regulations and processes were not always consistent across the professions. To minimise the anomalies that were possible, each Board had an observer from another Board with which it had professional similarities. For example, the Physiotherapists' Board had an observer from the Occupational Therapists' Board and vice versa. This procedure provided the opportunity for some sharing of ideas across the Boards but ultimately each Board still had the power to decide whether or not to adopt the processes or rules of another Board. Any anomalies that did exist resulted in registrants being treated differently by some Boards than by others which could be perceived by them as being disadvantaged.

Modernisation of regulation

Several of the Allied Health Professions and the CPSM itself had campaigned for a number of years to make changes to state registration and to protect professional titles. The need for protection of title by law had long been recognised as a need in helping to protect the public from unqualified practitioners. Additionally, because of the complex mechanism of changing regulatory legislation through an Act of Parliament and the time taken to do so, there was an urgent need to bring the rules determined by the 1960 Act up to date, especially in the area of fitness to practise. The only sanctions that could be applied to a registrant in the determination of a disciplinary hearing were to either remove a practitioner from the register or keep him or her on it. There was no flexibility to allow for the circumstances pertaining to the allegation to have any bearing on the determination. In addition, there were no rules related to or processes by which the health of the registrant could be considered.

In the mid-1990s the government commissioned an independent review of the PSM Act and in 1998 the government published its comments on what it expected of regulatory bodies in the future.[5] It was considered vital to successful statutory regulation that they should work in partnership with the government, the NHS and patient/client groups to further strengthen the existing professional self-regulatory systems. In addition, it was expected that regulators would be open, responsive and publicly accountable. The government also decided that the structure of regulatory bodies needed to be more streamlined to be more effective and efficient.

It was decided that, in order to expedite appropriate changes to the regulatory legislation, Orders in Council be provided in the Health Bill leading to the Health Act 1999. This would then allow the Privy Council to have the authority to amend, by Order, any existing legislation by which healthcare professionals were regulated. The Orders were made so as to allow the legislation framework to be kept up to date, taking into account both the public's expectations and the professions' views, without the need for primary legislation.

Subsequently, the 1960 PSM Act was repealed and replaced by an Order establishing a new health professions council that had the powers to register those already registered with the CPSM and to recommend other professional groups to be included on its register. The new Council would have a wider remit than its predecessor that would include protection of professional title, health procedures, wider disciplinary sanctions and linking CPD with re-registration.[6] It would also include a mandate for openness, responsiveness and accountability.

The Health Professions Council (HPC)

Following the repeal of the 1960 PSM Act a new regulatory body, the Health Professions Council, was established by means of the Health Professions Order 2001. This regulatory body commenced its preliminary activities in 2001 as a shadow organisation to undertake preliminary work in the development of HPC while the CPSM continued its regulatory activities until the Orders in Council received royal assent in 2002 when its powers ceased and those of HPC came into being.

HPC is an independent, UK-wide regulator of health professionals. It works on the principle of statutory professional self-regulation. It is accountable to the public, its registrants, government via the Privy Council, to whom it reports, and to other key stakeholders such as professional bodies, employers and education providers. It is not part of the Department of Health or the National Health Service. Many of its registrants are employed in the independent sector. It is a self-financing corporate body and as such corporate governance is high on its

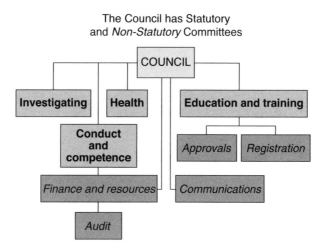

The Council has Statutory
and *Non-Statutory* Committees

Figure 9.2 HPC structure

strategic priority list. The rules for HPC were prepared during 2002–2003 and finally approved by government in July 2003. Until that point the rules of the CPSM continued to be used.

Structure of HPC

HPC consists of the Council and four statutory committees (*see* Figure 9.2).[6] It may also have non-statutory committees to assist the Council in discharging its function as a regulator.

Council

The Council comprises both registrant members and lay members. The principle underpinning the total number of members is that the number of registrant members should always exceed the number of lay members by one. Additionally, each professional group must have a member from its part of the register and an alternative member from the same part of the register who acts as a full member of Council in the absence of the registrant member. The lay members are defined as those people who are not on the register nor have ever been so. They come with expertise from all backgrounds and are appointed through the office of public appointments process, by the Privy Council.

Registrant members of Council and the alternative members are appointed by Council following election by their relevant profession. The lay member appointments, however, are made by the Privy Council. Each member's term of office is for a period of four years. To ensure a UK-wide representation on Council there must be at least one member from each of the four countries and that member must work wholly or mainly in the country concerned.

The Council is led by a President who is elected by and from Council for a period of four years. If the chosen President is a registrant member, another registrant member from the same part of the register and an additional lay member will be appointed to Council.

Statutory committees

These are the committees that must be established by HPC according to the Health Professions Order.

The four statutory committees are the Education and Training Committee and three Practice Committees which are the Investigating Committee, the Conduct and Competence Committee and the Health Committee. The Chairman of each committee is elected by and from its membership and must be a member of Council.

The Education and Training Committee must have at least one member from each part of the register, one person appointed from each country in the UK and one lay person who represents the interests of users of the services of registrants. The majority of the membership of this committee should be qualified and experienced in professional education provision, funding or assessment.

The Practice Committees consist of registered members and lay members, one of whom must be a registered medical practitioner. The number of registered members may exceed the number of other members by one. The interests of the four countries of the UK are also taken into consideration when committee members are appointed. No-one may be a member of more than one of the Practice Committees.

Non-statutory committees

The Council may appoint as many non-statutory committees as it deems necessary for the organisation to perform its duties efficiently and effectively. At the line of writing there are currently five such committees: the Finance and Resources Committee, the Audit Committee, the Communications Committee, the Registration Committee and the Approvals Committee. Each of these committees has a membership that includes both registrant and lay members and may appoint members from outside Council that have relevant expertise.

All external appointments to the statutory and non-statutory committees are subject to the guidance of the Commissioner for Public Appointments.

Panels

In addition, the Practice Committees, which have a strategic function in HPC's activities, have the authority to establish panels through which they can implement the processes to consider allegations related to their duties. Hence, there are Investigation Panels, Health Panels and Conduct and Competence Panels.

Each panel is constituted according to the professional field of the registrant concerned and the nature of the issue. Thus the membership comprises at least one member from the same part of the register as that of the registrant under consideration and at least one lay member who is not a registered medical practitioner, none of which are Council members. In the case of a Health Panel there must be one or more registered medical practitioner. The number of registrant members of a panel may exceed that of lay members. No member of Council may chair a Practice Panel.

The Education and Training Committee does not have panels but has a pool of Visitors on which it can draw appropriately to participate in the approvals process for programmes leading to the eligibility for registration. Similarly, the

Registration Committee's work in relation to international applicants for registration is undertaken by appointed assessors.

The people who participate in panels, the approvals process and the assessment of international applications for registration include registrants, lay people, medical assessors and legal assessors and are referred to as 'Partners' of whom there are over 360. These are all appointed by the Council using the public appointments process.

Professional liaison groups (PLGs)

The Council or its committees may, at any time that it is considered appropriate, set up PLGs to undertake project specific work necessary to the development of its functions. These groups are made up of members of Council with the relevant expertise and interest and may invite any external person whom they feel would be able to additionally contribute to their work. PLGs have a limited lifespan and a specified budget. Once their objectives are achieved the PLGs are disbanded.

The executive team

The Council is the strategic hub of HPC, making decisions and declarations concerning its intentions in fulfilling its duties as a regulator (*see* Figure 9.3). The executive team led by the Chief Executive and Registrar is responsible for putting in place processes to achieve the Council's objectives. Each committee has a team of people who work to implement the strategy developed by the committee.

The Chief Executive, who is appointed by Council, has the responsibility of ensuring that the register is up to date and that it is accessible to the general public. He is also the overall manager of the team of people that undertake the day-to-day work of the organisation and is responsible for the quality of service provided by the organisation. External standards of quality assurance are used such as those of the International Standards Office (ISO) 9001-2000 and the Plain English Society. He is also the accounting officer and is responsible to Privy Council for the financial status of the organisation.

Strategic intent

The Council as the strategic hub of HPC declared that its intention was to create an independent healthcare regulator with a leading reputation, using the following six guiding principles.

1   Protection of the public.
2   Communication and responsiveness.
3   Value for money and audit.
4   Transparency.
5   Collaboration.
6   Provision of a quality service.

In all Council or Committee deliberations the notion of *protecting the public* is always the prime focus. All its strategic and operational planning and process developments are done with users of registrants' services at the forefront of HPC's mind.

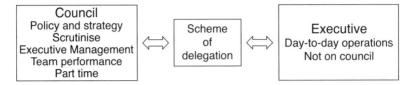

Figure 9.3 Role of Council and Executive

Council has created a Communications Committee and appointed staff with expertise in the fields of communications because, even though it is required by the legislation, Council is of the firm belief that, in order for it to be effective in achieving its prime aim, it must raise awareness of its objectives and processes to all its key stakeholders. HPC has, thus, produced brochures and leaflets, produced an Annual Report, placed advertisements in popular magazines, broadcast on radio, and continues to extend its range of publicity activities.

One of the committee's first tasks was to identify its key stakeholders:

- carers
- patients; clients; users
- consumer associations
- trade unions
- government
- special interest professional groups
- members of the public
- professional bodies
- registrants
- employers
- education providers.

The Communications Committee has developed a strategic plan whereby HPC can inform and receive comments and recommendations from all interested parties. The features that were considered in the planning were that implementation should be cost-effective, targeted and follow themes that were appropriate to the stage of development of HPC. The organisation has consulted widely across the whole of the UK on all its proposals for its standards and rules as they have been developed. Consultation exercises have not been localised to paper and information technology but members of Council have met with stakeholders at face to face events around all four countries. HPC will continue this process as revisions are made in the future. Council holds 'listening events' on a regular basis and an Annual General Meeting, where again members of Council come into direct contact with stakeholders. In addition, the Chief Executive, the president and members of Council regularly meet with those interested in the work of HPC.

A website has been developed that publishes new proposals, the Standards, results of fitness to practise hearings, details of Council members and much more information about HPC including how to make contact with the organisation www.hpc-uk.org. The communications strategy of HPC is being reviewed and revised constantly to ensure that Council fulfils its obligation, as stated in the legislation, to inform and educate registrants and the public about its work.

Council, through its executive team, has put in place specifically designed information technology to enable its responsiveness to be effective and efficient when anyone makes contact with it, either in the UK or abroad. It is essential that those requiring registration have their applications dealt with swiftly. HPC must always be in a position to be responsive to changes in healthcare delivery that may impact on its strategic planning and its processes. The legislation allows HPC to have some flexibility in developing its strategy and processes that enables it to respond to such external changes without the need for introducing new legislation.

HPC is conscious of its responsibility in relation to fulfilling its role in an economical way. Registrants, who provide the financial support for the organisation, require value for money. With this in mind, scrutiny of the fiscal aspect of HPC is very important. The Finance Committee has oversight of the finances on a regular basis and a report of its activities is received by Council at each of its meetings. The Finance Committee recommends to Council long- and short-term plans for HPC's work along with an annual budget set by the Chief Executive and the Finance Officer. In addition to the required external audit of accounts, Council has established an internal audit committee whose additional role is to undertake regular risk analyses to ensure that HPC is not faced with unanticipated large amounts of expenditure.

Transparency of the work of HPC is essential and forms part of its communication strategy. Additionally, all Council and committee meetings and fitness to practise hearings are open to the public. Additionally, minutes of Council and committee meetings and transcripts of fitness to practise hearing are published on the website.

HPC could not be effective if it were to work in isolation. It is committed to collaboration with a wide range of external bodies and groups. Regular meetings are held with professional bodies, the Department of Health, other healthcare regulators and education providers. HPC's objective of becoming a leader in the field of regulation could not be achieved without guidance, advice and professional expertise from external sources.

HPC aims to provide a quality service to all its stakeholders. This can only be achieved by reviewing its strategy and processes on a regular basis with the expertise of all interested parties. Lessons are constantly being learned and modifications are made in response to them. However, major reviews become necessary for HPC to meet the challenges of the ever changing world in which it exists.

HPC's purpose

The realisation of HPC's aim of public protection is primarily through the following key processes.

1 Approval of programmes of education and training for entry to the register.
2 Establishing and operating a register.
3 Setting standards.
4 Intervening where a registrant's fitness to practise is alleged to be below standard.

Approval of programmes of education and training

This duty is undertaken by the Approvals Committee. The process consists of the assessment of programmes against the standards of proficiency and the standards of education and training. Proposed programmes or major modifications proposed for an existing programme are considered in two parts, Firstly, documentation regarding the programme is submitted to the Approvals Committee for scrutiny. Visitors appropriate to the profession or professions concerned are appointed by the Committee to assess the document and subsequently to visit the education provider to clarify any issues. The Visitors will then make their recommendations to the Approvals Committee. Withdrawal of approval of an existing course may take place if the education provider fails to meet any conditions of approval as were thought necessary.

Ongoing monitoring of approved programmes will take place mainly through scrutiny of reports of the education provider and others, such as the Department of Health, and where it is considered necessary another approval process will be entered into.

The register

This is the responsibility of the Chief Executive and Registrar. Admission to the register is open to those people who have followed an approved education and training programme in the UK and have received the qualification recognised by HPC as appropriate to that programme. Each applicant is required to self-certify that they meet the HPC's standards of proficiency. International applicants and those people returning to practice after a period of absence must satisfy HPC that they meet the standards of proficiency that it has set. In addition, all new registrants and those re-registering must provide evidence of good health and good character and pay the required registration fee. Re-registration is required biannually and, additionally, will be subject to the registrant meeting the standards of CPD.

Currently there are approximately 170 000 names of practitioners on the HPC register; not all are resident in the UK.

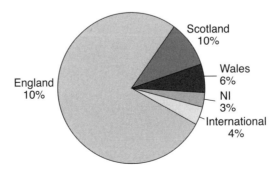

Figure 9.4 HPC registrants by nationality

HPC currently regulates 13 Professional groups.

1 Arts therapists
   - art therapists
   - drama therapists
   - music therapists.
2 Biomedical scientists.
3 Chiropodists and podiatrists.
4 Clinical scientists.
5 Dietitians.
6 Occupational therapists.
7 Operating department practitioners.
8 Orthoptists.
9 Paramedics.
10 Physiotherapists.
11 Prosthetists and orthotists.
12 Radiographers – diagnostic and therapeutic.
13 Speech and language therapists.

Some of the groups contain more than one related profession as in the case of the arts therapists. The number of registrants within each professional group varies, with physiotherapists having the greatest number and prosthetists and orthotists the least.

On average there has been a 4.5% growth in the number of registrants each year since the register was first created. International migration is increasing and it is very important that 'problem' international applicants are detected. To this end the applicant must provide HPC with a letter of good standing. HPC has also developed good co-operation and communication with many other international regulators to ensure that regulators worldwide are notified of sanctions made against registrants.

CPD and re-registration

Council has agreed that CPD should be linked to re-registration and has set the standards of CPD against which registrants will be judged. The re-registration

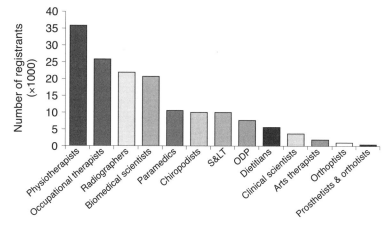

Figure 9.5 Number of HPC registrants

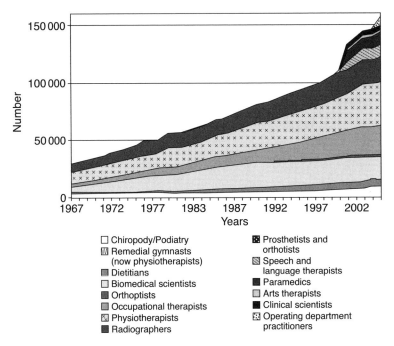

Figure 9.6 Health professions' growth

form will require self-declaration that the individual has met the standards as set by HPC. A random sample of approximately 2.5% of those re-registering will be required to submit evidence to support the declaration. This will then be scrutinised by partners in the relevant profession who have the expertise related to the CPD presented.

New professions

Over the next few years the register will grow considerably since its legislation does not restrict the number of professions it may regulate. There are many groups that have expressed an interest in being regulated by HPC, for example:

- Applied psychologists.
- Dance movement therapists.
- Medical illustrators.
- Clinical perfusionists.
- Clinical physiologists.
- Clinical technologists.
- Healthcare scientists.
- Sonographers.
- Sports therapists.
- Sports rehabilitation therapists.
- Psychotherapists.

The process of assessment for regulation of such groups consists of two stages. The first stage involves HPC and Council making an assessment of an application set against ten criteria. This involves scrutiny of submitted documentation and a presentation to Council by representative members of the relevant profession.

Once Council is satisfied with the application, it makes a recommendation to the Minister that the said profession be regulated. The DH then continues the process by consulting widely on the proposal and finally Privy Council decides reapplication.

In addition, even when HPC has not received an application for regulation it has the power to recommend regulation of a specific profession where necessary.

Protection of title

Market research has indicated that the public requires specific professional titles to be protected. It also demonstrated that the number of titles protected should be limited to help public recognition.[6]

From July 2005, the use of titles reserved for us by registrants has been illegal if used by non-registrants. Previously anyone or indeed everyone could call themselves a physiotherapist, for example, whether or not they were qualified and judged safe to practise. It is now a criminal offence to do so and HPC has the authority to take people to court, who falsely use such a title or imply that they have the required skills and knowledge of that profession. HPC is in the process of communicating widely on the sanctions related to misuse of titles of its registrants.

Previously, a registrant could use the term 'State Registered' or SR in association with the professional title. This is being actively discouraged by the HPC for those professions where 'grandparenting' has been completed.

'Grandparenting'

This is a process that is triggered when a new profession comes on to the register and, thus, has its chosen titles protected. It sets aside the normal education and training requirements but applicants need to demonstrate that they have been practising, lawfully, safely and effectively for a minimum of three years prior to applying for registration. These submissions are scrutinised by members of that profession who have recognised qualifications for registration and a decision made as to whether or not the applicant should be registered. The period for applications through the 'grandparenting' process has a limited life span of two years from the opening of the register for that profession. There is a fee for this process to be undertaken, in addition to the registration fee.

Standards

As required by the legislation, HPC has set standards following wide consultation on each of them. These are to be used by registrants and stakeholders for guidance about the expectations of the HPC.

Standards of conduct, performance and ethics[7]

These apply to all registrants and prospective registrants, for example students undertaking a programme of study that leads to eligibility for registration with HPC. They are common to all the healthcare professionals that are registered with

HPC in every respect. These standards include guidance on conduct such as 'maintain high standards of personal conduct', performance, for example 'keep accurate patient, client and user records', and ethics, e.g. 'behave with integrity and honesty'.

Standards of proficiency[8]

These standards set out the threshold level of competence for entry to the register.

There are two components. There are those standards that are common to all the professions such as those of communication skills and those that are specific to each individual profession, that is, the skills and knowledge that are required to undertake a particular profession. The standards express the expectations of HPC, the skills required to practise and the knowledge that underpins those skills and their application. The development of these standards was a multiprofessional project involving a great amount of input from expert registrants and professional bodies.

Standards of education and training[9]

These set out the standards for the education and training of prospective registrants. They underpin the delivery of the relevant programmes leading to a qualifier's eligibility for registration with HPC. They are used together with the standards of proficiency in the approvals process for recognition of education providers and their programmes. They are sufficiently flexible to be used either in the approval of a programme for a single profession or for multi- or interprofessional programmes. They have been developed through a PLG which, like the standards of proficiency, had a major input from registrants with expertise in education, others with expertise in education and the professional bodies.

Standards of continuing professional development[10]

Another PLG was established to develop these standards that once again involved a wide range of expertise from both within the HPC and from other organisations external to it. These standards give guidance of what the HPC considers CPD to be, the various modes of learning and how it will link CPD to re-registration. The standards are to be supported by the provision of guidelines for registrants and employers on what HPC expects in the way of evidence of having undertaken some CPD for the two-year period prior to re-registration. Although the content of any learning must be relevant to the registrant's current post the amount of CPD is not necessarily of such importance. What is of importance is how the learning has impacted on the registrant's practice.

Fitness to practise[11]

The fitness to practise process commences when an allegation is made against a registrant. Allegations may come from a wide range of sources such as patients or carers, an employer, or one or more of the registrant's peers. Such allegations are often handled in parallel with other organisations.

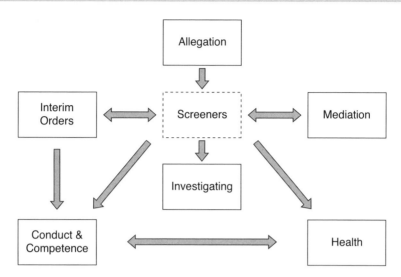

Figure 9.7 Fitness to practise process

The aim of the Practice Panels when assessing cases is to determine if they need to take action to protect the public. It is important, however, to balance that with the human rights of registrants. The Health Professions Order sets out the type of allegations regarding a registrant's practice that HPC can consider. These are:

- misconduct
- lack of competence
- a conviction or caution in the UK for a criminal offence
- a conviction elsewhere which, if committed in England or Wales, would constitute a criminal offence
- physical or mental health
- a determination by another health or social care regulator.

HPC may also respond to allegations regarding fraudulent entries to the register.

The Investigating Committee Panel

HPC's powers allow for the appointment of screeners to decide if the allegation should go to the Investigating Committee. However, Council has agreed that all allegations go directly to the Investigating Panel as the need for prior screening has not been proven to be necessary.

It is the responsibility of this panel, on receipt of an allegation, to consider whether there is a case to answer. The documentation is considered in private and should it agree that there is a case to answer it may:

- recommend mediation
- refer the case to the Health Committee Panel where there is considered to be a question about the registrant's health
- refer the case to the Conduct and Competence Panel.

Cases of fraudulent entry to the register are not dealt with alongside cases relating to fitness to practise. They are dealt with through a different Investigating Committee Panel as they are not related to practice issues directly. This panel would direct the registrar to remove or amend the entry on the register, as necessary.

The Health Committee Panel

The role of the Health Committee Panel is to consider any cases referred to it by the Investigating Committee Panel or the Fitness to Practise Panel. It considers whether the registrant's practice has been impaired by mental or physical ill health. In addition, it may consider any application for restoration to the register. This panel may then refer the case either to the Fitness to Practise Panel, where there is no evidence of ill health affecting the performance of a registrant, or, where health problems are confirmed, may make a recommendation to instruct the registrar to suspend the registrant from the register for a period of time or the panel may decide there is no case to answer.

Fitness to Practise Panel

These Panels have responsibility under the guidance of a legal assessor on legal matters. There are a range of sanctions that can be applied to the determination if the case is proven. These are applied using the principles of proportionality and reasonableness. The sanctions are:

- to take no further action
- to impose conditions of practice for no more than two years
- to direct the registrar to suspend the registration for a period of not more than one year
- to direct the registrar to take the registrant off the register.

In cases of suspension of registration or conditions of practice the case is reviewed with a view to the possibility of re-instatement on the register.

Appeals against the decision of the Fitness to Practise Panels can be made through the courts.

Interim suspension orders

In certain cases an interim order may be issued. This may only be introduced where continued practice is perceived to be a threat to the safety of members of the public, to serve the interests of the public in some other way or to serve the interest of the registrant. Such an order may impose conditions of practice or it may suspend the registrant until such time as the case is heard. The order lasts until a final decision on the case has been reached.

The Council for Healthcare Regulatory Excellence (CHRE)

Background

The NHS Plan, the consultation document *Modernising Regulation of the Health Professions* and the report of the Bristol Royal Infirmary Inquiry (the Kennedy Report) all highlighted the need to provide a common framework across all the healthcare regulators.

This proposal became reality in April 2003 by the establishment of a body entitled the Council for the Regulation of Healthcare Professionals (CRHP) with a UK-wide remit. This was brought about through the NHS Reform and Health Care Professions Act 2002. In 2004 the Council agreed to change its name to The Council for Healthcare Regulatory Excellence with the intention of reflecting the nature of its work more accurately.

The Council consists of 19 members. There is one representative from each of the nine UK healthcare regulators and ten lay members. It has an executive team that has the role of implementing the Council's strategy.

Mission statement

Its mission is to protect the public interest, promote and achieve excellence in relation to regulating healthcare professionals.

The role of CHRE

The role of this overarching body is to contribute to developing professionally led regulation in healthcare to protect the public.

Funding and accountability

The Council is funded by the DH and is accountable to the UK Parliament.

Responsibilities

These are set out in the Act which gives CHRE the powers to:

- promote the interests of the public and patients in relation to regulating healthcare professions
- promote best practice in healthcare regulation
- develop principles for good, professionally led regulation of the healthcare professions
- promote co-operation between regulators and other organisations.

The powers allow for CHRE to undertake an annual review of the performance of each of the healthcare regulators, compare performances of different regulators, recommend changes in the processes used by regulatory bodies, identify examples of good practice that currently exist and highlight factors that interfere with good practice.

It also has a clearly defined role in the scrutiny of 'undue leniency' in determinations made as a result of regulators' fitness to practise hearing. It has the power to refer such cases to the High Court for further adjudication. It can only look at the decisions that are made at the hearing stage. CHRE has no powers to look at those cases where an initial decision that there is no case to answer has been made.

There is a need, in the eyes of the public and others, that all registrants should be dealt with similarly, and this makes a good case for sharing of good practice across regulators.

Currently there are two project groups that have been established by the government to review healthcare regulation across the whole spectrum following the publication of the Shipman Report. There is the Chief Medical Officers group to review medical regulation and the Foster review group for the remainder of the professions. This is disappointing in principle as by separating medical regulation from the others there seems to be an immediate barrier to harmonisation of regulation. It is fair to say, however, that there are links between the two groups so sharing of good practice should occur.

Regulation and protection of the public have never been perfect but are getting much better due to a more open approach to regulation. It is fundamental that if regulation in healthcare is to be effective there has to be trust in the regulating bodies given by both registrants and members of the public. The public needs to be assured that all efforts are being made to protect them from the few deviants each profession has. It is important to remember that by far the majority of healthcare professionals are responsible people who do put their patients first. However, it is always the few deviants who are brought into the limelight by the media, creating an impression that all healthcare workers are not to be trusted. The truth of the matter is that most of them are.

References

1 The Health Professions Order 2001: Health Care and Associated Professions: Health Professions. London: The Stationery Office; 2001.

2 Norman S. Partnership: professional regulation. *Nursing Management*. 1999; 6(4 July/August): 33–7.

3 *Professions Supplementary to Medicine Act 1960*.

4 CPSM. About the Council; 2000.

5 Department of Health. *A First Class Service: quality in the NHS*. London: HMSO; 1998.

6 HPC. HPC, Presentation. London: HPC; 2005.

7 HPC. *Standards of Conduct, Performance and Ethics*. London: HPC; 2002.

8 HPC. *Standards of Proficiency*. London: HPC; 2002.

9 HPC. *Standards of Education and Training*. London: HPC; 2004.

10 HPC. *Standards of Continuing Professional Development*. London: HPC; 2005.

11 HPC. *Annual Report: Fitness to Practise*. London: HPC; 2005.

Chapter 10

From clinical governance to integrated governance

Amanda Squires

Introduction

The Commission for Health Improvement (CHI) independent reviews of clinical governance in over 300 NHS trusts across the UK between 2000 and 2003 identified considerable deficits in AHP arrangements. The fundamental problem seemed to be weak representation at a strategic level and lack of confidence in influencing strategic decisions which were barriers to the involvement of AHPs in the clinical governance agenda.

This resulted in AHPs being marginalised in core developments, both strategic and operational.

Whilst clinical professionalism was widely acknowledged, AHPs often seemed unable to take professionalism in the wider management sense beyond the clinic door. This lack of confidence inhibited the ability to influence, constructively challenge and suggest innovative ways of working.

The NHS 'quality' agenda: 1990

Healthcare has become a universal political priority as a result of its impact on national economy, the risks to health shared by the community, and a moral responsibility for equity of care within societies regarded as developed. The welfare-style NHS, created in 1948 to meet these economic, social and moral requirements, typified the expectations of the British post-war culture.

Since the Second World War interest had been raised in the universal concept of quality by a combination of factors including economic competition, environmental concerns and activity of the quality gurus in the manufacturing sector. Quality management arrangements progressed through quality control (product checked at the *end* of the process and accepted or discarded) with the next stage being actually learning from what was found[1] (*see* Figure 10.1).

The next stage was quality assurance (by employee observation and appropriate action during the process) depicted by Deming,[2] who added the 'action' component to Shewhart's cycle, becoming known as the 'Plan/Do/Check/Act Deming Cycle' (*see* Figure 10.2).

By 1990, changing influences, especially raised public expectations from experience in the competitive retail sector, resulted in political focus on British welfare services and the subsequent introduction of market style provision. The aim was to enable provision of care to become customer- rather than service-led

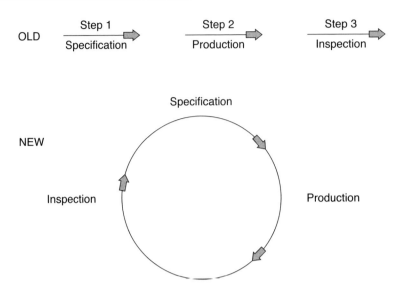

Figure 10.1 Linear and circular quality control. Adapted from Shewhart[1]

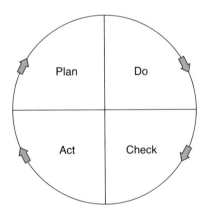

Figure 10.2 The Deming quality assurance cycle

and to reduce public expenditure. The government underestimated public suspicion its motives in creating a healthcare market; fears that it would lead to rationing; and above all the continuing appeal of the NHS to most of the British public.[3] There appeared to be support for improving quality and efficiency but that market principles were not the answer, where focus had been on cost and activity.

The concept of clinical governance: 1998

The 1997 reforms aimed to make the NHS 'modern and dependable'[4] with statutory responsibility for clinical performance allocated to chief executives. Governance, a 'system of governing', has been an accustomed term in commerce

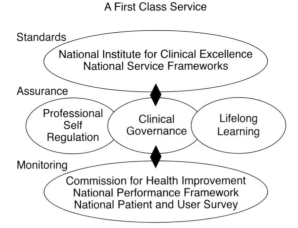

A First Class Service

Setting Standards

National Institute for Clinical Excellence (NICE): wide membership to produce cost-effective clinical practice guidelines.

National Service Frameworks: for best organisation of services.

Assurance

Clinical governance process to assure clinical decisions.
Lifelong learning: tools for effective, high quality care.
Professional self-regulation: sets, enforces and ensures professional and clinical standards.

Monitoring

Commission for Health Improvement (CHI): rolling programme of independent reviews, focused reviews, with power to intervene.
National framework for assessing performance: to monitor delivery.
National survey of patient and user experience: monitor experiences; results could trigger reviews.

Figure 10.3 Setting, delivering and monitoring standards

but has only relatively recently been used in UK healthcare. Clinical governance was introduced in 1998 in the White Paper, *A First Class Service: quality in the new NHS*[5] as part of a comprehensive approach to improving quality in the NHS (*see* Figure 10.3).

Clinical governance was defined[5] as:

> . . . a framework through which NHS organisations are accountable for continuously improving the quality of their services and safeguarding high standards of care by creating an environment in which excellence in clinical care will flourish.

The Clinical Governance Support Team was established to help organisations implement clinical governance, offering support, information and lessons learnt across the country.[6]

Although the focus was on clinical care in an attempt to redress the power balance, it was envisaged that in the future, well managed organisations would be those in which financial control, service performance and clinical quality were fully integrated at every level.[7]

CHI was established by the Health Act 1999 with the remit to monitor and help improve the quality of healthcare provided by the NHS through a cyclical four yearly review of their clinical governance arrangements and investigating service failures. It undertook the former function by a national programme of clinical governance reviews where review teams assessed how well clinical governance was working throughout the NHS by making enquiries at corporate and directorate levels and in clinical teams within NHS trusts. Eight review areas, or pillars, were identified by the Commission.

1 **Patient, carer, service user and public involvement:** How patients, carers, service users and the public have a say in decision making about health service delivery, policy and planning.
2 **Risk management:** The systems to understand, monitor and minimise the risks to patients and staff and to learn from mistakes.
3 **Clinical audit:** The regular systematic review of procedures against defined standards leading to action to address any identified problems.
4 **Clinical effectiveness:** Ensuring that the approaches and treatments used are based on the best available evidence.
5 **Staffing and staff management:** The recruitment, management, and development of staff and the promotion of good working conditions and effective methods of working.
6 **Education, training and continuing professional development:** The support available to enable staff to be competent in doing their jobs, whilst developing their skills and the degree to which staff are up to date with developments in their field.
7 **Use of information:** The systems in place to collect and interpret clinical and other information and to use it to monitor, plan and improve the quality of patient care.
8 **Strategic capacity:** How the organisation is leading and implementing clinical governance.

Other individuals and organisations have promoted different components/pillars, but the common factor is always how the components interrelate for a comprehensive approach. So that, for example, using the CHI components, effective leadership style would influence the culture whereby clinical audit programmes would be developed with users, be based on information from complaints and risk assessments, be included in a staff training programme with staff appraisal to identify progress and further development needs.

CHI selected trusts for clinical governance review by using a structured sampling technique to ensure geographic spread. Pathways, teams and sites were chosen within a trust on the basis of analysis to act as a sample of the trust's clinical governance activity.

The purpose of the review was to answer:

• What is it like to be a patient/service user?
• What are the systems and processes in place for safeguarding and improving the quality of care?

- What is the capacity in the organisation for improving the patient/service user experience?

The aim was to test whether clinical governance arrangements were working at grass roots level. This was undertaken by peer review through recruited and trained NHS and lay reviewers, supported by a team of CHI staff. Following a report on the review, the trust produced and was required to act on a plan from the findings. The results of the review and progress on actions contributed to trust star ratings.

The National Audit Office[8] stated that the clinical governance review process had had many beneficial impacts including that clinical quality was more mainstream; there was greater accountability for clinical performance; and there were more transparent and collaborative ways of working. However, there was a need to improve the way lessons were learnt from the reports and ensuing action plans, and also across the NHS.

A consistent finding has been the lack of integration of the components of clinical governance, some of which were exemplary on their own, but largely failed to contribute to comprehensive quality of services. It was noted above that mature clinical governance should be how the components interrelate for a comprehensive approach to service improvement.

An evaluation of the first 175 reviews[9] indicated that:

- NHS organisations were reactive rather than proactive.
- There was a lack of organisation-wide policies.
- Learning was not shared between and across organisations.
- Communication was not effective.
- There was a lack of sharing from the strategic to the operational level and between clinicians.

The findings also showed that of the seven components, four were of most concern.

1 **Risk management:** Many trusts were poor at managing potential risks; staff feared reprisals on reporting failures; staff shortages and poor attendance at mandatory training events increased the risks.
2 **Staffing and staff management:** Trusts had poor workforce planning and career development; there was poor management of locum and bank staff; and widespread failure to regularly check professional registration.
3 **Patient involvement:** Very few trusts were routinely involving patients and relatives in development of services and policies; shortage of information to patients on their care; barriers to making complaints.
4 **Use of information:** There was poor access to and use of information and some breaches of confidentiality.

Recurring AHP themes from the first 329 CHI reports[10] were as follows.

- **Staffing and staff management:** Well organised, some examples of good leadership, appraisal and PDP in place, widespread staffing shortages in most AHP professions, no shared vision of what a future integrated workforce could look like.
- **Education training and CPD:** Poorer access to training than other clinicians.
- **Audit research and effectiveness:** Lack of understanding of audit and EBP

structures within organisations so conduct these activities in isolation from other disciplines and fail to report activities.
- **Strategic capacity:** Weak representation at a strategic level.

This last point is probably the most significant, as such strategic leadership could address integrated workforce plans, equitable access to training and relevant contribution to organisation-wide audits (*see* Chapter 5).

Clinical governance reviews introduced a culture of external peer review of governance arrangements and consequently sought to listen to public concerns and engage managers – a necessary first step. If continuous quality improvement – the goal of clinical governance systems and processes – is to become a reality in healthcare organisations the understanding of the underlying concepts needs to be improved and embedded throughout organisations and the separate elements or pillars seen as an integrated whole.

In 2004, the Manchester Centre for Healthcare Management published their review of effectiveness and future of clinical governance reviews.[11] This showed that there was widespread acceptance of recommendations which mostly focused on systems, processes and management, which were addressed by trusts in their action plans and were mostly implemented. Recommendations included that the process for selecting organisations for review should enable resources to be targeted more effectively on areas of risk; recommendations should be implemented; and that reviews should be less cyclical to avoid similar cyclical peaks in performance.

In addition, trusts, PCTs and SHAs consistently reported on the resource burden of responding to data requests of the many regulators visiting them, some in parallel. This included the volume of requests; the perceived usefulness of some of the data requested; the duplication and inconsistency of requests; and the lack of co-ordination between various regulatory and other bodies.

Beyond clinical governance: 2006

While quality control and quality assurance can be achieved, being definable, quality *per se* by its responsive nature to changing needs can never be achieved. However, a culture of continuous quality improvement is achievable where employees continuously seek to satisfy the changing needs that matter to the individual rather than being carried out purely for monitoring purposes.[12] This concept is particularly attractive to autonomous practitioners who can assure managers, colleagues and the public that routine work is carried out correctly, leaving opportunities for exciting research and development which in themselves may result in best practice standards from which to progress further.

Continuous quality improvement aims to define and at least meet, if not exceed, ascending and expanding expectations. The new position becomes the minimal standard and continuous quality improvement can again move ahead. This ascending motion has been depicted by the Deming Cycle ratcheting quality up the incline of expectations, securing each improvement in a standard with audit and review programme (*see* Figure 10.4).[13]

National Standards for the NHS were published in 2004[14] which include a framework for both NHS and social service authorities to use in planning their services towards integration, and standards which all organisations should achieve in delivering NHS care. These standards are in seven domains.

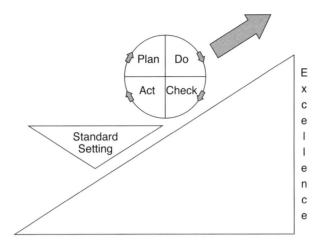

Figure 10.4 Ascending quality improvement Adapted from Koch, 1990[13]

1 **Safety:** Patient safety is enhanced by the use of healthcare processes, working practices and systematic activities that prevent or reduce the risk of harm to patients.
2 **Clinical and cost-effectiveness:** Patients achieve healthcare benefits that meet their individual needs through healthcare decisions and services based on what assessed research evidence has shown provides effective clinical outcomes.
3 **Governance:** Managerial and clinical leadership and accountability, as well as the organisation's culture, systems and working practices, ensure that probity, quality assurance, quality improvement and patient safety are central components of all the activities of the healthcare organisation.
4 **Patient focus:** Healthcare is provided in partnership with patients, their carers and relatives, respecting their diverse needs, preferences and choices, and in partnership with other organisations (especially social care organisations) whose services impact on patient well-being.
5 **Accessible and responsive care:** Patients receive services as promptly as possible, have choice in access to services and treatments, and do not experience unnecessary delay at any stage of service delivery or of the care pathway.
6 **Care environment and amenities:** Care is provided in environments that promote patient and staff well-being and respect for patients' needs and preferences in that they are designed for effective and safe delivery of treatment, care or specific function, provide as much privacy as possible, are well maintained and are cleaned to optimise health outcomes for patients.
7 **Public health:** Programmes and services are designed and delivered in collaboration with all relevant organisations and communities to promote, protect and improve the health of the population served and reduce health inequalities between different population groups and areas.

Each domain contains core standards based on existing requirements that the NHS is expected to be meeting already. There are also developmental standards which indicate the expected direction of travel in line with increasing user expectations, moving towards the excellence goal depicted in Figure 10.4. The concept is of integrated governance, rather than separate clinical and other functions which impact on each, rarely interrelate and have gaps or duplication of effort. It can only be hoped that CHI reports which identified such failings have been taken seriously throughout trusts and that new assessments under the Healthcare Commission will show evidence of lessons learnt within AHP areas.

Integrated governance has been described as:

> Systems and processes by which Trusts lead, direct and control their functions in order to achieve organisational objectives, safety and quality of services and in which they relate to the wider community and partner organisations.[15]

The approach is led by organisational objectives for clinical and other requirements, has systems to support them and information supporting key indicators on which to monitor and improve. It is proposed that current governance systems are not abandoned but form the building blocks of this new approach. It was expected by the Department of Health that the framework for integrated governance rolled out in April 2005 with implementation over the following two years.

The private and voluntary sectors are already required to meet minimum standards.[16] The Healthcare Commission has a duty to inspect independent (private and voluntary) registered practices annually. With an increasing number of NHS patients being treated in the private sector at NHS expense, it makes sense to have an integrated approach to these standards covering both sectors. This will happen over the next two years.

The Healthcare Commission has defined elements of the standards to assist organisations to assure themselves that they are meeting the core standards. The Commission requested organisations to declare their compliance with the standards and report exceptions; it corroborates this against other information, e.g. stakeholder views; patient and staff surveys and published reports. Where there is concern that a core standard is not being met the trust will be approached for further evidence and some trusts selected at random will be required to provide additional evidence on declared compliance. Interventions are proposed at various levels of intensity – from virtual, e.g. data checking, telephone contact to visits, with the option of onward referral to investigation if there is concern about potential failure of an organisation putting patient safety at risk. Reports will be made of Healthcare Commission findings and followed up.

In addition, to address the issue of resource burden on trusts, one of the Healthcare Commission's statutory functions is to co-ordinate the activity of other bodies which inspect healthcare by seeking to use the same information where possible, integrate inspection programmes, share findings and co-ordinate action planning.

The Core Standards Assessment is one of several products that the Healthcare Commission will use to identify the position the trust has on its route to continuous improvement, helping to facilitate this aspiration. Other products include improvement reviews and investigations.

Opportunities and threats for the Allied Health Professions

The reviews of clinical governance activity provided for the first time a national, independent picture of the AHP contribution. The message may not be welcome, and other disciplines also have much to learn. The opportunity now is for these issues to be taken seriously at national and local professional levels; appropriate changes made and embedded within professions that want to change; and progress monitored by the reports coming out of future national, independent assessments. The key to success would seem to be effective strategic representation of a group of staff actively working together (*see* Chapter 5). It is irrelevant to patients, trusts, national government and inspectorates what colour collar edge therapists display. The complexities of care pathways to meet increasingly complex health and social care situations require a truly integrated, interdisciplinary, interagency and innovative approach from all disciplines. It can only be hoped that AHPs will at least be actively involved, if not actually lead some of this work (*see* Chapter 6).

Conclusion

In the last 15 years, the NHS has experienced a transformation in terms of its approach to quality improvement as the needs of the society it serves have changed. From a service which was largely protected from external observation, it first experienced competition, then largely qualitative peer review and now enters objective self-assessment against objective and comprehensive standards. AHPs make up a very large and potentially influential part of healthcare provision, especially when this includes the private, social service and education sectors (*see* Chapters 1 and 4). Moving the government agenda forward together across disciplines and sectors is essential. Integrated implementation of the good practice recommendations within this series of books would significantly contribute to integrated governance requirements. Allied is, after all, defined as united.

Acknowledgements

Jo Dent, AHP Adviser, Healthcare Commission
Neil Prime, Development Manager, Healthcare Commission
Lisa Robinson, Criteria Development Team, Healthcare Commission

Disclaimer

The views expressed in this chapter are the personal views of the author and are not necessarily the views of the Healthcare Commission.

References

1 Shewhart WA. *Statistical Method: from the viewpoint of quality control*. New York: Lancaster Press; 1939.
2 Deming WE. *Out of the Crisis*. Cambridge: Cambridge University Press; 1982.
3 Rivett G. *From Cradle to Grave: fifty years of the NHS*. London: King's Fund; 1998.

4 Department of Health. *The New NHS: modern, dependable.* (Cm. 3807). London. Stationery Office; 1997. www.dh.gov.uk.
5 Department of Health. *A First Class Service: quality in the NHS.* London: HMSO; 1998.
6 Clinical Governance Support Team. www.cgsupportr.nhs.uk.
7 Scally G, Donaldson L. Clinical Governance and the drive for quality improvement in the new NHS in England. *BMJ.* 1998; **317**: 61–5.
8 National Audit Office. *Achieving Improvements Through Clinical Governance.* London: National Audit Office; 2003.
9 Commission for Health Improvement. *Emerging Themes from 175 Clinical Governance Reviews.* London: Commission for Health Improvement; 2002.
10 Internal document, Healthcare Commission; 2003.
11 Benson L, Boyd A, Walshe K. *Learning From CHI: the impact of healthcare regulation.* Manchester: University of Manchester; 2004.
12 Beckford J. *Quality: a critical introduction.* London: Routledge; 1998.
13 Koch H. *Total Quality Management in Healthcare.* Longman: UK; 1992.
14 Department of Health. *National Standards, Local Action: Health and Social Care Standards and Planning Framework.* London: Department of Health; 2004.
15 Deighan M, Cullen R, Moore R. The development of Integrated Governance. London: NHS Confederation; 2004.
16 Department of Health. *Independent Health Care: National Minimum Standards Regulations.* London: The Stationery Office; 2002.

Chapter 11

Research in the clinical setting

Ann Moore

Introduction

This chapter sets out to describe the current context of research in the clinical setting and summarises what has led to an increase in clinically based research. The chapter then explores the relationship between research, evidence-based practice, audit and evaluation. Later in the chapter the concept of a research-focused clinical culture is developed, including the implications of this development for clinicians, their managers and those taking up new consultant therapist roles. Within the chapter the process of research is briefly described, together with an introduction to research ethics and research governance. The chapter also addresses potential barriers for clinicians wishing to engage in research and discusses the need for the identification of learning needs in relation to research. The range of opportunities that exist for learning development in the area of research skills and the support mechanisms that are potentially available within higher education institutions, professional bodies and the NHS, to enhance and build research capacity in the workplace, are described.

The development of research in the clinical setting

Over the last two decades the AHPs have been gradually developing a workforce which is equipped with knowledge, understanding and, in the main, practical abilities to underpin research activities. This development has been fuelled by the move of AHP education into higher education institutions (HEIs) and the entry level qualifications for AHP practice and entrance to relevant registration councils being set at honours degree level or above. These developments have meant that the AHPs have been in a transitional state for some years, with many honours degree graduates entering the clinical setting with enthusiasm for research-related activities and accepting of an evidence-based practice culture, whilst other clinicians who qualified before the advent of degrees and who may not have access to continuing professional development activities in the area of research have been potentially left feeling unprepared, unsupported and intellectually vulnerable and challenged by the advent of the evidence-based practice movement and the growth in clinically based research activities.

Masters level courses have proliferated over the last two decades for AHPs, fuelled by the need for continuing professional development for honours degree graduates. Masters level courses have also been accessed by those who have not necessarily achieved degree level qualifications during their initial education and training period, but who had proved that they were academically capable of masters level work by other means. With most masters degree courses demanding the successful completion of a discrete body of research work, together with the completion of supporting research methodology modules, the proliferation of masters courses has led to a major increase in numbers of the Allied Health Professionals who have developed skills necessary to underpin research within the clinical setting and to support evidence-based practice.

The readiness for research activity in the workplace and growth in capacity has been further enhanced by the increasing numbers of AHPs completing doctoral programmes and making a significant contribution to new knowledge. The numbers completing doctoral degrees have increased dramatically in the AHPs over the last decade, indicating the growing level of interest and enthusiasm for research within these professions. This pattern of academic growth and an associated expansion in research activities and research outputs by clinicians has been mirrored in other parts of the world, particularly in Australia and in the USA.

Academic readiness for research in the clinical setting has been emerging as the call for evidence-based practice in healthcare has become louder.[1,2]

The government White Paper *The New NHS: modern, dependable*[3] announced within its three main areas for action a new system of clinical governance in the NHS and primary care settings to ensure that clinical standards are being met and that there are processes in place to ensure continuous improvement backed by a new statutory duty for quality in the NHS trusts.[3]

The Clinical Governance Framework was set out in the Secretary of State for Health's paper *A First Class Service: quality in the NHS*.[4] This emphasised: clinical effectiveness, evidence-based practice, the application of national standards and clinical guidelines and clinical audit, together with a number of other issues related to staffing, for example, continuing professional development, team working and appropriate staffing levels. Many of the features of this framework depend on sound research evidence for their underpinning and future development. This chapter therefore has been written to address the issue of research in clinical practice from both personnel and statutory requirement perspectives.

Definition of terms

It is useful at this stage to define terms here as several types of investigations can sometimes be confused with each other. These terms are research, audit and evaluation.

Research has been defined as 'any activity undertaken to increase knowledge'. It is 'the systematic investigation of a problem, issue or question'.[5]

Put another way, research is all about creating new knowledge, for example, knowledge about whether new treatments work or whether certain treatments work better than others. Research findings form the basis of nationally agreed clinical guidelines and standards and as such can contribute to the determination of what is best practice.

Clinical audit (the type of audit conducted by AHPs) is the systematic critical analysis of the quality of clinical care that is taking place. It can include collecting information in the clinical and managerial setting relating to how and when diagnoses are made, clinical decisions about treatment, the use of resources and the outcome of care from the service provider's and the patient's perspectives.[6]

The results of audit are systematically analysed in order to inform future practice and, importantly, improve the quality of practice. In other words audit could be said to be another way of finding out if what is happening is what should be happening in the clinical setting. There are obvious links here with evidence-based practice and the use of clinical guidelines.

There are also links between audit and research in that audit may often involve the measurement of achievement against measurable standards. Where possible, these audit standards should be based on research findings.[7] Sometimes it is necessary to conduct some research in advance of audit (pre-audit research), for example, to enable standards to be set prior to an audit taking place. It is also sometimes essential to carry out an audit prior to research taking place (pre-research audit) in order to establish, for example, what level of outcome might normally be expected following the use of a standard intervention. This may then help to determine the sample size to be used in the research activity or, indeed, the nature of the participating population to be used in a clinical trial.

There are some similarities between audit and research; for example, both involve answering a specific question relating to quality of care and both can involve the use of the same methods, for example, focus groups, questionnaires and observation. It has been suggested that research is concerned with discovering the right thing to do and audit with ensuring that what is done is right.[8] All NHS trusts now have a research governance policy which clearly identifies the differences between audit and research for their employees and others wishing to conduct research within the trust setting.

Evaluation, on the other hand, is the use of scientific method and the rigorous and systematic collection of research data to assess the effectiveness of organisations, services and programmes in achieving pre-defined objectives.[9] The aim of evaluation is to record not only what changes occur (i.e. audit) but also what led to those changes occurring.[10]

In the face of uncertainty as to whether a project is research, audit or evaluation, clinicians should always consult their local Research and Development (R&D) Officer or Manager for advice as the nature of the project will determine the nature and level of appropriate NHS trust approval for the project to be undertaken. In the case of research taking place in the clinical setting, it is the researcher/clinician's duty of care and also that of their manager to ensure that appropriate ethics and research governance approval has been obtained before commencing on the project and therefore managers have an important advisory role in relation to the nature of projects and their applicability to their local clinical setting.

Evidence-based practice

Evidence-based healthcare has been defined as 'the conscientious explicit and judicious use of current best evidence in making decisions about the care of individual patients'.[11] Another definition of evidence-based practice adds to the above definition by acknowledging the paucity of research evidence available at the time to underpin practice. The definition is therefore broadened to the following: 'evidence-based practice is the conscientious explicit and judicious use of current best evidence in making decisions about the care of individual patients integrating individual clinical expertise with the best available external clinical evidence from systematic research'.[2] Notably, this definition also empha-sises the importance of the clinician's expertise in the decision-making process concerning the use of evidence.

A number of terms have arisen in association with evidence-based practice: for example, evidence-based healthcare, evidence-based decision making, evidence-based patient choice, evidence-based management and evidence-based commis-sioning. These terms are important as they indicate the very broad nature of evidence required to underpin practice in a wide range of healthcare settings and situations. They also give clear indications of the scope of research activity that needs to occur in order to underpin AHPs' clinical practice.

The strength of evidence that is available is categorised based on the hierarchy of strength of evidence shown in Box 11.1.[2]

Box 11.1 Hierarchy of strength of evidence[2]

1 Strong evidence from at least one systematic review of multiple well-designed randomised controlled trials.
2 Strong evidence from at least one properly designed randomised con-trolled trial of appropriate size.
3 Evidence from well-designed trials without randomisation, single group pre–post cohort, time series or matched case-controlled studies.
4 Evidence from well-designed non-experimental studies from more than one centre or research group.
5 Opinions of respected authorities, based on clinical evidence, descriptive studies or reports of expert committees.

The major concern that most AHPs have with the hierarchy of evidence is that there does not appear to be enough evidence on which to base all aspects of practice. In particular, there are certainly not enough well-designed randomised control trials or systematic reviews to support all aspects of practice. However, it should be acknowledged that the hierarchy does allow for the use of expert opinion and that many aspects of day-to-day clinical life can feed into this category, for example, clinical audit and systematic data collection as well as expert opinion from clinicians who are recognised as being experts in their field.

There is also disquiet amongst some professions and some members of indi-vidual professions who firmly believe that the randomised control trial is not necessarily going to provide the best evidence to underpin their practice. There is no doubt that in an attempt to be demonstrating good practice in research activity some researchers have designed, in the past, randomised control trials which best could be described as being ill-informed. It is clear that many of the AHPs are moving towards studies which embrace a multi-method approach to answering a series of related research questions in order to give as full a picture as possible, provide sound evidence that will be deemed to be robust and that will truly inform practice. These multi-modal approaches to research will often include some experimental research, together with more qualitative evidence.

The introduction of evidence-based practice and the hierarchy of evidence has been described as a 'paradigm shift' for many employed in the healthcare setting. In other words, evidence-based practice constitutes a big change for the way in which healthcare providers function. This shift to evidence-based practice has meant a decreased emphasis on intuition, unsystematic clinical experience and pathological rationale as sufficient grounds for decision making and stresses the examination of evidence from clinical research.[12]

Evidence-based practice has considerable implications for healthcare staff and healthcare organisations as implementing evidence-based healthcare requires change which may be required at a number of levels, for example, at an organisational level, at departmental level or at individual staff levels. The changes are very likely to be interdependent.

With the implementation of evidence-based practice certain assumptions about the clinical workforce have been made:

• Clinicians have acquired and use critical appraisal skills in order to evaluate research papers.
• Clinicians keep up to date with new literature and hence the newly published evidence.
• Clinicians have easy access to the best available evidence.
• Clinicians have time allocated to access the evidence.
• Clinicians will access up-to-date evidence and inform patients about the current evidence supporting their treatment.
• Clinicians have time built into their consultation periods to fully brief patients on the available evidence.
• Evidence-based practice is in day-to-day use and is supported by appropriate infrastructures, for example, adequate timetabling for literature searches and patient consultations.
• Clinicians have access to databases and/or library resources in order to download evidence.
• Clinicians have access to training opportunities which will support evidence-based practice, for example, training on critical appraisal of literature, internet searches, research methods, etc.

Finally, there is an intrinsic assumption that there is at least some evidence in place to support every element of practice. Clearly in many areas of practice this is not currently the case and hence there is a need to grow the evidence by virtue of increasing robust research activity and following this up with adequate dissemination of findings. There is also a need for clinicians to comply with the definitions of evidence-based practice proposed above.[2,11] In other words to use evidence judiciously, relating to the individual patients and their needs, and where published evidence does not exist, then the results of systematic data collection and expert opinion must be utilised until stronger evidence becomes available.

Some suggestions for approaches to the management of evidence-based practice in the clinical setting have been made.[13]

• There should be a culture of finding, appraising and using research-based knowledge for all staff (including managers).
• All staff should have practical skills in appraising the evidence.
• Information should be available in an easily accessible form, ideally using a computer.

- An emphasis should be placed, particularly by managers, on asking what is the evidence for 'this proposal' or 'this decision'.[13]

In addition, essential components of an evidence-based service have been identified.[13]

Organisations need to have the capability to generate research evidence and the flexibility to incorporate it into practice.

There should be individuals and teams within clinical practice who are able to find, appraise and apply research into routine clinical practice.[13]

In order for evidence-based practice to be integral to the clinical working culture, it is important for managers to offer their support in the following ways.

Conduct an assessment of the staff cohort and their attitudes towards any issues they have relating to evidence-based practice and in response work up a strategy for achieving behaviour change if necessary.

Allow staff to have protected time to access evidence and to discuss their appraisal of the evidence. This can only help to fuel a positive research culture.

If possible, provide funds for specific evidence-based practice projects.

Try to ensure that clinicians have access to their evidence needs; for example, negotiate appropriate opening times for the hospital library, try to have computers available in the department for internet searching. Plan for future developments with regard to IT where palm-held computers and lightweight laptops linked to the internet may become the norm for clinicians.

Ensure that clinical information systems are appropriate and accessible for use in evidence-based practice.

Ensure access to training opportunities on critical appraisal and the application of research into practice.[14]

Barriers to the implementation of evidence-based practice

These mechanisms for promoting evidence-based practice relate directly to the barriers which have been identified in the implementation of evidence-based practice by clinicians.[15] These include the following.

- The size and complexity of the research which may appear to clinicians to be too daunting.
- Difficulties for clinicians in developing evidence-based practice clinical policy. In other words, how do clinical teams decide judiciously what evidence to employ and which to abandon? Basic decisions need to be made such as who has time to search for the literature and who will appraise it.
- Clinicians may also experience difficulty in applying the evidence because they may have poor access to the best evidence available and to clinical guidelines.

There may, in addition, be organisational barriers in the implementation of the evidence; for example, there could be resource issues relating to equipment that has been found to be useful in the management of certain conditions which is too costly for services to purchase. There may be differences in philosophical approach at an organisational level to implementation of certain kinds of research evidence into practice. Lack of CPD opportunities for staff can be a tremendous barrier to their personal development in terms of under-standing what evidence-based practice is all about, developing the skills necessary to appraise the evidence and acquiring the skills and competencies necessary to implement new and emerging interventions as more evidence becomes available [15]

There appear to be a number of effective measures which can be taken in order to promote behavioural change in respect of the use of evidence-based practice amongst clinicians and these measures include outreach visits and either manual or computerised reminders. In addition, multi-faceted interventions which con-sist of two or more of the following measures may be effective: audit and feedback, reminders, local consensus processes or marketing.

Finally, interactive educational meetings, where staff can engage in much discussion about evidence, are often helpful. There are, however, some inter-ventions which seem to have little or no effect and they may include didactic educational programmes and educational materials, for example, clinical guide-lines and handouts in hard copy.[16]

Stages of evidence-based practice

It is important when facilitating evidence-based practice to focus on one area of practice at a time and not try to do too much. Following a staged route is preferable as shown in Figure 11.1.

In this figure the important overlap between audit, research and evaluation is indicated. The question defined may emerge from a local practice audit. Research evidence will be accessed and appraised and findings implemented into practice that is then carefully evaluated.

It may be useful now to reflect on the term 'clinical effectiveness', which can be defined as 'the extent to which specific clinical interventions when deployed in the field for a particular patient do what they are intended to do, i.e. maintain and improve health and secure the greatest possible health gain from the available resources'.[17] Therefore clinical effectiveness is another perspective to evidence-based healthcare and is a measure of the 'six Rs':[18] the right person, doing the right thing, in the right way, in the right place, at the right time and obtaining the right result.[18]

Clinical guidelines are a growing and integral part of evidence-based practice. Guidelines consist of a set of systematically developed statements aimed at assisting the practitioner and the patient in making appropriate decisions about individual healthcare. The key features of guideline developments include the rigorous and systematic searching, reading and appraisal of the evidence and taking into account the hierarchy of evidence. Also integral to guideline development is the consideration of what the implications of the evidence are for clinical practice, i.e. is the evidence relevant for a local population or specific

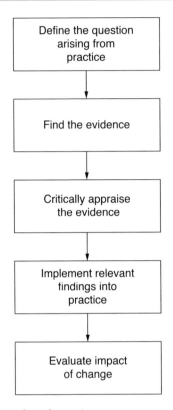

Figure 11.1 Stages of evidence-based practice

circumstances? It also involves weighing up the strength of the evidence and assessing the benefits, risks, costs and possible harm of implementing the evidence into practice. Clinical guidelines should provide a tool containing a description of the best available evidence and recommendations for practice and a resource for patients providing the basis for patient/clinician shared decision making. Guidelines should be used and interpreted locally in order to improve patient care. For a detailed explanation of evidence-based practice, the reader is referred to Herbert et al., 2005.[19]

The multi-faceted role of the Allied Health Professional

We now need to consider research activity in the clinical setting, but before doing so it is useful to reflect on the balance of activity that is now expected to take place within the clinical setting involving clinicians on a day-to-day basis. These activities include administration, clinical practice, placement education, research-related activities, management, CPD activities, social engagement within staff groups of the same discipline and with other disciplines.

The complexity of the clinician's role has grown and research-related activity is just one part of this complexity. As such, it is probably worth acknowledging that the development of a research sub-culture within clinical services is a desirable thing to do within the broad health service culture that represents everyday practice and to also acknowledge that the more developed this sub-culture is, the

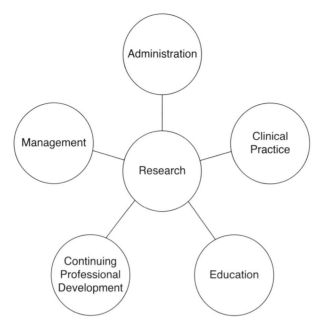

Figure 11.2 Multi-faceted clinical activity

more enhanced will be the quality of healthcare within the service, since a research sub-culture can obviously have an impact on many elements of healthcare activities.

Figure 11.2 indicates the central importance of research and research-related activities to every element of the clinician's role. These activities within the clinical setting can encompass a range of activities from systematic data collection through to clinical audit, evidence-based practice, evaluation and research.

Research and research-related activity in the clinical setting

Having addressed the related research activities we will now turn to research and its place in the clinical setting.

Clearly not all clinical staff can engage in research activities at any one time. It is time-consuming and therefore a costly activity. As was seen earlier in the chapter, it is necessary for all staff to engage with research findings in relation to evidence-based practice and all staff can contribute to the formulation of relevant and robust research questions via audit, systematic data collection and through observation of their own and others' practice.

Some clinicians, perhaps in association with higher degrees, will engage in mainstream research activities and some clinicians will also engage in their own research, particularly those in clinician/researcher posts and consultant posts. The question is, how can they be facilitated to carry out their research activities in the clinical setting? Managers in some circumstances may wish to facilitate research activities in their services in a range of ways.

- Giving personal support to the individual conducting the research.
- Allocating time, funding, staff, hardware/software and other resources to enable research to take place.
- Giving approval for research to take place in the department and giving written confirmation of this support for research governance purposes.
- Enabling the research by getting other staff 'on side' and therefore creating positive momentum for the project.
- Seeking out appropriate collaborators/mentors/supervisors in the local NHS trust or HEI settings.
- If competent and confident in the research process themselves, managers may well take on a research supervisory role in projects within their services.

Key elements of research supervision

Supervisors need to be aware that the supervisee will have expectations of the supervisory process and it is wise to agree how the process will work at the beginning of the supervisory period, perhaps with the formulation of a learning contract which specifies each party's responsibilities.

There is a chance that the supervisor may act as a role model for a young researcher, therefore it is important that supervisors appear to take research seriously in their own working lives. Supervision is rather like teaching and different researchers will respond to different types of supervisory approach. It is useful to establish early on in the supervisory process how the supervisee thinks and works and is best motivated. Constructive feedback is always welcome in a supervisory relationship and destructive feedback does nothing for the researcher and even less for the supervisory relationship. Research has its highs and its lows and younger researchers often need help in keeping their morale high. It is important for supervisors to try to understand their supervisees' problems, whether they are emotional or intellectual. Supervisors need to try to identify learning support needs of their supervisee early in the research process; for example, statistical help and support may be necessary, as may help with submissions for ethics approval. It is important that supervisors realise that they will not have all the skills that every supervisee requires in relation to the projects being supervised and therefore it is important to be able to negotiate help from other individuals within the trust or in a local HEI as necessary to fully support the work in hand.

It is therefore clear that supervisors, or potential supervisors, need to assess their own limitations in terms of knowledge and skills at regular intervals to ensure that the researcher is getting the help that they need and deserve.

Key elements of the supervisee's role

1 Supervisees should make regular contact with their supervisor and keep them informed of progress by the submission of written reports. It is vital that this communication is effective so that issues which arise within the research process can be identified early on.
2 Supervisees must take responsibility for their own learning and identifying their own learning needs which may then be discussed with the supervisor.

3   All supervisees and researchers within the workplace have a responsibility to comply with professional, ethical and research governance codes of practice.

The research process

To ensure a consistent and thorough approach to research, researchers will usually operate within a framework termed the research process. Three important features of research have been identified: research challenges the status quo, it is creative, and it is systematic.[20]

A systematic approach to research is vital, particularly in the health sciences, as research in this area is not easy since, more often than not, it hinges on human participation and this can create difficulties because human behaviour is extremely complex, variable and difficult to isolate and measure. In addition, clients/patients who are the subject of research may not be functioning optimally and this adds to the complexities of behaviours within the research process. Some individuals may not wish to participate in research and some individuals may have to be excluded from the research project for various reasons. This can create difficulties when large numbers of subjects are needed for a specific research study.

For all research studies involving patients, hospital staff, patients' relatives, patients' tissue or organs and clinical records, ethical issues will need to be considered very carefully before the research can commence. Therefore it is vital that a systematic approach to research is adopted.

The research process in outline

The research process itself includes a number of distinct stages as shown below:

- Identifying the research topic area.
- Reviewing relevant literature.
- Selecting and formulating a research question or problem.
- Investigating the feasibility of the proposed project.
- Stating the aims and objectives of the study.
- Design of the study.
- Choice of methods.
- Choice of the methods of analysis.
- Development of proposals for funding (if appropriate).
- Proposals for ethics and research governance approval.
- Writing communication documents.
- Construction of instruments and schedules.
- Pilot studies/reliability/validity studies.
- Research governance and ethics approval.
- Data collection for the main study.
- Data analysis.
- Write-up of the findings.
- Dissemination of the findings.

Identifying a research topic area

Clearly it is useful for any researcher to know whether anyone has carried out the sort of research work proposed before. If so, the researcher can learn from the successes of other projects and also learn from their mistakes which are often flagged up in the limitations of the study section in research papers. Limitations of research projects are also sometimes to be found in published review commentaries. The research topic area can be defined broadly without a literature review, but the only way to produce a good research question is to engage with the literature at an early stage in a research project. This means carrying out internet and on-line library searches using key words to identify research in the area. It also means, in some instances, searching the grey literature and hand-searching conference proceedings and other types of publications which are relevant. Researchers in the health service should seek advice from their library staff if they are unsure about conducting a literature review.

Reviewing the relevant literature

When first embarking on a research project, the first stage should consist of conducting a literature review. This enables the researcher to:

- identify whether this type of research has been done before, which will enable the present study to be placed in the context of other research in the field and allows the study to be placed in a theoretical base
- identify problems that other researchers may have had in this area of research – it may be that the research can then improve on other people's work, having identified lessons learnt in the limitations of previous studies
- Identify a component or components, for example, a validated questionnaire or a specific application of a measurement device, that can be built in to the present proposed study.

Sometimes it can be very reassuring to know that the study that is being contemplated will address the problems in hand since others have successfully used the approach that is being considered in the past.

The literature may indicate that the researchers should change their emphasis in terms of the project in that others may not have been successful in using the approach that is being considered. This will save a lot of wasted time, effort and emotional energy.

The literature may indicate research approaches and research designs and methods which may be helpful at this stage.

The researcher may, having reviewed the literature, be prompted to change the topic area as the literature may highlight a dearth of evidence or theoretical base to justify such a project taking place.

A thorough literature search also enables the researcher to challenge their own and others' professional beliefs, often exposing evidence which has not come to light before.

What literature should be accessed?

- Articles in peer review journals.
- Articles in non-peer review journals.

- Research published in textbooks.
- Government documents, for example, government white papers which may set the political context for a study.
- Census surveys, for example, the OPCS surveys which can help the researcher to identify what a representative sample of the population might consist of.
- Grey literature may also be accessed to identify opinion leaders and their ideas and thoughts concerning the topic area proposed.

It should be noted that some qualitative researchers prefer not to carry out an in-depth literature review at the beginning of a project as it is believed that the knowledge of the literature may in some way bias the researcher's approach to the participants and their own interpretation of the data.[21]

Having reviewed the literature, the researcher will now have a clear idea as to whether it is the right time to carry out the research proposed. In other words, is anyone else researching in this field who may be just about to publish research results? This can often be identified from peer-reviewed papers published in conference proceedings in the field. If publication in a peer-reviewed journal is imminent, then it may be worth waiting until the publication is in the public domain, since the results may prevent the researcher from 'reinventing the wheel'. A detailed search of the most recent conference proceedings in the researcher's specialist area to see what research is currently ongoing is very important, particularly in fast-moving areas of research. It is also advisable to speak to experts in the field to see if they are aware of any research which is ongoing in the proposed area.

The literature review will also highlight whether the researcher has sufficient knowledge of the subject area to underpin the research and the tools which will be needed to conduct the research, for example, data collection methods and methods of analysis. It should also raise questions in the researcher's mind about whether they have the appropriate clinical and research competencies to undertake the project. This may indicate the need for further personal development before the research can commence. It is important always for researchers to ask themselves an important question at the beginning of a research process: 'Do I know what I don't know?'.

The literature review can give the researcher confidence that the project may be worthwhile doing and will add to the profession's/subject area's body of knowledge and that it indeed may be relevant to practice. In some cases the literature may indicate the contrary.

Clearly, it is important to decide whether there is a sufficient body of knowledge to support a research hypothesis, i.e. is there any information available on which to base a research project of this nature? If not, then the researcher may have to rethink their approach and go back to basics, perhaps collect some baseline data in a systematic way in order to begin to generate a small coherent body of knowledge on which to base more profound research work.

It is useful at an early stage in a project, following literature review, to discuss the project with an expert in the field as their thoughts may be vital in moulding a project in an appropriate way to produce rigorous and meaningful findings (*see* Figure 11.3).

The researcher, at this stage, should now question their own motives for carrying out the project and have come to a decision as to whether the research is of real interest to them. Taking on a project which is of little interest to the

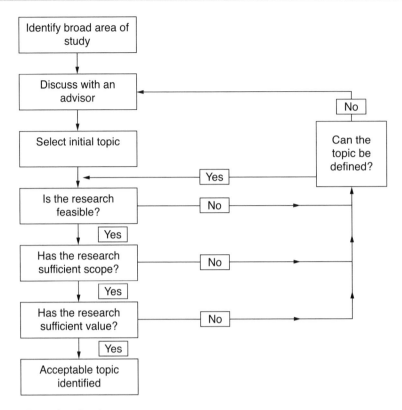

Figure 11.3 Topic selection

researcher personally will be demotivating and, if the researcher has little interest in the project, then they will hardly be in a position to inspire colleagues who may have to have some involvement in the project. Also, at this early stage of the project, it is very sensible to consider the expertise that will be needed to carry out the project and whether this expertise needs to be gained by additional training or could be bought in by individuals expert in the field for the duration of the project. However, both these scenarios have cost implications for the service and therefore need to be explored early on. It may well be, of course, that these resources could be available through collaboration with other services or institutions.

Characteristics of a good research problem

- It must be clearly, simply and precisely stated.
- It must be limited in scope so as to be realistic.
- It must be consistent with some, but not necessarily all, of the known facts, ie underpinned by some subject knowledge.
- The problem must be verifiable in principle and practice.

Investigating the feasibility of the project

Below is a checklist of feasibility issues which the researcher needs to engage with before embarking on the research.

- Is an appropriate venue for the research available?
- Are appropriate people available to help with the conduct of the research, particularly where the effects of an intervention are being explored? In this context, those collecting measurable data should not be the same individuals as those carrying out the intervention.
- Researchers need to ascertain if their project is going to take place within their own service and whether colleagues in the service will co-operate in the data collection if necessary and appropriate. A research-positive culture in existence is likely to help this situation, otherwise the project could run into difficulties due to resistance or just through apathy. It is useful to bring colleagues on side before a project starts by involving relevant colleagues in discussions and decision making with regard to the project and its design at an early stage and important to include in these discussions the possible benefits for the service and colleagues in participating in this research work.
- Are enough clients/patients available to make the study viable in the time available to the researcher? If the researcher is utilising a clinical trial design a power calculation needs to be carried out in order to ascertain how many subjects will be needed to demonstrate a significant difference in outcome. If the researcher is wishing to conduct a study on a rare condition, then it may take many years to recruit an appropriate number of subjects which may not be feasible. An alternative is to consider a multicentre approach to the study.
- Is administrative support available for the study? Most studies need administrative support in relation to patients' records and appointments and the like. This support may be available, but it needs to be negotiated at the start of any research project.
- Is there time to do the research? There is no doubt that research often takes more time than the researcher has contemplated. Negotiation of time for research activity to take place needs to be considered at an early stage in the project and the time negotiated should include time for the preparation for the project, data collection, data analysis, write-up of the project itself and dissemination of the findings.
- Is funding needed? Possible costs for a research project include the following: personnel costs in terms of data collection and administration costs, cost of additional equipment, for example, measurement devices used in data collection. It may be possible to hire this kind of equipment or to borrow it from a distributor or perhaps collaborate with another organisation which has such equipment for the purposes of the research.

   The cost of consumables, for example, stationery, electrodes, pharmaceutical products, for a project needs to be considered at an early stage.

   Patients should be offered payment for their time and travel costs if they have to attend at times additional to treatment requirements. This needs to be borne in mind by the researcher in terms of financial costs of the project.

   Statistical input for analysis may need to be costed in. In addition there may be costs associated with dissemination of the project findings; for example, conference fees, travel costs, publication costs and other project costs such as photocopying and postage should not be forgotten about.

External funding

Sometimes a project is just too costly to be run in isolation within a single NHS department and external funding could therefore be considered from professional bodies, registered charities, research councils and the Department of Health. It is also worthwhile considering an approach to the local NHS trust to see if any funds are available from the R&D committee.

Identifying and defining the research question

The next and vital stage in any research project is to develop the research question. This takes a considerable amount of time, but is vital in the research process. The research question often arises from a disturbance in practice recognised by the clinician or researcher or a curiosity which simply occurs to the researcher. Alternatively, the research question may be stimulated by the literature, previous research, clinical audit, systematic data collection findings or a simple observation of practice.[22]

The complexity of developing a solid research question has been recognised[22,23] and it has been suggested that researchers should develop a list of possible relevant research questions which are then evaluated against a number of criteria related to the researcher themselves, the literature, resource availability and some other additional questions.[23] Once these criteria have been evaluated, then a priority research question will emerge.[23]

A complex relationship exists between the research question, the underpinning theory, the literature, and the research methodology.[22] Methodological principles will dictate whether certain research designs and methods are inappropriate or appropriate.[21]

The research design represents the overall plan and structure of a piece of research;[22] research methods are the specific techniques to be utilised in the research activity, e.g. sampling method, data collection methods and methods of analysis. Sim and Wright[22] classify research questions into three types: exploratory questions, descriptive and normative questions, and explanatory questions.

1 Exploratory questions set out to find out what is happening, to seek new insights, to ask questions and to assess phenomena in a new light. For example, an explorative question might be, what barriers do professional doctorate graduates face when researching in clinical practice?
2 Descriptive and normative questions provide a descriptive account of a phenomenon within an established framework of knowledge. For example, what factors influence interprofessional learning within a high-dependency cardiorespiratory setting?
3 Explanatory questions tend to be highly specific and set out to test a hypothesis. For example, there is no significant difference in right and left cross-sectional areas of multifidus muscle at L4-5 areas of the lumbar spine as measured by ultrasound imaging in elite high jumpers.

It is important to realise that any approach to research manifests the researcher's philosophical perspective on reality and how knowledge of the world can be gained in a legitimate way. Epistemology is the philosophy of knowledge and a research approach will be based on an epistemological perspective. There are several major philosophical perspectives on research: positivism, critical rationalism and phenomenology. The detailed discussion of these approaches is beyond the scope of this chapter, but the reader is referred to Sim and Wright.[22]

Research design

The research design is developed to reflect the chosen approach to the research and indicates how the research question will be answered. Research design necessitates consideration of what information will be examined, i.e. what data will be collected, when it will be collected, how it will be collected, who will be involved in data collection, what variables will be investigated, in what conditions will data collection take place and what methods will be used for the analysis of the data.

Data collection methods also include methods of sampling. There are various types of methods of sampling.

- Random sampling, where every subject in the population concerned has an equal chance of being selected for the study; for example, a sample of all patients presenting with multiple sclerosis in the South of England.
- Stratified sampling, which uses a sub-population for sampling; for example, using a 10% sample of all patients with multiple sclerosis from each NHS trust in the South of England.
- Cluster sampling, where a sample of NHS trusts in the South of England is taken and then a percentage of patients who have a diagnosis of multiple sclerosis will be recruited from each of these trusts.
- Another example of sampling is quota sampling which is used in market research which is where, randomly, subjects are chosen who fulfil certain criteria, so for example, market surveys may include white Caucasians aged between 40 and 60 who have professional backgrounds.
- Lastly, there is convenience sampling where subjects who are locally available are recruited to a particular study. Convenience sampling often has its difficulties because the researcher may well be known to the possible participants which in itself could create some bias.

Subject recruitment

In designing the study consideration must be given to how participants will be recruited, how many will be needed, including the justification of this number (for example a power calculation must be produced if indicated by the data collection methods and design).

Inclusion and exclusion criteria need to be drawn up before each project in order to reduce the risk for individuals participating in the research and also to avoid confounding variables, which may influence the results of the study, for example, certain age groups, certain levels of mobility, etc.

It is also necessary to decide how participants will be allocated to intervention groups if appropriate (particularly if the research design includes randomisation).

It is useful to identify extraneous variables early on in the process which may influence the results of the research and try to minimise them if at all possible; for example, in an experimental design room temperature may be a factor with some experimental work which may involve strenuous exercise. Standardisation of drug therapies may also be appropriate for some clinical studies.

Design of the data analysis

The type of analysis to be used to convert the raw data into meaningful data should be decided at the design stage of the research process and will depend on the research design used, and the type of data collected.

A statistician should be consulted at an early stage in order to plan appropriately.

Construction of instruments and formal communications

At the design stage, simple questionnaires may need to be designed and piloted (it should be noted that questionnaire design can be a challenging intellectual process, particularly if the questionnaire is designed to collect qualitative data). In many cases designing a questionnaire can constitute the whole research project itself and questionnaire design should not be undertaken lightly and without advice. Simple questionnaires involving the collection of demographic data and hard facts are more simply designed, but the need for clarity and non-ambiguity cannot be overemphasised. Importantly, any questionnaire that is produced for research purposes must be piloted and if the questionnaire is designed to collect more than simple demographic data, then the questionnaire needs also to be tested for validity, sensitivity and reliability.

Other instruments and formal communications which should be designed at an early stage in the research process include forms for recording observations during examination or treatment processes, examination forms, systematic data collection forms, interview schedules, consent forms and participant information sheets. The participant information sheet should clearly explain the research project to participants and must be written in lay terms. Many NHS trusts and R&D offices have their own standard consent forms and proforma for participant information sheets. Normally they will include the title of the project and its aims, an introduction to the project, where it will take place, who will be involved and what participation will mean to the individual concerned, when they will need to attend and for how long, what they can expect to happen and the fact that they can withdraw from the project at any time without any consequences. The information sheet should also indicate the researcher's contact details and their supervisor's/manager's contact details if appropriate.

Research governance and ethics

Five fundamental ethical principles and related issues in research involving participants have been set out by Sim and Wright.[22]

1 Respect for autonomy
   - the need to gain informed consent
   - the need not to deceive participants
   - the need not to exploit participants
   - the need to respect confidentiality and privacy.
2 Respect for persons
   - the need to give informed consent
   - the need not to exploit participants
   - the need to ensure that research procedures do not undermine a person's dignity or self-respect.
3 Beneficence
   - the need to carry out research whose findings will benefit members of society
   - the need to disseminate such findings.
4 Non-maleficence
   - the need to avoid causing harm or distress
   - the need not to breach anonymity or confidentiality
   - the need not to raise unrealistic or unfulfillable expectations in research participants.
5 Justice
   - the need not to use vulnerable individuals in research
   - the need to ensure that the benefits and burdens of research are distributed fairly.[22]

All those involved in research, either at a researcher, supervisor or management level, need to abide by these ethical principles.

In October 2004 the DH (UK) introduced the Research Governance Framework for Health and Social Care. This framework aims to clarify who has responsibility for the dignity, rights, safety and well-being of any human participants in research and to ensure that any research proposal is worthwhile, of high scientific quality and represents good value for money.

All research carried out on NHS property using NHS facilities or involving NHS service users, their organs, tissues or data or users' relatives or carers and NHS staff, requires a NHS governance approval before the research can be carried out.

The full research governance document can be found at: www.dh.gov.uk/ PolicyAndGuidance/ResearchAndDevelopment/fs/en.

This document also includes a comprehensive list of useful websites related to research governance and ethics issues.

Ethical standards and principles are integral to the Research Governance Framework. Every NHS trust in the United Kingdom has been asked to draw up plans and procedures for the implementation of the NHS Research Governance Framework. As a result, each trust may operate slightly differently, but each will have a local interpretation of the Research Governance Framework and will have produced a Research Governance Framework Policy Document for trust use. (This document should be available from the R & D manager or officer of each individual NHS trust.) This document will set out the responsibilities for governance within the NHS trust. In addition, each trust will relate to a Local Research Ethics Committee and all research proposals must be approved by a Local Research Ethics Committee (LREC) under the governance policies. In some NHS trusts LREC approval must be gained before the paper is submitted for research governance approval to the trust's R & D committee. In other trusts the full proposal for research governance approval must be submitted before the ethics committee views the documentation. It is wise to contact the LREC secretary or research governance officer in order to ascertain what the local procedures are.

The research governance documents clearly set out the responsibilities of all the key people involved in the research process including participants, researchers, principal investigators, research funders, research sponsors, universities, organisations providing care, care professionals and responsibilities relating to ethics committees.

As far as managers of healthcare professionals who are involved in research are concerned, a section of the governance document of particular importance to them is the summary of main responsibilities of organisations providing care. Managers are advised to study the governance framework carefully so that they understand their responsibilities within the governance framework system. At the very least, if research is being undertaken in a service and is self-funding, the NHS trust will need to agree to take on the sponsorship of the project and in this case arrangements will need to be put in place:

- Confirmation that proper arrangements for initiation, management monitoring and financing of the study are in place.
- Ensuring access to adequate resources is available.
- Allocating responsibilities for management monitoring and reporting.
- Ensuring arrangements are in place to meet the Research Governance Framework requirements.
- Ensuring systems are in place for detecting significant developments.

In addition, it is the responsibility of all care professionals to:

- ensure the care and well-being of service users participating in research
- ensure that permission and approval have been granted for the research
- ensure that research complies with the Research Governance Framework
- ensure that research protocols are followed to the letter.

The process of gaining ethics and research governance approval can be quite a time-consuming business in some localities and researchers and managers should plan for potential delays whilst waiting for approval.

Progress after gaining ethics and governance approval: pilot and feasibility studies

At this stage the researcher needs to try out the prepared instruments and design and test the feasibility of data collection. It may also be necessary to conduct reliability and validity studies at this stage. There are various types of reliability, which can be divided into equivalents (interrater reliability and alternative forms reliability), stability (intrarater reliability) and internal consistency (split half reliability, item analysis).[22]

Validity relates to the data collected during research. Data are said to be valid when they represent what they purport to represent or, put another way, a piece of measurement equipment is said to be valid when it measures what it purports to measure. There are various forms of validity: face validity, content validity, criterion-related validity and construct validity.

Not all research designs will require reliability and validity studies to be undertaken, but pilot studies which, in effect, offer rehearsal opportunities are advisable to ensure the smooth running of a project from both the participant's and the researcher's perspectives.

Time may also need to be given at this stage for training of those involved in data collection in order to standardise the approach to data collection.

Data collection

Having planned the research study carefully and thoroughly, data collection should go smoothly. It is useful for every researcher to keep a research project diary and also it is necessary for them to keep thorough records of all data collection and events that take place throughout the project for research governance purposes.

Analysing the data

There are many computer packages that are available to help with data analysis, depending on the nature and type of data collected. The type of analysis to be carried out should have been decided at the project design stage and if so analysis should now go smoothly.

Writing up and dissemination

Having completed the research project, there is a need to let others share knowledge of the research project, its design and its findings. In many ways research does not exist until someone else knows about it!

Individuals can choose a variety of mechanisms for dissemination purposes. Which mechanisms are chosen largely depend on why the individuals wish to disseminate the work; for example, is dissemination required to influence local practice, to influence national practice or international practice?

Local dissemination

For local dissemination, various methods can be used and this is a good place to start as it gives the researcher the opportunity to sound out local opinion about the robustness of the project and the implications of the research findings with a local audience before involving individuals at national or international level. It is particularly useful for young researchers who are still developing confidence in delivering conference papers.

Mechanisms for local dissemination can include in-service workshops, lectures and seminars, short paper-based reports and publications in local trust newsletters and/or on bulletin boards. Small group tutorials with staff and students can also help, particularly if the findings have practical implications.

National dissemination

Presentations at national conferences, of a unidisciplinary or multidisciplinary nature, can be vital to any researcher's development as the feedback gained as a result of presenting can often be formative in developing other research ideas or developing the research further. For new researchers, making a poster presentation can be less intimidating than delivering a peer-reviewed verbal presentation. Publishing in professional journals is a good way of disseminating research when it is of fundamental importance to the practice of a single profession. Publishing findings on the NHS trust's website can also be a way of attracting attention to the project and engaging with others who may be interested in this research area. In addition, professional special interest group events are a useful forum for discussion of findings at a national level.

International dissemination

International conferences offer an important opportunity for young researchers to engage with those who are more experienced in this field of research and in their own subject area. Both poster presentations and platform presentations are available to young researchers and many international conference organising committees now offer a mentorship process for young and upcoming researchers in order to help them with formulation of their abstracts for submission. In addition, publishing in peer reviewed high-quality international journals is an excellent way of engaging with the research community and for getting feedback from expert peer-reviewers of the paper concerned. There is no substitute for publishing in internationally peer-reviewed journals, as the presence of a paper in such a medium will often fuel academic debate at a more global level.

Dissemination of research is part of the responsibilities identified within the Research Governance Framework document and it could be argued that there is a moral obligation for researchers to publish results of studies for which a number of individuals have given up their time to participate in.

In addition, many of the health professions have relatively low evidence bases and every shred of evidence is vital to expanding the evidence base and may hold many valuable messages for the discipline, for researchers and also for those engaged in practice.

Dissemination skills

There are a number of textbooks which deal with dissemination skills in depth, but Jenkins et al[23] is recommended as a reference source for those interested in finding out more about scientific writing, presenting research papers and preparing conference posters.

Implementing research into practice

Implementation of the findings of research into local clinical practice by clinician/ researchers can be a challenging task. Implementation of research into practice is the essence of evidence-based practice, but when the research evidence has been created locally by a local researcher, acceptance of findings which go against routine clinical practice, by local and experienced clinicians, can be a painful process as it constitutes a large paradigm shift and feels uncomfortable.

Smooth implementation of evidence demands a positive acceptance of new research findings by clinical staff and time to create avenues and opportunities for change. Staff also need to be motivated to change practice by being exposed to the potential positive benefits of change. The researchers, who are, after all, opinion leaders, may need emotional and practical support in their efforts to implement change and this can often be gained through mentorship and/or clinical supervision.

The changes to be implemented may require additional resources; for example, it may mean that more staff training has to be arranged, more equipment may need to be purchased and perhaps the implications may mean longer patient/therapist contact time. In considering change, the positive and negative features of the potential change must be weighed up carefully in order to gauge the real costs of implementation in terms of quality of patient care, staff morale and departmental efficiency.

Support for research

For the AHPs, the obvious focus for research support is the local HEIs. However, there are other avenues that may be considered.

1 Experienced researchers may exist, based in the clinical setting in the researcher's own or another discipline, and with approval these individuals could be used for supervision or mentorship purposes.
2 The local NHS trust R&D office may provide networking opportunities within the trust or within local HEIs for the researcher, but will also give advice about research governance and ethics issues.
3 The AHP consultant roles encompass clinical specialism, education, management and research and these clinicians are advised to form links for research purposes with local HEIs and as such can act as an important research link between the clinical and academic settings. Often these consultants may be developing their own research profiles and registering for a doctoral degree within the local HEI. As they learn and begin to research into local practice, then the research culture within departments will begin to grow and other staff may be encouraged to become involved in research activities. Consultant AHP posts are potentially the most significant development for the therapies' research culture in the last decade.

Higher education institutions and research in the clinical setting

HEIs provide a number of key opportunities which can support research growth in clinical settings, as follows.

- Top-up degrees for diplomats offering grounding in research methods and statistics as well as evidence-based practice.
- Standalone masters modules which can include research methods, statistics and evidence-based practice and other modules relevant to the clinical research interests of individuals.

- Masters degrees offering clinical specialism or generic qualifications. Masters degrees offer research training modules, for example, research methods, statistical analysis, as stated above, but other modules offered will carry a heavy evidence-based approach to teaching and learning. Masters students also have the opportunity to undertake a moderately sized research project under expert academic supervision and many of these studies are publishable and therefore can feed into the evidence base of the relevant profession. Following completion of masters degrees, publication rates for clinicians are disappointingly low, indicating that clinicians need encouragement to disseminate their research findings from within their own practice base.
- Doctoral programmes. The PhD is the traditional postgraduate research route. Students registered for these degrees often study in relative isolation supported by an academic supervisor or supervisory team. Most universities offer learning opportunities which complement and support the programme of research work. The PhD process is designed to enable the student to experience all aspects of the research process by exploring a narrow focus of research in extreme depth. Typically, a PhD study will include a thorough appraisal of literature, a number of pilot studies including appropriate validity and reliability studies, and a main study. For clinicians studying this route their thesis would normally include an in-depth discussion of the clinical relevance of the study concerned. PhD registration, however, is commonly taken up by academics who wish to develop their expertise, or by clinicians who wish to move into academia. The relative isolation of the traditional PhD route is increasingly less attractive to clinically based researchers.
- A relatively new development for the AHPs is the professional doctorate degree. These degrees are validated at doctoral level and usually consist of a four-year programme of work. These degrees, in contrast to the PhD, are designed for clinicians who wish to research into practice and at postdoctoral level remain in practice and carry on developing their research activities in this scenario. Typically, a programme would consist of four years with mandatory attendance at regular intervals within a cohort of students. The content and notion of these attendances vary from institution to institution, but the final two years are usually dedicated to the production of an extensive research thesis.
- Professional doctorate degrees are ideal for researcher/clinicians or for the new consultant AHPs. The positive advantage of these programmes is the cohort/peer support, the regular attendance mode and the emphasis on research actually designed to influence practice.
- HEI-based seminar/workshop programmes. Most higher education institutions will have a programme of research-based seminars and workshops which are often open to local clinicians. They enable academics and clinical colleagues to share ideas and debate recent advances in research within their own organisations.

Supervision

Most HEIs will have research-active staff who can offer expert support and advice to clinicians who wish to undertake research, but who are not intending to register for a higher degree. Supervisors' fees, however, will need to be negotiated on a one-to-one basis.

Mentorship

It is an advantage or indeed in some cases mandatory for consultant therapists to acquire a mentor based in an HEI who can advise on research development opportunities, research activities, dissemination opportunities and research culture development in the workplace. Mentorship, however, needs to be negotiated with the local higher education institution in terms of fees and staff availability.

Research collaboration

Staff in HEIs are keen to collaborate with clinicians in research activities, but again, early discussion is advisable. Strengths lie in this kind of collaboration as each party brings different experiences and expertise to the whole process.

Other research support available for clinicians

- R & D Officers/Managers within the NHS can often help with research governance issues and perhaps with information about local funding opportunities.
- The Secretary or Chair of the Local Research Ethics Committee can also help individuals with queries with regard to proposals for ethics approval.
- NHS Research Support Development Units (NHS RSDUs) are under contract to the Department of Health to provide research training and support for NHS staff. The local Research and Development Manager within each trust will be able to provide contact details for the nearest NHS RSDU.
- Primary Care Research Networks have been established, often based in higher education institutions and again under contract to the DH. They provide support and training for members of the NHS staff based in primary care settings who wish to undertake research. Again, Research and Development Managers should have contact details for their nearest PCRN.
- Professional Research Support Groups. Many AHP are developing research networks in order to increase research capacity and to improve the uptake of the use of evidence in practice; for example, the Chartered Society of Physiotherapy has just funded the development of the National Physiotherapy Research Network. This network will establish a series of research 'hubs' across the United Kingdom which will offer support and advice to local clinicians and help them network with higher education institution-based academic researchers in order to increase research capacity. These hubs will also actively encourage and welcome multiprofessional participation in the hub activities.

Potential barriers to research development within the clinical setting

In a study of barriers to research activity by nurses it was suggested that in order to achieve successful change in practice with regard to nurses utilising evidence, nurses needed time to read and apply research, authority to change practice, critical appraisal skills, an understanding of statistics and support from their managers and peers.[24] It is clear that productive research groups have been characterised by the following.

- They have clear organisational goals.
- They emphasise research.
- They have a distinctive culture.
- They have a climate of respect paired with intellectual jostling.
- They conscientiously socialise new members.
- They have sufficient resources (especially manpower).
- They have accessible resources.
- They have a flat organisational structure with a leader who facilitates group productivity through participatory governance, who is experienced in research and plays an important, though not predominant, role in individual researchers' planning and who keeps organisational goals visible.[25]

It is probably important that individuals understand that the primary benefit of incorporating research into CPD is an improvement in patient care since by increasing the awareness of the substantial benefits to be gained through research, clinicians will be more likely to incorporate research findings into practice, thereby providing the most efficient care for their patients.[26] It has been suggested that a clinical working environment which encourages the evaluation of practice and research-related activity is a potential facilitator of change in accepting research as commonplace.[26]

In a study of GPs in Queensland, Australia, researchers found that the GP environment and the culture within the general practice were barriers to involvement in research. Enabling factors, however, included access to academic mentors, access to information resources and opportunities to participate in reputable, relevant and established research activities.[27]

In America, researchers recently[28] found that American physical therapists have a generally positive attitude towards evidence-based practice and are interested in increasing their skills and the amount of evidence used in practice. The beliefs, skills and behaviours examined were related to age and years since qualification. Younger and more recent graduates expressed more positive attitudes and had greater skills and confidence relating to accessing and critically appraising information. The use of online databases to search literature related to computer access at work and at home. Lack of time was the biggest barrier to using evidence-based practice.

In assessing the barriers to clinical research in physical therapy, some authors have concluded that the inability to give up revenue-producing time and lack of administrative and financial support are major barriers to clinical research taking place.[29]

In AHP/services which include staff of a range of ages, experience and qualifications, a review of the barriers to involvement in research put forward in the 1980s by Ballin *et al*[30] still holds some considerable relevance. The barriers that were identified at that time were:

- unfamiliarity with the research process
- unfamiliarity with the use of statistics
- lack of administrative, financial support
- lack of equipment and facilities
- lack of a research consultant
- inability to give up revenue-producing time
- unwillingness to make research a higher priority
- lack of external funding
- lack of consistent patient load
- lack of administrative, philosophical support
- unwillingness to give up personal time
- lack of research ideas
- lack of referrals
- lack of library facilities
- lack of interest.[30]

Many of these issues are still live today, but managers may wish to consider each of Ballin's categories in turn and identify what progress has been made in their own clinical settings in each of the areas listed.

Summary

There is no doubt that evidence-based practice is here to stay, but it can only occur if sufficient evidence is available to support practice. Therefore, there is a need and a desire to increase the amount of clinically based research activity within the workplace, and several initiatives that have been highlighted within this chapter are already contributing to the increase in research capacity within the AHPs.

For some individual clinicians, there will always be some apprehension about research. This is epitomised by the following quotation:

> Research is a high-hat word which scares a lot of people! – It needn't. It is nothing but a state of mind, a friendly, welcoming attitude towards change. It is the problem-solving mind contrasted with the let-well-alone mind. It is the composer mind instead of the fiddler mind. It is the tomorrow mind instead of the yesterday mind.
>
> Kettering[31]

References

1 Rosenberg W, Donald A. Evidence based medicine: an approach to clinical problem solving. *BMJ*. 1995; **310**: 1122–6.
2 Bury T, Mead J. *Evidence-based Healthcare: a practical guide for therapists*. Oxford: Butterworth-Heinemann; 1998.
3 Department of Health. *The New NHS: modern, dependable*. London: HMSO; 1997.
4 Department of Health. *A First Class Service: quality in the NHS*. London: HMSO; 1998.
5 Bailey DM. *Research for the Health Professional*. Philadelphia: FA Davies; 1991.

6 Secretary of State for Health, Wales, Northern Ireland and Scotland. *Working For Patients*. London: HMSO; 1989.

7 Barnard F, Hartigan G. *Clinical Audit in Physiotherapy: from theory to practice*. Oxford: Butterworth-Heinemann; 1998.

8 Smith R. Audit and research. *BMJ*. 1992; **305**: 905–6.

9 Shaw C. Aspects of Audit I: the background. *BMJ*. 1980; **280**: 1256–8.

10 Bowling A. *Research Methods in Health: investigating health and health services*. Buckingham: Open University Press; 2002.

11 Sackett DL, Grey JAM, Haynes RB, Richardson WS. Evidence-based medicine, what it is and what it isn't. *BMJ*. 1996; **312**: 71–2.

12 EBM Working Group. Evidence-based medicine: a new approach to teaching the practice of medicine. *JAMA*. 1992; **268**: 2420–25.

13 Muir-Gray JA. *Evidence-based Healthcare: how to make health policy decisions and management decisions*. Edinburgh: Churchill Livingstone; 1997.

14 Swage T. *Clinical Governance in Health Care*. Oxford: Butterworth-Heinemann; 2000.

15 Haynes B, Haines A. Barriers and bridges to evidence-based clinical practice. *BMJ*. 1998; **317**: 273–6.

16 Bero LA, Grilli R, Grimshaw J. Closing the gap between research and practice – an overview of systematic reviews and interventions to promote the implementation of research findings. *BMJ*. 1998; **317**: 465–8.

17 NHS Executive. *Promoting Clinical Effectiveness: a framework for action in and through the NHS*. London: Department of Health; 1996.

18 Graham G. Clinically effective medicine in a National Health Service. *Health Director*. 1996; **June**: 11–12.

19 Herbert R, Jamtvedt G, Mead J, Hagen K. *Practical Evidence-based Physiotherapy: informing practice with high quality clinical research*. Oxford: Elsevier Science Limited; 2005.

20 Domholdt E. *Physical Therapy Research*. Philadelphia: WB Saunders Co; 1993.

21 Straus A, Corbin J. *Basics of Qualitative Research: techniques and procedures for developing grounded theory*. 2nd ed. Thousand Oaks: Sage Publications; 1998.

22 Sim J, Wright C. *Research in Healthcare: concepts, designs and methods*. Gloucester: Stanley Thornes Limited; 2000.

23 Jenkins S, Price CJ, Straker L. *The Researching Therapist*. Edinburgh: Churchill Livingstone; 1998.

24 Bryar RM, Closs J, Baum G *et al*. The Yorkshire BARRIERS Project: Diagnostic analysis of barriers to research utilisation. *International Journal of Nursing Studies*. 2003; **40**: 73–84.

25 Bland CJ, Ruffin MP. Characteristics of a productive research environment: literature review. *Academic Medicine*. 1992; **67**(6): 385–97.

26 CSP Development Group. Physiotherapy research and CPD. *Physiotherapy*. 1996; **82**(1): 58–63.

27 Askew DA, Clavarin OAM *et al*. General practice research: attitudes and involvement of Queensland general practitioners. *Medical Journal of Australia*. 2002; **177**(2): 74–7.

28 Jette DU, Bacon K, Battie C *et al*. Evidence-based practice: beliefs, attitudes, knowledge and behaviours of physical therapists. *Physical Therapy*. 2003; **83**(9): 786–805.

29 Connolly BH, Lupinnacin S, Bush AJ. Changes in attitudes and perceptions about research in physical therapy amongst professional physical therapist students and new graduates. *Physical Therapy*. 2001; **81**(5): 1127–34.

30 Ballin AJ, Breslin WH, Wierenga KAS *et al*. Research in physical therapy. *Physical Therapy*. 1980; **60**(7) 888–95.

31 Kettering CF. Research. In: Boyd TA, ed. *Profit of Progress*. New York: BP Dutton & Co Incorporated; 1961.

Chapter 12

The discipline of strategic thinking in healthcare

Jon Chilingerian

Introduction

This chapter has been written for those who lead healthcare services or hope to in the future. Some of the conceptual and methodological challenges associated with good strategic thinking are considered. The purpose is more of an opening up of a discussion of the subject and not a bundle of 'how tos'. Although the demands and constraints on leaders can introduce many complications for strategic thinking, strategic management will benefit if the six pillars of strategic thinking discussed are firmly established.

Strategic thinking helps us to interpret what a pattern of investment decisions (time, talent, and money) means for the capabilities of an organisation. The shape and form of these decisions reveal what the organisation has initiated and institutionalised in terms of tacit knowledge, specialised skills, trust relationships, social capital and the depth of experienced clinical leadership. When the realised strategy becomes a true strategic service vision, when it has truly become embedded in the culture, management practices and behaviour of the organisation, it becomes very hard for others to imitate.

Strategic activity in healthcare is on the rise worldwide. In recent years, hospital and clinic mergers, innovative alliances, and the outsourcing and spinning off of new (and old) clinical services exemplify this rise in strategic activity. The increase in strategic thinking in healthcare also includes making decisions about the mix of medical pathologies, patients and care processes, improving the service process and repositioning care programmes aimed at local, regional or international patients.

In the United States there were 153 hospital mergers in the 1980s and 176 hospital mergers in the first seven years of the 1990s.[1] During the last decade, more than 100 private hospitals in Western Europe merged or were acquired within single domestic markets such as England, Germany, or France.[2] Ownership structures have also changed as some public hospitals have become private hospitals or have hired private management companies. Technological, demographic, regulatory and/or consumer forces have led medical groups, clinics and hospitals to shape the new rules of healthcare competition.

Some healthcare organisations have begun to identify global markets for their brand.[3] For example, in 2000 Johns Hopkins National University Hospital International Medical Centre opened an oncology unit in Singapore and in 2004 the Mayo Clinic opened a cardiac disease unit in Dubai. Bumrungrad Hospital, founded in Thailand in 1980, was one of the first hospitals to focus on attracting foreign patients, caring for over 300 000 non-Thai patients each year.[4]

Between 1997 and 2001, Sweden's Capio acquired hospitals throughout Europe including 17 in Sweden, 12 in Norway, three in the UK, 12 in Spain, one in Switzerland and one in Denmark. India-based Apollo Holdings established clinics in Kuwait, Qatar, Saudi Arabia and Bangladesh, and are targeting more clinics in Dubai, Bahrain, Nigeria, Tanzania, Ghana, Singapore, Philippines, London, and Chicago.[5] These strategic innovators are reinventing the industry by becoming Europe, Asia and Africa's leading independent providers of general hospital services, specialty hospitals and diagnostic clinics.

There are several ways to undertake these strategic activities:

- Building the capacity and managing for cultural consistency.
- Acquiring other organisations and offering the service faster and more effectively.
- Forming alliances and offering a less costly but expedient service.

These decisions require the practice of strategic thinking and planning as a discipline, i.e. a rigorous approach and methods for inquiring, identifying, selecting, and implementing courses of action in the pursuit of long-term strategic goals and objectives.

While health leaders are involved in many aspects of organisational life, above all they are judged on the quality of their strategic thinking and planning. The ultimate test of leadership is adapting healthcare organisations to novel and unexpected events by making strategic changes successful. The following examples illustrate a typical mix of decision challenges for healthcare managers:

- Planning a merger of four local hospitals into one entity.*
- Developing and launching a breakthrough care process or clinical service.*
- Deciding which care programmes should be established as focused factories.*
- Planning major capacity expansions for diagnosis and surgical treatment centres.*
- Increasing research grants for the transplant surgery programme.
- Establishing real-time MRI units for surgical procedures.
- Solving primary care access issues.
- Optimising clinical staffing.

Not all of the managerial decisions listed above are strategic. On the one hand, some of the decisions listed above necessitate adaptive responses to changes in the 'marketplace' and pressures in the task environment. One the other hand, the decisions with the asterisks (*) have more permanent effects over longer time periods[6] and require strategic thinking. These problems involve high stakes, uncertainty or ambiguity, complexity or novelty, differences of opinions and a long-term commitment of effort, talent, money, reputation or other assets.

While these types of strategic changes can have a direct impact on healthcare quality and costs, organisation goals and employee work life, poor planning and/

or execution of these strategies can alter or destroy an organisation's future. These decisions require a strategic thinking process. The discipline of strategic thinking is not about a 'widely accepted organising structure and a growing body of empirical knowledge';[7] rather it is meant to convey a rigorous thinking process to organise tacit knowledge and existing information and to move from intuition and unchallenged assumptions to learning from experience.

Although the strategic intent of hospital mergers may be to stem the growth in costs or create better healthcare services, mergers can also lead to a clash of cultures, inefficiency and organisational failure. The case described in Box 12.1[8] illustrates the point.

Box 12.1 Case history

In 1996, two major US hospitals with two very different cultures merged into one entity. Hospital A was a warm, caring, yet high performing academic teaching hospital sponsored by the Jewish community. Hospital B was a high performing general hospital, with strong Protestant roots. Although the strategy was called a 'merger of equals', the academic hospital took control over most of the front stage, clinical departments.

The physicians at Hospital B said, 'We merged with Hospital A'. The physicians at Hospital A said, 'We acquired Hospital B'. Soon afterwards, the environment became increasingly competitive; budgets were tightening and costs controls were needed, many clinicians resigned and many loyal patients went elsewhere. By 2000, the merged hospitals' organisational practices were labelled 'cumbersome and inefficient', and the hospital was losing 50 million a year. Despite a staff of 1200 physicians, annual revenues over one billion, and a very strong reputation for quality, the merged hospital had lost its strategic focus and was close to disintegrating.

In 2002 the new CEO saw that hospital management had acquired incapacity to make and execute strategic decisions. Within two years the new leader restructured, taught the clinical leaders how to think strategically. During this time he taught the clinical leaders how to align operational strategy with the corporate strategy, he put a new team in place, and redesigned the strategic decision-making process. The CEO created several ground rules for strategic thinking such as 'voice your concerns during the meeting, not afterwards' and 'challenge assumptions in a respectful way'. As of 2006, the hospital continues to be successful and to contribute to the community.

The case illustrates several important lessons. First, merging two great hospitals may sound like a good strategic move but someone must organise a thinking process to anticipate the inevitable pitfalls of a merger. Without executive leadership teaching everyone the discipline of strategic thinking, any potentially 'great' strategic move can fail. Second, mergers require a consistency and alignment among three levels of strategy: corporate, competitive, and operating strategy. And third, the discipline of strategic thinking must consider how culture and organisation influence successful implementation of any strategic change.

Why do organisations exhibit different behaviours and results when facing similar environmental conditions? Strategic behaviour is not highly associated with the 'requirement of the environment' but is largely determined by the quality of the strategic thinking process.[9,10] This chapter addresses several strategy questions that should be understood by every healthcare manager. What does strategic thinking and planning in healthcare mean? What are the demands and constraints on strategic thinking? What are the pillars of effective strategic thought? What are some of the avoidable errors that healthcare leaders can make during strategic policy making and planning?

A word about strategy and management

Recently a clinical director presented the strategic problems that his medical centre had been confronting over the last decade.[11] He said:

> In 1997 when we were having a serious financial crisis, we hired strategy consultants to help us to restructure and to restore confidence. At the time we had been losing patients to local community hospitals. The medical centre reorganised into patient-centred care programmes and made many changes that resulted in service quality improvements, as well as improved hospitality and patient friendliness. Following these changes, the situation improved by 1999.
>
> After restructuring, we were afraid that the physicians would leave the hospital. Patient volume increased, and the financial situation improved. But then we experienced bed capacity problems and a serious shortage of nurses. Moreover, the increase in volume not only brought additional patients but a more complex patient mix that consumes the most expensive clinical resources: support services, intensive care beds, and operating room time.
>
> The strategic question is: Are we in a vicious cycle that will lead to future financial problems?

The quote reminds us that although the 'ostensible strategic problem' is discovering a better way to relate the organisation to the environment from an economic perspective, the 'real problem' is unanticipated consequences of implementing strategic changes – a problem of strategic thinking and organisational behaviour.

Healthcare organisation must confront these issues because they are embedded in a task environment, which refers to anything relevant 'out there' that can affect (or can be affected by) an organisation's desired long-term goals and performance. Every healthcare delivery system establishes its own strategic service domain that implicitly or explicitly targets the type of illnesses and diseases covered and type of populations served and formulates how the services will be delivered. Therefore, strategy is the way decision makers respond to a 'task environment' that results in a skilled sequence of activities intended to achieve long-term goals.[12]

The task environment can be local, regional or international and includes: patients and their families, referring clinicians and employees, medical suppliers, rivals and/or competitors for patients and resources, government and regulatory agencies, unions and professional associations, and the like. A successful strategy not only creates long-term value for patients and employees, but also creates

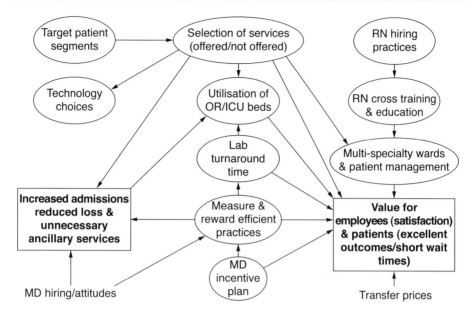

Figure 12.1 Hospital strategy as a skilled activity sequence

strategic visions that are hard to imitate. Some strategies are hard to imitate because they result from *ad hoc*, incremental, decision making.

Like it or not, looking at your pattern of investments over time, a strategy emerges. Figure 12.1 is an example of what a hospital looks like in terms of developing a skilled activity sequence. The question is: how well can you manage these strategic decisions?

These decisions often involve three levels of strategy: corporate, competitive and operating strategy.

1 **Corporate strategy:** refers to a healthcare organisation's choice of 'businesses' or clinical services and populations and how these businesses or services are managed. Corporate strategies include managing medical devices and suppliers, creating clinical standards, branding the name, transferring skills and sharing activities, vertical integration, diversification, mergers, alliances, partnerships, etc.

2 **Competitive strategy:** refers to how an organisation will create value in a given market by meeting the needs of patients and consumers, while meeting the needs of the clinical and non-clinical employees and the organisation as a business.

3 **Operating strategy:** refers to the formulation of policies, processes, technologies, human resource practices and the organisation of work, people and resources that influence the way the service is seen by patients and the results achieved on a day-to-day basis.

The challenge for strategic thinking is to align all three levels of strategy into an effective activity system.

Figure 12.2 Five dimensions of star quality. Source: Chilingerian.[13]

In exploring how to compete, a fundamental question is: What creates value for patients? From a patient perspective, perceptions of value can take many forms. One source of value for patients is perceived quality; however, quality is not a simple concept but best understood in terms of five underlying dimensions shown in Figure 12.2.

If we analyse a cardiac surgery programme in terms of these five dimensions, patients might want the following results.

1 Excellent outcomes:
   • low recurrence rates: less than 1% over last ten years
   • complications rates less than 0.5%
   • on average patients go back to work sooner.
2 Extremely high patient satisfaction – exceeding patient expectations:
   • 98% are extremely satisfied with the care and 2% 'merely' satisfied
   • excellent pain management
   • 100% willing to recommend the service again.
3 Efficient decision making:
   • high degree of co-ordination of patient care across operating units
   • average cost per case is less than the average local community hospital
   • quick diagnosis to treatment
   • optimal involvement of the patient in the care process.
4 Some amenities:
   • short waits once admitted
   • excellent dining services and food.
5 Excellent relationships, psychological support and information:
   • high degree of trust and confidence
   • clinical staff time spent answering questions
   • annual patient reunions/long-term relationship.

The essence of an effective healthcare strategy is finding a path that creates long-term value for patients, employees and the organisation. Value, when viewed from the patient perspective above, can be defined as the results achieved (outcomes) plus the service experience (e.g. service process, amenities, relationships, decision-making efficiency) divided by the sacrifices (e.g. wait time,

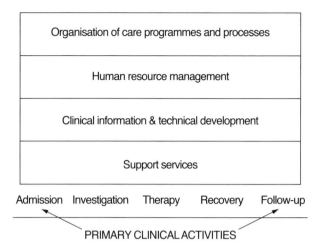

Figure 12.3 Primary clinical and non-clinical activities

inconveniences, diagnostic uncertainty, disrespect, amount of pain) plus the out-of-pocket costs of acquiring the services.[13,14] Value creation depends on the quality of relationships and reputation that a service delivery organisation has with organisations, groups and individuals in a given task environment.

In healthcare, there are two sources of strategic advantage.

1   The basic clinical activities are performed.
2   Choice of the mix of medical specialties.

In healthcare basic clinical activities are: admission, investigation, therapy, recovery and follow-up. Cardiology, pathology and general practice are examples of medical specialties. Porter[15] argues that strategy is different from operational effectiveness which he defines as performing basic activities better than your competitors. The essence of strategy is strategic positioning which, when applied to healthcare, is when a decision-making unit offers different medical services and/or performs the basic clinical activities in novel or unique ways.

Seeing the task environment as global suggests some distinct advantages in adapting or integrating medical specialties and/or clinical activities, Figure 12.3 identifies the five primary clinical activities and four secondary activities.

In addition to offering a medical specialty, a healthcare organisation that wants an international presence has to think about how to co-ordinate these nine activities internationally. Can these nine activities be done differently? Can the primary clinical activities be positioned (and perceived) as 'better services'?

Strategic thinking requires a consideration of the separate and unique char-acteristics of an organisation's situation and the development of a series of interrelated activities tailored to the constellation of those features that are present. While strategy is often thought of as deliberate choice to improve the long-term success of an organisation, in practice strategy can be an accumulation of trends and adaptive actions taken over time without much deliberation or conscious purpose.[16,17,18] For some health organisations, strategy might also require challenging standard practices, re-writing the rules, or re-inventing the theory of health services. The following case exemplifies how good strategic thinking effects long-term success for the organisation and consumers.

An example of effective strategic thinking

In 1972, Dr James Black, a scientist working at a British lab for the pharmaceutical company SmithKline, discovered a new class of anti-ulcerants called H2-antagonists.[19] In 1976 SmithKline launched the new drug called Tagamet (or cimetidine), which by 1981 accounted for 780 million dollars of SmithKline's sales. They were excited and optimistic because they understood the theory of the business – the pioneer with the patent has a distinct advantage over all competitors and this was a blockbuster drug.

Between 1976 and 1986, the results were not what the strategic planners at SmithKline anticipated. By 1986, SmithKline's competitor in the United Kingdom, Glaxo Holdings plc, despite being priced 20% to 75% higher, overtook Tagamet in global sales with a 'me too' drug called Zantac. It was Zantac not Tagamet that became the first drug to earn one billion dollars in global pharmaceutical sales, despite the fact that when the Food and Drug Administration approved Zantac they said it offered 'little or no' contribution over Tagamet. In 1989, as Dr James Black was awarded a Nobel Prize in Medicine for cimetidine, Zantac dominated the world-wide market taking 42% of the global market, beating Tagamet's sales in Italy, UK, the United States, France, and Japan.

How could Glaxo be so 'consistently lucky'? Alternatively, what went wrong for SmithKline? How could SmithKline, with first mover advantage, patent protection, and a Nobel Prize, have lost the battle for global sales? This case holds many lessons for strategic thinking. In the early 1980s the US was 37% of the worldwide market. Tagamet easily captured 90% of sales in the United States.

Strategic thinking must make sense of temporal patterns as changes (such as sales) unfold. People have difficulty seeing and interpreting developments over time.[20] Between 1982 and 1989, Glaxo was taking away SmithKline's business yet SmithKline's managers appeared not to notice until it was too late.

In 1972, when Glaxo heard about Dr Black's discovery, they decided to improve on Tagamet. In 1978 they began clinical trials in 20 countries and in 1981 they launched Zantac. When Glaxo's research revealed that physicians saw Zantac as a 'me too' drug with no added medical benefit, the marketing decisions makers wanted to follow the assumptions underlying the prevailing theory of the industry – if it is an inferior product then price it 10% below Tagamet's daily treatment cost. The CEO of Glaxo agreed that Zantac added no medical outcomes benefit, but the simplified once-a-day dosage regime and the lack of side effects made the drug far more convenient and safe. The CEO insisted on charging a 75% higher price. Based on published studies, they positioned their drug as having superior effectiveness with the tag line: 'faster, simpler, and safer'. Finally, Glaxo had a much stronger international sales force, by creating co-marketing strategic alliances with companies in Japan, Germany and France.

There are two explanations. First, by challenging classic marketing assumptions about price strategy, Glaxo analysed the competitive situation better than SmithKline. Second, the early commercial success of Tagamet led SmithKline to become 'inattentional blind'. While distorted interpretations of performance trends is a widespread phenomenon, as illustrated by the Bristol Royal Infirmary Inquiry Final Report,[21] high-spirited organisations like SmithKline, with a proud and successful history, are more likely to display psychological denial and cynical reactions to incremental bad news. Clearly in this case strong leadership gave the strategic planners permission to challenge old assumptions. The lesson for strategic thinking is to train everyone to challenge assumptions about the task environment. Strategic thinking about healthcare organisations is not exceedingly complex if the basic steps in strategic thinking are followed.

A new framework for strategic thinking: demands, constraints, and choices

When healthcare leaders talk about strategic planning aimed at furthering the objectives of the health system, often they base their decisions on intuitive judgement, which is compressed experiences and/or perhaps an ill-defined 'gut' feeling for current trends. Evolutionary psychologists have observed that the human brain, developed during the Stone Age, works against 'average' managers trying to resolve complex strategic problems.[22,23] If managers are under time pressure they cope with uncertainty by either taking random actions or becoming paralysed by processing too much information.[24,20]

The human brain may have its limitations, but cognitive psychologists argue that there is hope for strategic thinking. Health leaders should bear in mind that:

> Real improvement can be achieved, however, if we understand the demands that problem solving places on us and the errors we are prone to make when we attempt to meet them . . .   Dorner[20]

Strategic thinking places such high demands on managerial attention that strategic planning processes are predisposed to make analytical mistakes. By understanding the faulty way that human beings solve problems, bad habits can be broken and managers can learn how to avoid the worst mistakes.

Figure 12.4 displays what has been observed by students of managerial behaviour: although managers make strategic choices, they are limited by the number of demands and the nature of the constraints.[25,26,27] Strategic demands are those activities such as meeting performance criteria that must be undertaken for legal reasons (because of national policy or legislation), the local community, clinical employees, and competitive pressures from other stakeholders. The characteristics of the demands reveal how easily the mind can grasp or comprehend the requirements of a strategic situation.

The search for high-quality decisions is always restricted or limited by constraints. Constraints define the 'permissible' combinations of solutions that meet the basic demands. The dominant constraints are determined by the situation but might include lack of expertise, the amount of time or executive attention available, 'lock out' due to prior resource commitments, organisational culture, the need for consensus due to the balance of power in an organisation, and the assumptions underlying the theory of the service.

Figure 12.4 also shows how strategic action and behaviours are limited by the constraints in a situation. Situation A and B are an opportunity to launch some new services such as a non-invasive MRI centre, a bone biopsy clinic, and a new eye clinic. Situation B has more constraints; for example, there is a senior registrar who has requested the bone biopsy clinic and threatened to leave if you do not start one this year. Since this physician is among the most productive staff, the search for a high-quality decision is constrained; it feels that there may be no

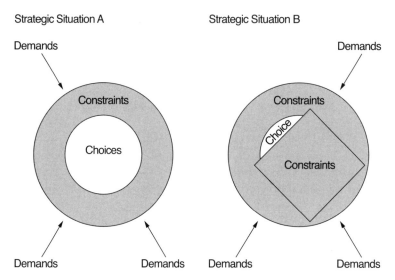

Strategic Situation A   Strategic Situation B

Demands   Demands

Constraints   Constraints

Choices   Choice

Choices   Constraints

Demands   Demands   Demands   Demands

Figure 12.4 Demands and constraints on strategic thinking

choice but to adopt the technology. Good strategic thinking can help to uncover the options for any alternative.

Although demands and constraints cannot be ignored, good strategic thinking can require decision makers to explore all the options that are available.

Generic strategic demands on leaders

Every strategic problem places unique requirements on decision makers. When we look beyond the particular strategic issues of any given healthcare organisation, we find at least four generic demands on leaders. The key demands that underpin strategic analysis include: time pressures, multiple stakeholder values, complexity and uncertainty. Each of these demand characteristics will be discussed briefly.

Time deadlines put pressure on decision makers. Strategic thinking can be more vigilant if there is an adequate amount of time available (neither too much nor too little). Psychologists tell us that when deadlines overwhelm people such that they perceive an imminent crisis, mounting fear and helplessness can lead to poor judgment.[24] On the other hand, when the issue is off in the distant future, there is less vigilance. *Stakeholder values* reflect an individual's understanding of 'what ought to be'. There is no easy way to deal with the problem of multiple values in healthcare. When the culture of a medical practice includes a high regard for individual autonomy, a belief in professional accountability, a high degree of collegiality, plus a strong 'business' emphasis, the goals and interests will be in conflict. Negotiation may be necessary to achieve a consensus. When there is no clear goal and the situation is unclear, the result is *ad hoc* incremental or 'repair service' behaviour.[20] Managers get in the habit of solving the problems that people bring. A manager guided by complaints may focus on the symptoms and miss the underlying disease. Consequently, when multiple stakeholders are involved, a process is needed to build commitment to a shared set of goals with clear criteria of success.

Another demand on a leader's strategic thinking is complexity. *Complexity* has been defined as a situation in which there are many interrelated variables with multiple feedback loops. The greater the quantity of variables and the inter-dependencies, the greater the system's complexity.[28] With complex, novel or unstable situations either we lack knowledge, skills and experience, or we reach the limits of human ability. When confronted with a new situation, one should look for the history that fits by finding analogies, and then clarifying 'likenesses' and 'differences'.[29] The approach and methods should be discovered while taking action, which requires 'reflective thinking'.[30]

A good example of a complex problem is thinking about the consequences of changing the mix of non-elective and elective surgical patients. One problem is managing patient flow when there are many interdependent work steps with randomness or statistical fluctuations. To think about this problem there are many elements. First there is the random arrival rates of acute patients that shifts the mix of clinical pathologies treated. There is also the utilisation of the fixed capacity such as operating rooms, intensive and regular beds. Three more variables include the talents of the clinicians, the variation in the service process, and the co-ordination of the activities throughout the care processes. The effect on performance of changing one or more of these variables is counterintuitive, making the hospital one of the most complex types of organisation known.

While complexity is real, it is also highly subjective. Since complex structures are hierarchical in structure and redundant, so the interactions among some sub-systems are weak, loosely coupled and trivial for any given problem.[31] For example, we can focus on co-ordination between two departments without analysing the physiological and psychological differences among the stakeholders. Simon[31] proposes that we can map the parts of the system and the parts that interact and collapse some of the complexity.

In science there is a presumption that strategic contexts and critical events can be measured or observed. The inability to visualise or observe an event or the consequences of change[20] with uncertainty being another demand on a leader's strategic thinking. In healthcare many do not have good information about clinical outcomes and satisfaction levels of various patient population segments and may have no information about clinical efficiency, service convenience or the amount of trust relationships between providers, patients and managers. Hence, some strategic decisions are made with a lack of knowledge about what will happen, because some events are difficult to measure or observe.

Generic strategic constraints on leaders

Every strategic problem places situational and generic constraints on decision makers. The time and effort required to work through strategic issues increase with the number of constraints on the problem. Three types of constraints will be highlighted: executive attention, wrong conceptual models, and the constellation of strategic sub-goals.

The first generic constraint on strategic thinking is the availability of *executive attention*. We live in a world that has an overabundance of strategic information. The internet has made information nearly a free good. The constraint is that healthcare managers are so busy that executive attention has become a scarce resource and a bottleneck for strategic thinking.[27] According to Cyert and

March,[32] each member of the organisation has more demands on their time and attention than they can handle:

> At any point in time, the member attends to only a rather limited subset of his demands, the number and variety depending again on the extent of his involvement in the organisation and on the demands of the other commitments on his attention.

External pressures, for example, competitive, legal or legislative, may decide the order of attention to strategic goals. However, people in organisations attend to certain parts of the environment and ignore other parts. Given the limits of executive attention, multiple conflicting values (or other conflicting demands) are rarely seen as a major problem for strategic thinking.

A second generic constraint on strategic thinking is choosing the *wrong reality model* or theory that explains performance. Forrester[28] described a reality model or theory as structural knowledge; that is, the decision maker's understanding of how the variables in a system are related in cause–effect relationships. Strategic decisions are constrained by structural knowledge and conceptual models and theories that may be wrong or incomplete.[20] In general, managers spend too much time staying current by updating information and too little time revising conceptual models.[31]

Every health service must answer three implicit questions: How do we create value for patients and employees? What is our ultimate destiny as a service provider? What makes our services distinct? The answers to these questions define the general theory that governs the performance of the service. The root causes of strategic failure are unchallenged assumptions about the variables that influence strategic thinking.[33]

A further constraint for strategic thinking is the existence of *multiple sub-goals*.[34] Every health decision is subject both to budgetary and resource constraints and many other sub-goals as well. Though one sub-goal may be singled out as the primary 'strategic goal' for political or cultural reasons, the other sub-goals will constrain strategic decisions. If policy makers choose improved access over efficient clinical decision making or better outcomes as the desired goal, the other two immediately become constraints right away or during implementation. So the managerial domain seeking to offer efficient access to care confronts the clinical service domain seeking to offer the best quality of care. Both domains are constrained by the requirement that the care process should not exceed the budget, otherwise either volume or some amenities must be reduced. Though clinicians and managers may not share the same primary goal, finding an alternative acceptable or 'satisfactory' to both parties translates sub-goals into constraints.[34] Therefore, every strategic decision is concerned with finding alternatives that satisfy a large set of constraints.

Although there are unique demands on strategic thinking there is always residual choice. In the next section six pillars of effective strategic thinking are introduced. Having the discipline to use these pillars to support strategic thinking will expand the range of alternatives and options and increase choice.

Six pillars of strategic thinking

People are programmed to begin strategic planning by advocating or talking about solutions, preferred alternatives or obvious strategies. Leaders must avoid

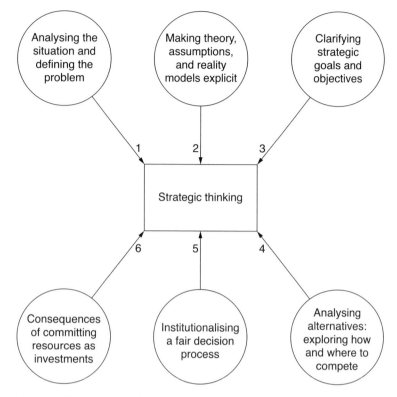

Figure 12.5 Six pillars of strategic thinking

premature discussion of strategic solutions for two reasons. The first is that people begin by strongly advocating one opinion. Assumptions and uncertainties in the situation become indistinguishable from known facts. A primary source of strategic mistakes is hidden assumptions.[33] Second, hidden assumptions will lead to two types of ineffective decision processes. If the decision makers have the same assumptions they will reach closure very fast without considering the full set of consequences; if they have different assumptions, the discussion will be never-ending and emotionally charged, at least until the deadlock is broken by abandonment or force.[35]

Strategic thinking shifts the group from premature discussion of solutions to an exploration and understanding of the problem, the assumptions and the goals, before deciding on the alternatives. By shifting everyone's focus from solutions to effective strategic thinking, the decision makers have a better understanding of what is at stake and who holds the various points of view. Although strategic thinking slows down the decision process, the pool of information is enlarged as people have more time to think around what the decision is really about.

Figure 12.5 identifies six pillars that support effective strategic thinking. These pillars are the foundations of strategic thinking. Each one will be discussed in turn.

Pillar one: analysing the situation and defining the problem

Strategic thinking must begin with an inquiry into the context or predicament of the decision makers along with the basic conditions that define the immediate situation. Managers begin by acquiring, focusing and analysing information and inferences about the situation. The goal is to separate the known facts from the assumptions and the uncertainties. Can anyone detect a pattern in how the situation is evolving? What are the time series or trends such as changes in patient attitudes, community demographics, demand for services, or new technologies?[36]

Although environments are complex, most strategic problems can be broken down into smaller problems. As Simon[9] has argued:

> . . . there are millions of variables that in principle could affect each other but most of the time don't . . . in most situations we face we can detect only a modest number of variables or considerations that dominate . . .

To determine some of the key issues and dominant variables it is necessary to engage the decision makers by beginning a round-robin conversation with their stories about the key trends.[29] Tichy[37] suggests asking thought-starter questions.

* What is the environment you are working in today and in the future?
* Given the environment, what is the 'business' theory today and tomorrow (see Pillar Two)?
* How well do people understand the business theory? What do you need to teach them to change the theory for tomorrow? How will you do that?

The leader asks each decision maker to think about these questions and to tell 'their' story about the current strategic situation using three basic rules.

1 Take the best information into account.
2 Tell (or write out) the story in three or four sentences.
3 Make sure the facts can be verified.

As the story unfolds, determine the timeline, by asking when it started.[29] The group can ask each other 'who', 'what', 'when', 'where' and 'why' questions. After these discussions begin, the information must be interpreted. If the narratives are complicated by uncertainty, exploratory tools are needed to make sense of the situation.

There are three other tools to help strategic thinkers define problems and analyse situations:

1 Stakeholder analysis.
2 SWOT analysis.
3 Problem reframing.

Stakeholders are individuals, groups, coalitions, and organisations internal and external to the decision makers and 'who either affect or who are affected by a corporation's actions, behaviour, and policies'.[38]

To undertake a stakeholder analysis, list all the internal and external stakeholders and identify their perceived stake or interest in the strategic situation such as needs, hopes, fears, and/or worries.[39]

There are three advantages in understanding stakeholder interests. First, this analysis helps to determine the full set of consequences and the possibility for reconciling various interests. Second, thinking about stakeholder interests provokes the question; what will it take to get people to accept this decision or see this decision as in their best interest? Third, it helps to identify the options within each strategic choice. Hence the analysis can help to make a connection between strategic thinking and strategic planning and implementation.

SWOT analysis identifies the strengths, weaknesses, opportunities and threats in the situation. Strengths are internal capabilities that enable and weaknesses are internal characteristics that prevent the organisation from performing. Opportunities and threats are external trends, ideas and events that create relative advantages and/or disadvantages.

The problem with SWOT analysis is that after all the relative advantages and disadvantages have been identified, decision makers end up with four lists. In order to make the SWOT analysis useful three questions should be raised.[41]

1 Where did the information on strengths, weaknesses, opportunities and threats come from?
2 How do we know they are correct?
3 Are they enduring and unchanging known facts or are they assumptions?

The group should go through the lists and separate each item into categories:

- Known facts.
- Interpretations.
- Uninformed opinions.
- Assumptions.

After a stakeholder and SWOT analysis have been undertaken, the problem or opportunity has been defined. Decision theorists have observed that defining a problem frames the situation and biases strategic thinking.[41] More importantly, the way a problem is framed limits the identification of alternatives.[42] They suggest writing down the problem, re-analysing the problem, considering other frames. Hammond et al[43] offer the following suggestion.

Begin by asking what was the triggering event? Then ask and answer four questions.

1 How have we framed the opportunity or problem we are trying to solve?
2 Which stakeholders or what conversations activated or provoked the need for a decision?
3 How are the two related?
4 Are there other ways to 'see' or reframe the problem?

One device to bring greater discipline to the analysis of situations is to separate known facts from uncertainties and assumptions.[29] The Oxford Dictionary defines a fact as 'a datum of experience as distinct from conclusions'. Facts are final and reliable realities, but there are several problems with facts. First, there is always a paradox: too many yet too few facts.[31] Often we know more about the recent past and not enough about the remote past.[36] Second, we may know a lot about activity this month, but very little about the conditions or processes that caused an increase or decrease in activity. We can count the number of visits but these do not speak for themselves. We can find statistical association among variables, but rarely attain real contextual knowledge about the past. To help organise the facts, we need a theory or reality model, the second pillar of strategic thinking.

Pillar two: making theory and assumptions explicit

Having begun an initial analysis of the situation and formulated a definition of the problem it is important to uncover the hidden theory or reality model. Theory is a constellation of many relevant or important variables in cause–effect relationships; that is, it identifies the critical variables that interact with a large number of other variables. Theory preserves the relevant facts and eliminates the irrelevant facts. Unconsciously, people may turn their backs on acquiring new information because a hidden theory ruled those facts out. If the business theory no longer fits the current reality or the facts of the situation, strategic failure is likely.

Theories are limited by the decision maker's definition of the problem situation and vice versa. In this sense, the theory of the business is like a trap designed to catch one type of animal.[44] Just as a lion trap will not catch a mouse or a butterfly, you design the trap based on the type of animal and you just might catch that animal. Theories are either incorrect owing to evidence to the contrary, or not yet known to be incorrect, but will eventually be proven wrong. It is important to make theory explicit.

Drucker[33] proposed that every successful organisation has developed an implicit theory of the business that is a proven formula that guides strategic actions. For any given situation, past experience has taught decision makers to differentiate variables that exert a strong influence on performance and success from the variables that exert little or no influence. They have learned that if they make small changes in those variables, outcomes can be influenced.

According to Drucker the theory of the business is based on aligning three types of assumptions.

1 Assumptions about the task environment (i.e. what society is willing to pay for).
2 Assumptions about core competencies (i.e. primary activities that the organisation must succeed at performing).
3 Assumptions about mission (i.e. how success is defined).

An assumption is an unconscious or tacitly expressed apprehension of the world. Assumptions are taken for granted to be evidence-based conclusions and therefore, final and reliable realities. Incorrect assumptions preclude some viable alternatives; consequently they are self-imposed constraints. Although many assumptions are hypotheses, and therefore tentative, hidden assumptions become unquestioned conclusions that block inquiry and promote advocacy. When people have rival hypotheses, facts can be used to test each hypothesis. If people hold different assumptions, facts do not resolve the issues but are drawn selectively to confirm what people assume.

Mitroff[38] was once brought in to help a healthcare organisation whose executive team were trying to solve some strategic problem. Although the decision makers had collected and analysed the same information, each faction reached different conclusions. What caused the deadlock? Mitroff discovered that each faction relied on different assumptions.

> More data only served to activate underlying differences. It did not test or resolve them, it only made things worse. We have a perfect example of where more can lead to less. Since for the most part the assumptions

remained buried and implicit, the groups themselves were largely unaware of what was happening. All they knew was that time and again they had disagreed and were immensely frustrated.

In healthcare organisations challenging assumptions is not always so straightforward. Financial information, budgets and other historical 'facts' explain success or failures. Since all of this information requires interpretation, even the hard facts are actually assumptions. Sometimes what we believe to be facts are only 'agreed-on' assumptions that we treat like facts to move things along. Assumptions provide people with psychological security that they can predict what will happen, or what to expect. Psychologists argue that since people avoid uncertainty, they may not accept the possibility that their assumptions may be wrong or incomplete.[20]

Identifying assumptions as hypotheses

The cure is not only to separate facts from assumptions, but to prioritise and challenge these assumptions. There is one trick to challenging assumptions. Having identified strengths (S), weaknesses (W), opportunities (O) and threats (T) in the SWOT analysis, ask everyone to take each item under SWOT and label it as either (1) a known fact or (2) an assumption. Next ask them to identify the most important or critical assumption in each of the lists. Next call this assumption a hypothesis and ask the group to think of rival hypotheses. Then allocate each person an imaginary £100 000 to invest and ask them how much of that £100 000 they would bet on the critical assumption. Review the assumptions according to the amount of money people would wager.

Pillar three: clarifying strategic goals and objectives

In every strategic problem there are a few key result areas that define success. Strategic goals are desired outcomes and objectives and help to specify a way to get there. In this sense, goals are the 'value premises that can serve as input to decisions'.[34] Therefore, when leaders undertake strategic thinking, nothing is more important than setting clear and engaging goals.

Goals play a role in problem solving because they define the purpose of the inquiry in terms of what people truly 'hope' to accomplish. Goals help to find the right alternative by answering the question: what would constitute a path to solving the problem? When we want to improve the quality or efficiency of a service, clear goals can become a guiding light for strategic activity.

When goals are unclear, managers will never know whether the goal has been attained.[20] 'To improve the quality of care' or 'to make the clinic more accessible' are examples of ill-defined and arbitrary goals. Consider the 'quality of care' goal: although it is vague managers will take a random series of actions to fix whatever complaints about quality arise. This is 'repair service' behaviour – unclear goals that lead to fixing whatever problems are brought forward. The potential consequence is fixing trivial quality problems and becoming a prisoner of the moment, which may mean ignoring underlying problems until they become catastrophic quality issues.

There has been a vast amount of research on the importance of defining explicit goals or criteria of success. There is clear evidence that specific and challenging goals lead to better performance than less difficult goals, but goal setting does not guarantee success, because goal setting has to think about the demands and constraints on decision making. Here are three techniques to establish goals.

One approach[43] is to engage all of the key decision makers in an idea-building and brainstorming session aimed at uncovering desires and concerns. Given the analysis of the situation, what do the decision makers really want? Ask the key decision makers to list their concerns, desires, hopes and fears. Ask them to clarify what they really mean by their concern or desire.

Hand out a summary of the stakeholder and SWOT analysis (Pillar One). What are the concerns and interests of the stakeholders? Have each person tell a story about the best-case and worst-case outcomes. How would we explain these outcomes to the stakeholders? Finally, what would be needed to explain the rationale to the stakeholders for an alternative?

Once a list of goals exists it is possible to develop a sense of the relatedness or unrelatedness among goals, and priorities if they exist. Some goals are a means to an end, for example, if a healthcare programme identifies the following goals offering results as important performance areas.

- Offering excellent health services to patients.
- Obtaining superior clinical outcomes.
- Limiting long wait times.
- Providing rapid responses to emergency situations.
- Ensuring all clinicians are experts in their sub-specialty.

Upon closer scrutiny we find that some of these goals are instrumental, that is, the means to get to some end, and others are terminal goals. The instrumental goals are: limiting wait times, providing rapid responses and ensuring clinical expertise. If achieved they will enable provision of excellent health services and obtain superior clinical outcomes.

One technique to help identify relationships among terminal goals and instrumental objectives is to ask the 'five whys'. The process works as follows: ask 'why' and when an answer surfaces, ask the second 'why' about the answer given, and continue until you discover the hierarchy of relationships among the key result areas. By asking 'why' do we want to limit long wait times, 'why' do we want to ensure all clinicians are experts, decision makers may discover that shorter waits and clinical reputations are related to customer perceptions of excellence but not related to other key results.

Once the constellation of concerns and desires surfaces into key result areas, they need to be converted into well-defined strategic goals. According to goal theory, strategic goals should have six characteristics.[46,47]

1 Begin with the word 'to' followed by an action verb aimed at producing a single key result.
2 Write in explicit language such that the goal can be measured.
3 Set goals that are difficult to reach but attainable.
4 Ensure the goals are logically related to the key performance areas and connected to the defined problem.

> 5 Specify four features of each goal: a target date, the people accountable, some quality standards, and maximum cost factors.
> 6 Establish a consensus that the goals are acceptable to the decision makers (see Pillar Five).

Pillar four: analysing alternatives: exploring how and where to compete

This pillar gets decision makers to think about strategic alternatives. Healthcare organisations have to think about two basic strategic questions: where to offer their services and how to offer the services. There are several tools that can be used to think about how to redesign healthcare programmes and activities. A complete discussion of these tools is beyond the scope of this chapter. To achieve strategic advantage, Porter[17] has argued that there are some basic strategic alternatives: strategies aimed at serving a mass market and/or strategies aimed at serving a targeted market segment. Two mass market strategies are cost leadership and differentiation. The advantage of cost leadership developing an activity system is that it produces a product or offers a service that is below the cost of similar organisations. The advantage of differentiation comes from increasing the perceived value of a product or service relative to the value of other organisations' products or services. Since there are only two generic strategies, having unique qualities or being very efficient due to a unique cost structure, if you have neither of these qualities you are 'stuck in the middle'.

Market segmentation strategies are sometimes called focus strategies and are targeted to meet the needs of a specific patient population. The advantage of focus is to achieve either cost leadership and/or a differentiation strategy.

Traditionally, general hospitals have been organised around medical departments: orthopaedics, medicine, surgery, paediatrics and departments such as laboratory services, radiology, therapy services, nursing departments, and so on. As a result, healthcare organisations and clinicians have a habit of 'doing everything for everyone' and their strategies have been limited. They neither achieve cost leadership or real differentiation. In healthcare, each clinical programme should develop focused strategy that strives to meet the health needs and wants of a specific patient population in a way that achieves both very high quality and efficiency.

To begin thinking about this aspect of strategy, it is helpful to organise the vast amount of healthcare information in new ways. For example, to develop insights and to organise their thinking about strategic alternatives, Intermountain Health System in Utah in the United States developed a new system for categorising their work. They identified 600 clinical work processes. Upon closer examination, they found that 62 care processes accounted for 93% of acute volume and 30 processes accounted for 85% of outpatient volume.[48] Moreover, after grouping work processes into nine clinical programmes built around the 600 tightly coupled work processes, they found that nine of the most common work processes in the cardiovascular clinical programme accounted for nearly 19% of the health system's inpatient and outpatient costs. By applying the Pareto Principle, they discovered that a minority of causes, inputs, and/or effort usually lead to good

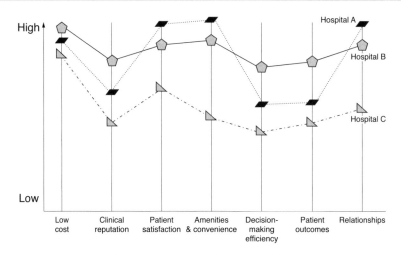

Figure 12.6 Value curves of three major providers of healthcare services

results. This helped Intermountain to achieve more with much less effort and to develop breakthrough strategic thinking.

Visualising quality and costs can also help strategic thinking. Kim and Mauborgne[49] advocate unlocking the creativity of people by showing a visual profile (or value curve) of the factors that influence competition and the location of current and potential competitors. The attributes assumed to be important to patients are low cost, clinical reputation of the hospital and attending doctors, as well as five consumer-driven dimensions of quality that have been elucidated by Axelrod and Cohen.[12] The five dimensions of quality are: patient satisfaction, amenities and convenience, decision-making efficiency, patient outcomes and relationships: information and emotional support.

Figure 12.6 depicts one Asian hospital's portrait of the competition's value curves.[4] Hospital B's physician-centred rather than patient-centric culture results in its poor performance in patient satisfaction, amenities and convenience and relationships. However, it dominates A and C on four key dimensions: cost, decision-making efficiency, patient outcomes and clinical reputation, reflecting its status as an academic medical centre. Hospital A is more expensive but dominates B and C on amenities and convenience, relationships, and patient satisfaction. Clinical reputation is moderate, reflecting its lack of publications and teaching and its approach of replication rather than innovation. Hospital C is inferior on all seven dimensions. In particular, its decision-making efficiency is assessed to be lower than A and B as the fee-for-service method of billing creates an incentive to perform a higher volume of procedures, investigations and longer stays in hospital.

Another simple tool to help strategic thinking is to observe the evolution of case mix trends in the healthcare organisation. Based on degree of complexity and severity of the health services provided, all clinical programmes could be segmented into three pathology categories from low to high: A, B and C. For example, in the case of medical centres, tooth extractions are simple, routine procedures and fall into an A category of care. On the other hand, the transplant programmes are very complex, dealing with many uncertainties, and would fall

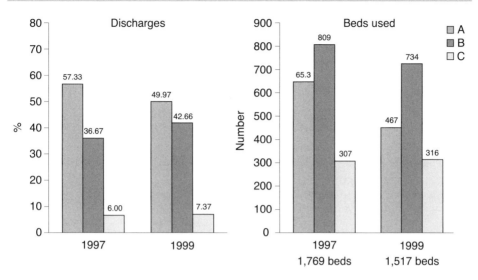

Figure 12.7 Evolution of pathology severity (A, B, C pathology)

into the C category of care. Category B represents moderately complex and resource-intensive patient care, such as cardiac surgery. Figure 12.7 shows how the evolution of pathology at one medical centre had been shifting from A to C care in terms of beds and admissions.[11]

ABC patient pathology is categorised by degrees of complexity, based on patient's resource utilisation, the co-ordination requirements, complexity of clinical findings, rarity of disease (requiring sub-specialty attention) and risk of complications. A-cases are the least complex, C-cases are the most complex (adapted from Chilingerian and Vandeckerckhove[11]).

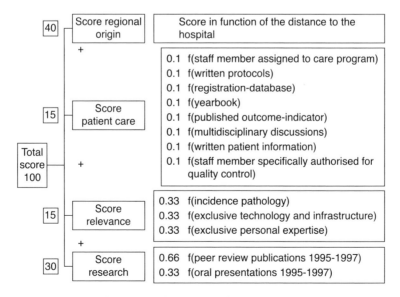

Figure 12.8 Strategic thinking in healthcare: profile score. Adapted from Chilingerian and Vandeckerckhove[11]

A comparative analysis of the care programmes' performance might help the clinical leaders to think more strategically about how the medical centre has been positioned. Figure 12.8 illustrates how one medical centre developed a system for comparing each care programme to all others on two dimensions:

1 The financial attractiveness or profitability of the service.
2 The clinical or academic profile.

The clinical profile was developed by the clinicians based on several dimensions:

- the average distance the patient travelled to the hospital
- the quality of patient care
- the research attached to the care programme
- the amount of expertise in relation to competitors.

Therefore some care programmes can be profitable and have a high profile, or less profitable and have a less distinctive profile.

Another hospital in Belgium began strategic thinking by organising their clinical work into 250 care programmes, such as transplantation, tumours and obstetrics. To take a more objective approach to making choices in medical strategy, the medical centre utilised portfolio analysis to evaluate all of the care programmes. Figure 12.9 illustrates how a portfolio approach can help healthcare organisations think about their competence priority and resources that they should give to the different clinical programmes in their portfolio.

Figure 12.9 reveals that obstetrics and transplantation are both financially attractive. Although transplantation has a high profile the obstetrics programme is not differentiated. Ambulatory care is neither distinct nor financially attractive. With the help of the next tool, decision makers can generate alternatives aimed at strategic changes; growth, improvement, outsourcing, etc.

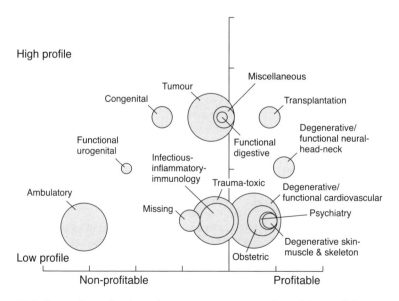

Figure 12.9 Strategic evaluation of care programmes. Adapted from Chilingerian and Vandeckerckhove[11]

When thinking about where to compete, Porter[17] argues that diversification, whether through acquisition, joint venture or start-up, has not been a successful strategy. He argues that before an organisation considers diversifying it must answer these questions.

- How attractive is the industry in terms of an organisation's ability to create value?
- What is the cost to enter this industry?
- Who will be better off after the decision?

Each question is a hurdle and each one must be passed. Consider the attractiveness of the industry in terms of ability to create value. There are five forces governing industry competition:[17]

1 Threat of few entrants.
2 Bargaining power of suppliers.
3 Bargaining power of customers.
4 Rivalry among others offering similar products and services.
5 Threat of substitute products and services in the future.

The collective pressure from these forces determines whether or not the industry is attractive. An attractive industry has high barriers to entry, modest buyer/supplier power, few substitutes and stable rivalry.

If the industry is attractive, then the second cost to enter this 'test' must be passed. The cost of the investment decision (which includes time, talent and reputation as well as money) must not 'capitalise' all future benefits. Again, if this second test is passed and the opportunity still seems very attractive, the 'better off' test must be passed. In the case of acquiring a new business or service, either the organisation or the new business must be better off after the acquisition. Given the current merger mania, this approach can be very helpful for healthcare organisations.

Another tool to help thinking about where to compete is shown in Figure 12.10. This figure identifies a matrix that guides strategic thinking based on the

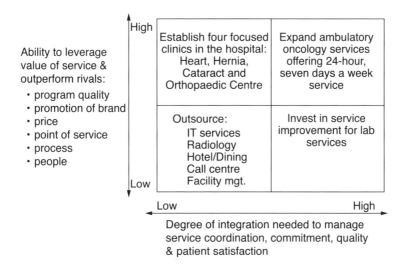

Figure 12.10 Rethinking the mix of services

ability to leverage the value of the service and outperform others, and the degree of integration needed to manage service co-ordination, commitment, quality and patient perceptions. This tool can help to identify four redesign activities:

1 what health services are core services
2 where to invest and improve
3 where to outsource
4 where to focus the strategy.

Figure 12.10 shows how a healthcare organisation can use this matrix to rethink the mix of services and develop a new strategic service vision.

Strategic thinking applied to international healthcare

Globalisation takes place if there is some distinct advantage in integrating medical specialties and/or clinical activities worldwide.[50] If healthcare organisations effectively transition into global players, they could have global access to: knowledge, financial capital and social capital. As Alsagoff[4] points out:

> An organisation that employs doctors in many geographical locations can exploit ICT to overcome the inertia of doctors to knowledge sharing or their incapability to husband and harvest widely dispersed information. More effective knowledge management accelerates the development of its medical specialties and clinical activities, which are important sources of advantage.

In other industries, large global organisations like Wal-Mart compete aggressively with low prices, depth of inventory and/or their unique product offerings. The incipience of global healthcare presents a credible threat to every country where a foreign provider could offer better value. Some foreign providers bring efficient clinical decision making, tacit knowledge and innovation, lower prices, or all four. For example, a South African cataract team was brought into a hospital in the National Health Service for six weeks to manage the backlog of patients. After six weeks the surgical team from South Africa eliminated a six-month backlog of cases, achieving clinical efficiency four to five times higher than the resident ophthalmology staff.

Like it or not, local healthcare providers will face even greater international competition in the future. Will small domestic healthcare providers stay the course, merge, go out of business, or get acquired? Will globalisation lead to national health policy restrictions of professional licences to practise or be open to global providers?

Whatever the outcome, health leaders have to think strategically about whether their organisations need an international strategy. Figure 12.11 is a tool to think about expanding on an international scale.[2] Each quadrant is a strategic approach to meeting local needs while integrating international health practices with domestic know-how. The strategy represented in the bottom left quadrant would merely buy or build a health facility in another country and would not draw on its home-oriented advantages by sharing services, transferring clinical or non-clinical know-how. If the hospital or faculty was successful, they kept it; if it was not, they divested. In the past, several hospitals that tried this international approach have not been successful.

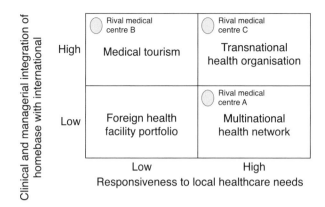

Figure 12.11 Thinking about a multinational strategy: standardisation versus adaptation. Adapted from Chilingerian and Savage[2]

The upper left quadrant emphasises scale efficiency with a high degree of co-ordination and integration between operating strategies and the delivery of clinical services. This may be where most healthcare organisations are today. For example, to create value in international one-stop shopping, medical centres must set up an integrated set of activities that includes: airport pick-up; appointment co-ordination; and leveraging the value of diagnostic, surgical and medical services.

The bottom right quadrant develops an alliance with local providers but attempts little or no integration with headquarters' operating strategies and delivery systems. The upper right quadrant achieves both clinical and managerial integration between the operating strategies and delivery of care while targeting their services and service concepts to meet local needs.

Figure 12.11 can also be used to develop an international growth plan. Doz, Santos and Williamson[51] theorise a three-phased approach to global organisation, based on the degree of standardisation versus customisation. In Phase One, organisations build on innovations and financial success of their domestic operations. Phase Two sees them expanding geographically into nearby markets, usually through leveraging local success in order to provide low-cost services. In Phase Three, they expand into more markets and balance local responsiveness with global integration. Alsagoff[4] used this approach in his analysis of medical centres A, B and C in Asia in order to develop an international growth plan (*see* Figure 12.11). Medical Centre C is a transnational healthcare organisation that established many hospitals outside of its home-base country and is integrated with its flagship. Medical Centre A is still a multinational health network, since its overseas hospitals are not well integrated with its home-base hospitals, while Medical Centre B is focused on medical tourism with little interest in meeting local needs.

Pillar five: institutionalising a fair decision process

When organising for strategic thinking, there are several questions that a manager/leader must answer.

1 Who has 'organisational rights' to be involved with this decision?
2 Who has the expertise to help us think about this decision?
3 Who should be consulted prior to or during the decision making?
4 Who will be informed of the rationale for decision and the expectations?

Once these questions are answered, the fifth pillar of strategic thinking is developing a collaborative problem-solving approach termed 'fair process'.[52] This is a pillar in which students of organisation theory have observed that strategic behaviour is not highly correlated with the so-called 'requirements of their environmental situation' but is contingent on the type of decision processes.[24,9,10] There are many varieties of ineffective decision-making processes; three will be highlighted.

The first ineffective decision process has been labelled 'group think'. This process focuses on a problem – however, the group is insulated from external scrutiny, displays strong advocacy as opposed to inquiry norms, and has a history of authoritarian leadership. The process leads to rapid convergence and the product is decision-making failures.[24,10] A second type of decision process identifies a problem, the group then begins what is perceived to be an endless discussion, until it is clear that a political deadlock is reached, and the only tangible product is the identification of 'friends and foes' rather than an effective decision. A third decision process is the so-called garbage can process, which begins with a solution in search of a problem.[53]

> Many things are happening at once; technologies are changing and poorly understood; alliances, preferences, and perceptions are changing; solutions, opportunities, ideas, people, and outcomes are mixed together in ways that make interpretations uncertain and leave connections unclear.

The decision context is characterised by turnover of decision makers, unclear preferences and measures of success, and no sure enough way to succeed. People permanently attach themselves to issues and, depending on who shows up, any solution can be associated with any problem. When there is an opportunity to resolve a problem, some set of the permanent issues takes over the debate and time is the source of order.

In contrast to the other decision processes, fair process has several characteristics. Fair process engages key people to analyse the situation resulting in a framing of the decision problem, explores and narrows the list of new ideas, explains the rational for decisions, setting expectations about roles and responsibilities, and implementing the strategy with an eye toward evaluation and learning.[54] Studies of decision making have found that commitment to strategic goals is directly related to the perception that the decisions process was 'fair' even if decision makers disagree with the final outcome or alternative selected. Commitment to strategic goals means that the key people are drawn to the strategic goals because they believe the strategy is important. Moreover, they will persevere to implement the strategic activity even when there are severe constraints.[55]

Consider the role of leadership. Strategic thinking management is not about strong and brilliant leaders telling people where we should go and why, it is all about framing and asking powerful questions and applying concepts and analytic techniques. It is presumptuous and arrogant for any top leader to tell people what they should aim for and how to deliver health services but asking 'what should we aim for?' and 'how can we can deliver health services?' are powerful questions.[56] Even in a crisis, the top leaders do not make strategic decisions unilaterally. The work of the leader is to establish the conditions that enable key internal stakeholders to develop a capacity for planning and execution, and to coach and facilitate a process to be sure that closure is always reached.

There are several behavioural principles involved in fair process. The first is the idea that while people are the source of novel ideas and strategic innovations, no individual can evaluate the added-value of their own contributions. A process is needed to determine whether everyone agrees and there has to be time to take a dialectical approach and build on the areas of agreement and allow the sources of disagreement to be aired.

A second principle of fair process is setting clear expectations about roles and responsibilities. As Kim and Mauborgne[52] argue: 'it matters less what the new rules and policies are and more that they are clearly understood'.

A third behavioural principle is the need to build (not request) commitment to a strategic direction. Commitment to strategic direction is enhanced when people believe that the strategy (i.e. skilled sequence of activities) is achievable, important and meaningful to the group or organisation.[55] When strategies are seen as achievable, people have more self-confidence. When people are self-confident they take on much larger strategic challenges. To make strategic goals important and meaningful to people, leaders must persuade, clarify and explain the rationale for the strategic choices selected. Goals assigned with a clear rationale as to why they are desirable and achievable can be as motivating as strategic goals arrived at via mutual participation.

Fair process combines two ingredients in a single process: rational process and interpersonal process. Rational process has been explained in the previous five pillars. To reiterate, it begins with an analysis of the situation and a clear separation of the facts from assumptions before alternatives and consequences are discussed. Good interpersonal process involves engaging people in an analysis of the problem: actively listening to various points of view, understanding the contributions of everyone, reviewing and summarising what has been said.

Management of the emotional aspects of decision making does not require controlling or suppressing inappropriate feelings, rather it requires accepting the inevitability of emotions and using emotion to motivate the group to commit to the shared goals that the group wants to attain.[57] The idea is to create challenge and dissent in a way that conveys 'I may not agree with you, but I do understand why this is important to you'. Ultimately, fair process will help the leader build commitment to the strategic goals and decisions.

Pillar six: consequences of committing resources as investments

A careful analysis of the situation, separating facts from assumptions, identification of strategic goals, and thinking about how and where to compete should identify where the organisation should invest time, energy, and talent. Since major strategic commitments are not easily reversed, the consequences of each alternative should be analysed against the strategic goals. However, each alternative has a set of consequences; some clear, others more ambiguous.

It is important to distinguish types of resource allocation decisions: expenditures and investments. Expenditures are irreversible prior decisions that accumulate and are consumed by annual operating budgets. Investments not only buy new tools, catheterisation labs, positron emission tomography scans and DaVinci robots, they also commit money, reputation and talent to an uncertain future.

Every organisation has an implicit strategy that results from a pattern of investment. There are two interesting outcomes of an investment pattern. First, you can become a prisoner of your past decisions. Commitment refers to major strategic decisions that affect resources in a way that influences future choices and limits opportunities.[6] For example, once an organisation has decided to develop or acquire a diagnostic treatment centre, launch a new MRI service, or add beds to the surgical intensive care unit, the menu of future options has been dramatically reduced. Strategic choices force a 'lock in', a cost based on a past strategic choice. Investments that sink clinical and managerial talent, human effort, capital, and reputation into uncertainty should not be made intuitively or impulsively.[58]

Strategy represents the capabilities that an organisation has built and how an organisation has been able to use those capabilities to create value. A pattern of investment also creates specialised skills, patents, tacit knowledge, unique work processes. A second outcome of a pattern of investments is that these specialised assets are hard to copy or imitate.

The sixth pillar of strategic thinking considers the 'full set' of consequences, as well as the risks and uncertainties before committing resources to a strategic direction. By definition, decisions are 'strategic' for two reasons: they are made without knowing exactly what is going to happen; and the decisions are 'important' because the decision involves a commitment with risk. Risk can be defined as a decision maker's exposure to a chance of a loss. The phrase 'chance of a loss' (or probability of loss) refers to the degree of belief that people have that the loss will take place.[59]

In considering risk, decision makers should ask each other what kind of resource commitment would be made.[60] Any strategic decision can be divided into:

- **large risks:** commitments that could have large payoffs in some scenarios, or large losses in other scenarios
- **sustainable risks:** commitments with a large positive payoff in some scenarios, or small losses in other scenarios
- **win-win risks:** a commitment that offers various benefits in virtually every scenario.

To understand the full set of consequences, strategic thinking must uncover the amount of uncertainty; the lower the amount of uncertainty, the better the understanding of the likely consequences. Uncertainty, as it is used here, is defined as a lack of sure knowledge about past, present or future events. Consequently, every strategic situation could be categorised by the amount of uncertainty in framing the problem and finding a solution.[56,59,60] Table 12.1 displays strategic situations by five classes of uncertainty. For example, in class 1, which represents the lowest levels of uncertainty, decisions are mechanical and do not require a great deal of strategic thinking. The problem is well-defined and

Table 12.1 Strategic situations by degree of uncertainty

Situation	Degree of uncertainty	Problem	Solution/Execution
Class 1	Low	Well-defined	Clear/straightforward
Class 2	Low–Moderate	Well-defined	Few discrete approaches
Class 3	Moderate	Several frames	Few discrete approaches
Class 4	High	Many frames	Many scenarios
Class 5	Ambiguous	Many frames	Unknown solutions

the trends are clear enough to be able to predict what might happen if a strategic opportunity is exploited. An example of low uncertainty would be determining the costs and benefits of shifting acute cases over to day surgery, such as simple inguinal hernias or eye surgery, or developing clinical guidelines for ACE (angiotensin converting enzyme) inhibitor therapy. There are other strategic situations that have much higher levels of uncertainty.

The second class of uncertainty problems can be framed and diagnosed easily but there are alternative methods and a few discrete consequences or outcomes, when one or more of the alternatives have a likelihood of a discrete success or failure. For example, developing clinical protocols for cardiovascular care, such as diagnosis and management of heart failure-systolic dysfunction.

The third class of strategic problems contains even more uncertainty. The problems can be framed in a variety of ways, and there are a few discrete alternatives available. For example, developing an integrated patient care management system that includes electronic protocols, electronic clinical charting, and a centralised patient data base.

Class 4 uncertainty has many ways to frame the problem and many ways to predict the outcomes based on the 'what ifs'. Few technical tools are available; the situation requires more of a pilot testing and learning approach. Class 4 problems are complex because the number of scenarios rises exponentially with the number of inputs.[59] For example, if there are 10 uncertain variables, each with only three discrete event outcomes, there are $3^{10} = 59\,059$ scenarios. In these cases it makes sense to develop three scenarios: a 'base' case, a worst case and best case. Each scenario should have a decision tree that makes the likelihood of the various outcomes or consequences more explicit. Examples of this type of uncertainty would be exploring opportunities to franchise hospitals, or expanding international healthcare delivery and medical tourism in developing countries in Asia.

Class 5 uncertainty has been called true ambiguity because 'multiple dimensions of uncertainty interact to create an environment that is virtually impossible to predict',[60] as unknown variables that would define the future. Examples would include developing public health programmes to respond to bombings or bioterrorist action. Fortunately, class 5 decisions occur infrequently.

In class 2, 3 and 4 there is trial and error and learning from experience. If assumptions are understood and made explicit, learning can occur. Although class 5 uncertainty is largely unstructured, managers should identify what is known, what is unknown but knowable, and how the trends (if any) have evolved over long periods of time.

Connecting strategic thinking with strategic planning for health services

Throughout the last section the six pillars have brought organisational strategy into sharp relief. Each pillar has something to contribute on that score. The pillars invite the decision makers to take adequate time to explore and reflect. After the six pillars of strategic thinking have been attended to, the care programmes must develop a service vision or plan for implementing strategic ideas.

Strategic planning relies on creative thought. In this sense, planning requires solving a simultaneous equation that considers how to formulate a service to meet the wants and needs of some target patient population. Planning also means imagining the consequences of implementing a strategy. How close will strategic activities get to the desired long-term goals? What organisational and cultural changes are needed to implement the strategy?

A brilliant framework developed by Heskett[61] can help to bring all of the work of strategic thinking into a bona fide plan of action. The strategic service vision is a way to organise people, process, and other assets to offer patients and consumers better value.

In health services there is an internal and an external service vision. The external refers to creating value for patients, their family and friends. The internal service vision refers to the creation of value for clinical and non-clinical employees. A service vision contains four basic elements: a targeted market, a well-defined service concept, a focused operating strategy and a well-designed service delivery system.[61] In addition to these, there are three integrative elements, woven through the model, that connect the four basic elements in order to become a fully developed framework for both planning and executing strategic thinking. These are: strategic positioning, leveraging of value over cost, and integration of strategy and systems. Although these integrative elements are a part of the overall strategic planning process, they also serve as a means to analyse a service and its level of success. The following discussion draws heavily on Heskett's work.[61] Each of the elements of the strategic service vision will be discussed.

Figure 12.12 showcases how all of these elements work together in an organisation's strategic service vision.

The first element of service planning is identifying a targeted market segment. Market segmentation groups categories of patients into smaller, stable, homogeneous groups. The size of a group should be large enough to provide an efficient service – 'critical mass'. Patients can be categorised by illness and further segmented by psychographics; personality, attitudes, lifestyles or demography; age, education, gender behaviour; or loyalty or utilise.

Market segmentation defines a distinct group of consumers who require special products or services. Segments can be based on needs and are evaluated both in terms of financial attractiveness and in a group of consumers identified by one or more characteristics that allows the organisation to design a product or service to meet their needs. Having a 'targeted' market is important because a service should not pretend to serve every need for every type of patient.[61] Patient segments can have both demographic and psychographic – actions prompted by thoughts and feelings of fear, pleasure, boredom, vanity and so on – dimensions

Four basic elements

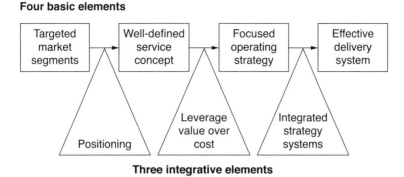

Three integrative elements

Figure 12.12 Strategic service vision. Adapted from Heskett *et al*[61]

in common. In healthcare there are disease segments: diabetes, cancer, asthma, sports medicine and care of the elderly, for example.

Beyond age, race and diagnosis, there are many new attitudinal and behaviour segments to consider. For example, discovering who are the 'most or least proactive' or 'most or least demanding' or 'most or least stoic' patients. Exploring which patients are capable of self-care, which patients may want a great deal of information and which patients want more convenience but may not be overly demanding; and which patients want fact-based reassurance but may have a tendency to overutilise care. Once patient wants and needs are understood, they connect with a well-defined service concept, the second key element of the service vision.

A service concept represents a bundle of ideas that is perceived by a patient segment to satisfy their healthcare needs. The service concept answers the question, 'What service are we providing?'. The concept also describes how the provider wants to be perceived and how the service will be perceived by key stakeholders. Heskett[61] states that a 'well-defined' service concept means that it is stated in terms of results that the organisation produces for its stakeholders, allowing them to evaluate the work. Because needs tend to be complex, service concepts are multidimensional and almost never unidimensional. A busy patient not only expects good outcomes, they want convenience, emotional support, and quick diagnosis-to-treatment. Hence a service concept translates these ideas into clinical results such as outcomes, information, relationships, amenities, convenience and efficient treatment.[13]

The targeted patient segments and well-defined service concepts are integrated by strategic positioning. Positioning answers three key questions.

1 What does a valuable service mean to your customers?
2 How does your service concept create value?
3 Can other providers meet those patient needs better than you?

Strategic positioning designs a service so it will occupy a meaningful and distinct place in the mind of the consumer. A position is more than branding, because it connects the service concept with the target market. It answers questions such as:

What is a good service in the eyes of patients in that segment? How well do competitors provide the service? Can the proposed service concept provide better?.

The third element of a strategic vision is 'focused' operating strategy that sets forth the way the service concept will be achieved and is the product of many decisions about operations, financing, marketing, human resources and control. Organisations should not focus on all of these things; rather, one or two of these operational strategies will be identified as strategically important. To integrate the service concept with the operating strategy the decision makers must leverage the value of the service over cost of delivery. Leverage, as it is used here, means the perceived value of a service is greater than the actual cost of delivering the service.

An organisation's service delivery systems are the necessary elements utilised to fulfil the organisation's mission. This system can include the clinical work processes, role of people, technology, equipment, facilities and procedures. Delivery systems should develop sufficient capacity and manage the quality of care.[61] Finally, the service delivery system should be integrated with the operating strategy; culture, people, clinical processes, and the like.

The formulation of the strategic service vision means leveraging the value for patients over the cost to deliver the service. Teboul[62] argues that the best way to understand the relationship between value and the service proposition is to analyse the fit between the two. Figure 12.13 plots the service proposition against the value proposition. In this example, the healthcare organisation established a new cardiac surgery centre that focused on eleven dimensions of the value proposition: rapid turn-around of tests, problem-free admissions, decision-making efficiency, excellent outcomes, convenience, continuity of relationships, easy communication with physicians, attentive nursing, highly co-ordinated care, state-of-the-art facilities and a highly skilled clinical team.

This healthcare organisation selected nine elements of the service delivery system and the operating strategy. One focus of the operating strategy is brand

Value for Patients		Marketing: Brand communication	Marketing: Selective recruitment	Operating strategy & work process: Electronic medical records	World class physician	Continuing education	Staff committed to goal	Telemedicine support	Human resources: Higher than average wages	Skilled primary nurse
Speed	Rapid turn-around of tests	○		○			○	○	○	
Speed	Hassle-free administration	○						○		
Quality	Decision-making efficiency	○			○				○	
Quality	Excellent outcomes	○			○		○			
Quality	Convenience	○			○					
Quality	Continuity of relationship	○					○			
Quality	Easy communication w/physician	○		○	○			○	○	○
Reputation	Attentive nursing	○					○		○	○
Reputation	Coordination of care	○				○				○
Reputation	State-of-the-art facilities	○		○	○			○		
Reputation	Skilful care team	○		○	○	○		○		○

Figure 12.13 Matrix for connecting patient value with service delivery

communication, which offers a wide range of promotional information and video cassettes that communicate the data on speed of service, quality, and reputation. Each of the other key elements of the service formulation connects with the value proposition. For example, the electronic medical record provides complete patient records, which helps ease of communication with physicians, rapid testing, the impression of a state-of-the-art facility and the skills of the care teams. The electronic medical record also supports the goal of excellent technical outcomes by allowing clinical staff and managers access to information such as rates of ventilator-associated pneumonia per 1000 days in the CCU, and unscheduled readmissions within 10 days.

The same type of matrix should be used to analyse the interaction between service formulation and value to the organisation; that is, clinical efficiency, costs and capacity utilisation. Likewise the same matrix should be used to analyse the interaction between service formulation and value to the employee; that is, employee satisfaction, employee growth and development, self-managing teams and an inclusive workplace.

Although this tool can facilitate the connection between strategic thinking and planning, the analysis of 'fit' can be difficult to comprehend. The connection may not be understood during transition or implementation and value creation for patients and employees is always somewhat hidden or undetectable. Nevertheless the ability to translate a service vision into value for patients, employees and the organisation runs to the heart of strategic thinking.

Conclusions

Strategic thinking is not about leaders establishing and persuading everyone to buy the new vision. It is all about framing and asking powerful questions and applying concepts and analytic techniques. It asks 'what should we aim for?' and 'how can we can deliver health services in the long run?'. Strategic thinking separates the known facts from the assumptions and uncertainties and develops a discipline to challenge assumptions about the environment, assumptions about the mission, and assumptions about what makes the organisation distinct from other organisations.

To analyse where and how to offer services, there must be a clear set of strategic goals and objectives. However, knowledge of strategic goals and objectives, while important, is not enough. Key stakeholders should be committed to those goals and therefore a fair process runs to the heart of evoking effective strategic thinking.

To undertake strategic thinking key stakeholders must make the reality model explicit. Reality models are based on presumed experiences, habit and organisational culture. The role of the leader in strategic thinking is to give people permission to be sceptical, to challenge assumptions and to learn from small failures. The manager/leader allows people to ask, 'how closely does the reality seen in here match the reality out there?'. These six pillars are the building blocks for effective strategic thinking and planning.

Finally, strategic thinking is not about the numbers, the big ideas, or the visions of brilliant leaders. Nor is it about a widely accepted applied theory and a growing body of empirical knowledge. Strategic thinking is a discipline that develops new habits and work practices rather than the application of scientific principles. The practice draws on analysing situations and learning from experience, making assumptions explicit, exploring how and where to compete, uncovering tacit knowledge, fair process, and diligence.

This view of strategic thinking and planning suggests that while the 'economics' of strategy is informative, it has little to do with the practice of strategic management. Moreover, although important, the successful match of a strategic service vision and the task environment is not a guarantee of competitive advantage. Strategic management takes discipline, leadership and hard work.

Acknowledgements

I want to thank all of my healthcare students at Brandeis University, all the executives and European health leaders who discussed these ideas with me in class. I am particularly grateful to Professor Dominique Heau at INSEAD in Fontainebleau, who allowed me to sit in on his class lectures on 'What is strategy?'. Dominique's classes inspired me and encouraged me to think about health strategy. I owe thanks, and thanks again, to Robert Jones and Fiona Jenkins for their incredible 'flexibility' in working with me.

References

1 Spang HR, Bazzoli GJ, Arnould RJ. Hospital mergers and savings for consumers: exploring new evidence. *Health Affairs*. 2001; **20**(July/August): 150–58.
2 Chilingerian J, Savage GT. The emerging field of international health care management. In: Savage GT *et al.*, editors. *International Health Care Management*. New York: Elsevier; 2005.
3 Burns LR, D'Aunno T, Kimberly J. Globalization in healthcare. In: Gatignon H, Kimberly J, editors. *The INSEAD-Wharton Alliance on Globalizing: strategies for building successful global businesses*. Cambridge: Cambridge University Press; 2003.
4 Alsagoff F. Singapore General Hospital: on local shores and beyond. Unpublished Masters thesis. Fontainbleau, France: INSEAD; 2005.
5 Apollo to recast medical tourism, targets Asia, US. *The Economic Times*. 2004; **18 Sept**.
6 Ghemawat P. *Strategy and the Business Landscape*. New Jersey: Prentice Hall; 2005.
7 Kay J. *Why Firms Succeed: choosing markets and challenging competitors to add value*. New York: Oxford University Press; 1995.
8 Roberto MA, Garvin DA. *Taking Charge of the Beth Israel Deaconess Medical Center (Multi Media Case)*. No. 303-058. Boston: Harvard Business School Press; 2003.
9 Simon H. *Reason in Human Affairs*. Stanford: Stanford University Press; 1983.
10 Janis I. *Crucial Decisions: leadership in policymaking and crisis management*. New York: The Free Press; 1986.
11 Chilingerian J, Vandekerckhove P. *Managing a Transplant Decision at University Medical Center Leuven*: (A). Fontainebleau, France: INSEAD; 2004.
12 Axelrod R, Cohen MD. *Harnessing Complexity: organizational implications of a scientific frontier*. New York: Free Press; 1999.
13 Chilingerian J. Who has star quality? In: Herzlinger RE, editor. *Consumer-Driven Health Care: implications for providers, payers and policy-makers*. San Francisco: Jossey-Bass, Inc; 2004.
14 Heskett J, Sasser E, Schlesinger L. *The Value Profit Chain*. New York: Free Press; 2004.
15 Porter M. What is strategy? *Harvard Business Review*.1996; **Nov/Dec**.
16 Mintzberg H. Patterns in strategy formation. *Management Science*. 1978; **24**(9): 934–48.

17 Porter M. *Competitive Advantage: creating and sustaining superior performance*. New York: The Free Press; 1980.

18 Roberton M. *Why Great Leaders Don't Take Know For An Answer: managing for conflict and consensus*. Philadelphia: Wharton School Publishing; 2005.

19 Angelmar R, Pinson C. *Zantac* (A). (European Case Program) Fontainebleau, France: INSEAD; 1992.

20 Dorner D. *The Logic of Failure: recognizing and avoiding error in complex situations*. Reading, Massachusetts: Perseus Book; 1996.

21 Kennedy I. *Learning from Bristol: The Report of the Public Inquiry into Children's Heart Surgery at the Bristol Royal Infirmary 1984–1995; Cm5207-1*. The Stationery Office, Norwich; 2001.

22 Ridley M. *The Origins of Virtue: human instincts and the evolution of cooperation*. New York: Penguin Books; 1998.

23 Nicholson N. How hard-wired is human behavior? *Harvard Business Review*. 1998; Jul–Aug; **76**(4): 134–47.

24 Janis I, Mann L. *Decision Making: a psychological analysis of conflict, choice, and commitment*. New York; The Free Press; 1977.

25 Stewart R. Demands, choices and constraints: a model for understanding managerial jobs and behavior. *The Academy of Management Review*. 1982; **7**(1): 7–13.

26 Mintzberg H. *The Nature of Managerial Work*. New York: Harper and Row; 1973.

27 Chilingerian J. *The Strategy of Executive Influence*. Unpublished PhD dissertation. Massachusetts Institute of Technology (MIT); 1987.

28 Forrester J. *Urban Dynamics*. Cambridge, MA: The MIT Press; 1969.

29 Neustadt RE, May ER. *Thinking in Time: the uses of history for decision makers*. New York: The Free Press; 1986.

30 Schon D. *The Reflective Practitioner*. New York: Basic Books, Inc; 1983.

31 Simon H. *The Sciences of the Artificial*. 2nd ed. Cambridge, MA: MIT Press; 1981.

32 Cyert RM, March JG. *A Behavioral Theory of the Firm*. New Jersey: Prentice Hall Inc; 1963.

33 Drucker P. The theory of the business. *Harvard Business Review*. 1994; Sep–Oct: 95–104.

34 Simon H. On the concept of organizational goal. *Administrative Science Quarterly*. 1984; **9**(1): 1–22.

35 March JG. *Decisions and Organizations*. Oxford: Basil Blackwell; 1988.

36 Carr EH. *What is History?* New York: Vintage Books; 1961.

37 Tichy NM. *The Cycle of Leadership*. New York: Harper Collins; 2002.

38 Mitroff I. *Stakeholders of the Organizational Mind*. San Francisco: Jossey-Bass Publishers; 1983.

39 Fisher R, Ury WL. *Getting to Yes*. Boston: Houghton Mifflin; 1988.

40 Geneen H., with Moscow A. *Managing*. New York: Avon Books; 1984.

41 Tversky A, Kahneman D. Rational choice and the framing of decisions. In: Bell D, Raiffa H, Tversky A, editors. *Decision Making: descriptive, normative, and prescriptive interactions*. New York: Cambridge University Press; 1988.

42 Russo JE, Schoemaker PJ. *Ten Barriers to Brilliant Decision Making and How to Overcome Them*. New York: Simon and Schuster; 1989.

43 Hammond J, Keeney S, Ralph L, Howard R. *Smart Choices: a practical guide to making better decisions*. Boston: Harvard Business School Press; 1999.

44 Cohen J, Stewart I. *The Collapse of Chaos: discovering simplicity in a complex world*. New York: Penguin Books; 1994.

45 Ackoff R. *The Art of Problem Solving*. New York: John Wiley and Sons; 1978.

46 Morrisey GL. *Management by Objectives and Results in the Public Sector*. Reading, Massachusetts: Addison-Wesley; 1976.

47 Olson DE. *Management by Objectives*. Palo Alto, California: Pacific Books; 1968.

48 Bohmer R, Edmondson A, Feldman LR. *Intermountain Health Care*. Boston: Harvard Business School Press. Case Number 9-603-066; 2003.

49 Kim, WC, Mauborgne R. *Blue Ocean Strategy: how to create uncontested market space and make the competition irrelevant*. Boston: Harvard Business School Press; 2005.

50 Porter M. *The Competitive Advantage of Nations*. New York: The Free Press; 1990.

51 Doz Y, Santos J. Williamson P. *From Global to Metanational*. Boston: Harvard Business School Press; 2001.

52 Kim WC, Mauborgne R. Fair Process: managing in the knowledge economy. *Harvard Business Review*. 1997; **75**(July-August): 65–75.

53 March JG, Olsen JP. *Rediscovering Institutions: the organizational basis of politics*. New York: The Free Press; 1989.

54 Van der Heyden LB, Randel CS. Fair Process: striving for justice in family business. *Family Business Review*. 2005; **18**(1): 1–21.

55 Latham GP, Locke EA. Goal setting: a motivational technique that works. *Organizational Dynamics*. 1979; **Autumn**: 68–80.

56 Heifetz R. *Leadership Without Easy Answers*. Cambridge, MA: Harvard University Press; 1994.

57 Gottman JM, DeClaire J. *The Relationship Cure*. New York: Three Rivers Press; 2001.

58 Heau D. Class lecture and notes at INSEAD: Fontainebleau, France; 2005.

59 Morgan MG, Henrion M. *Uncertainty: a guide to dealing with uncertainty in quantitative risk and policy analysis*. New York: Cambridge University Press; 1992.

60 Courtney H, Kirkland J, Vigurie P. Strategy under uncertainty. *Harvard Business Review*. 1997; **November–December**: 67–79.

61 Heskett J. *Managing in the Service Economy*. Boston: Harvard Business School Press; 1986.

62 Teboul J. *Le Temps des Services: une nouvelle approche de management*. Paris: Editions d'Organisation; 2002.

Chapter 13

Entrepreneurial action for social change: a primer for healthcare professionals

Tia Gilmartin

Introduction

In recent years, entrepreneurship has received much focus in political, academic and social circles.[1,2,3] It is estimated that between 20%[4] and 50%[5] of the population engage in some form of entrepreneurial behaviour. According to Brenkert[6] entrepreneurship has generated attention for four main reasons. First, entrepreneurship has been linked to the creation of millions of new jobs and a range of new products or services. It is interesting to note that the bulk of these new products, services and jobs are generated by small- and medium-sized ventures.[2] Second, entrepreneurship has been linked with significant alterations in how people live. A few examples of entrepreneurial ideas that have changed our lives in significant ways include automobiles, supermarkets, mobile phones and personal computers. Third, entrepreneurship is seen as a way for people to exercise their self-determination and self-control. Whitehead[7] identifies the ability to exercise one's imagination, creativity and courage to develop new ideas as distinguishing features of entrepreneurship. Finally, entrepreneurship is said to lead to greater efficiency in meeting people's needs and wants. Through the process of opportunity identification, entrepreneurs identify and fill gaps in existing products or services.

Derived from the French verb *entreprendre*, to undertake, entrepreneurship is behaviour guided by a value system that celebrates continuous change. The entrepreneur is defined by his or her ability to continuously search for change, respond to the change, and exploit it as an opportunity. The successful entrepreneur:

> . . . tries to create value and make a contribution. Successful entrepreneurs aim high. They are not content simply to improve what already exists, or to modify it. They try to create new and different values and new and different satisfactions.[8]

Effectively, entrepreneurship is the means by which innovation in the form of new products, services or organising patterns is identified, developed and brought into being.

The driving forces of entrepreneurship are ideas, people and money. In recent years entrepreneurial action has been offered as a solution to developing more effective healthcare systems.[9] Entrepreneurial action in healthcare can take on many forms ranging from individual healthcare professionals (HCPs) starting their own practices or businesses; healthcare delivery organisations refocusing their strategy to develop a range of services that address the root causes of poor health or gaps in existing services; or the development of collaborative public–private partnerships to build capacity and self-reliance in communities, especially among poor or marginalised groups.

HCPs in their roles as practitioners and leaders can play a part in creating new contexts for health and healthcare service delivery. One criticism levied against healthcare professionals is a resistance to align professional self-interests with organisational goals that balance business and social responsibilities of healthcare service.[10,11] Healthcare leaders and their organisations face economic pressures to use scarce resources in the most effective manner; changing citizen expectations about healthcare service and quality, and the growing burden of chronic disease or diseases associated with lifestyle and relative affluence. In this context, HCPs are in a unique position to apply their knowledge, skills and insights into the strengths and weaknesses of the existing healthcare system to respond to these pressures and create sustainable change.

The purpose of this chapter is to introduce principles and practices of entrepreneurship. Given the role of healthcare organisations and professionals in society, a specific emphasis is placed on identifying and developing entrepreneurial ventures for social change. This chapter is organised in three parts. Part 1 provides an overview of the key concepts of entrepreneurship. Part 2 focuses on the unique aspects of social entrepreneurship, and finally, Part 3 concludes with an overview of the entrepreneur's key tool, the business plan. A number of resources for interested social entrepreneurs are also included.

At the completion of this chapter, the reader will be able to:

- describe the concepts and principles of entrepreneurial activity and differentiate the unique focus of social entrepreneurship
- compare and contrast a number of strategic decision-making tools to manage social enterprises
- describe the components of the entrepreneur's key tool, the business plan
- identify key criteria to assess the strengths and weakness of a new venture/business idea.

Concepts and principles of entrepreneurship

Peter F. Drucker[8] describes the entrepreneur as someone who exploits the opportunity that brings about change. It is interesting to note that an entrepreneur does not necessarily need to invent a new product or service. Instead, the entrepreneur is skilled at scanning the environment for new ideas and acting as a change agent by bringing together diverse groups of stakeholders. The distinguishing feature of the entrepreneur and entrepreneurial action is the willingness to act boldly, sometimes without the availability of resources in hand, and to assume risk for the success or failure of a new venture.

Typically, an entrepreneur is someone who works outside the boundaries of a traditional organisation. However, the boundaries of creativity, opportunity identification and action for change can also occur within existing organisations. Pinchot[12] originated the term 'intrapreneur' to describe people who use their creativity to make changes within an organisation while remaining an employee. Stevenson and Jarillo[13] extended this thinking by focusing on the behaviour of managers and leaders in established organisations as a source of entrepreneurial action. They distinguished the entrepreneurial manager from the administrative manager. The entrepreneurial manager pursues opportunities without regard to resources currently controlled. Conversely, the administrative manager focuses his or her activities on preserving the status quo or creating stability in between periods of change and growth. Both types of leadership and management action are needed to sustain entrepreneurial ventures (*see* Box 13.1 for a comparison of these leadership styles).

Box 13.1 Principles and practices of social entrepreneurship

1 Change agents in the social sector
   - Reformers and revolutionaries with a social purpose.
   - Attack underlying problems, rather than treating symptoms.
   - Seek to create systematic changes and sustainable improvements.
2 Adopting a mission to create and sustain social value
   - Social mission is fundamental to the venture.
   - Making a profit, creating wealth or serving the customer is part of the model as a means to a social end.
   - Social impact is the gauge of success.
3 Recognising and relentlessly pursuing new opportunities
   - Not exclusively driven by perceptions of social need or compassion.
   - Have a vision of how to achieve improvement.
   - Persistent and determined to make their vision work.
4 Engaging in a process of continuous innovation, adaptation and learning
   - Break new ground, develop new models, and pioneer new approaches.
   - Need not be inventors – need to be creative in applying what others have invented.
   - Engage in a continuous process of exploring, learning and improving.
5 Act boldly without being limited by resources currently in hand
   - Do not let limited resources keep them from pursuing a vision.
   - Not bound by sector norms or traditions.
   - Develop resource strategies to support and reinforce a social mission.
   - Take calculated risks to manage the downside and reduce the harm that will result from failure.
6 Exhibit a heightened sense of accountability to the constituencies served and for the outcomes created
   - Take steps to ensure value creation.
   - Have a sound understanding of the constituencies you are serving.
   - Correctly assess the needs and values of the people you serve and the communities they live in.
   - Understand the expectations for your 'key stakeholders'.
   - Assess progress in terms of social, financial and managerial outcomes.

Entrepreneurs are defined by the following functions.

• Innovation and creativity.
• Bearing risk for society or bearing uncertainty.
• Spotting and acting on opportunities.
• Bridging between sectors, fields, and resources.
• Leadership to create something new or bring about change.[14]

One strand of entrepreneurship research focuses on describing individuals who are able to create something of value from practically nothing. This work has focused on understanding personal characteristics;[15] experiences with starting and sustaining new ventures;[16,17] techniques used to identify new business opportunities;[18] and the role of personal networks and information exchange to spark new business ideas.[19] From this work a number of beneficial personal attributes for entrepreneurs can be identified. These include the ability:

• to make decisions independently
• to take risks in order to achieve a clear set of goals
• to plan ahead
• to be flexible and adaptable to unexpected changes and opportunities, ready to deal with ambiguity and uncertainty
• to get things done on time
• to take advice from others
• to be persistent
• to communicate well, and
• to know when and when not to compromise.[20]

Gartner[21] suggests that describing entrepreneurship in terms of the individual misses half of the story. The other half of the entrepreneurship story involves the identification and exploitation of opportunities. Entrepreneurs as compared to their traditional management counterparts are skilled in seeing opportunities for change where others may only see problems, a lack of resources or abilities. An opportunity in this context is a 'feasible profit seeking, potential venture that provides an innovative new product or service to the market, improves on an existing product/service, or imitates a profitable product/service in a less-than-saturated market'.[22] Furthermore, an opportunity has the qualities of being attractive, durable and timely and is anchored in a product or service that creates or adds value for its buyer or end user.[23] Entrepreneurial opportunities are recognised by virtue of the entrepreneur's knowledge, expertise and beliefs about existing products, services or market need.[24] Drucker[8] identified six main sources from which entrepreneurial opportunities arise. These are:

1 the unexpected success, failure or outside event
2 the incongruity between reality and 'what ought to be'
3 innovation based on process need
4 change in the sector (industry) or market structure
5 demographics – population change, changes in perceptions, mood and meaning
6 new knowledge – both scientific and non-scientific.

For example, HCPs can establish consultancies within or outside the health system to offer services focusing on appropriate clinical care, research, skill and knowledge development for other HCPs, teaching patients and their families self-care techniques or programme management.[20] Entrepreneurial opportunities for healthcare delivery organisations include developing effective chronic care services and supporting organisational systems; establishing health and wellness services to promote population health; or being the first in a geographic region to offer a new surgical procedure or medical technology.

Entrepreneurs bring diverse stakeholders together to capitalise upon an identified opportunity for a new product or service. The key ingredients of successful entrepreneurial activity include ideas, people and money. Ideas for new businesses are plentiful but very few of these will turn into successful new ventures.[25] The potential entrepreneur can sit around his or her kitchen table and generate a list of new business ideas that range from the ultra innovative to the mundane. While the boldness of entrepreneurial action can be confused with rashness, entrepreneurship is an exacting and calculated practice. The distinguishing skill of the successful entrepreneur is the ability to both generate an idea and critically screen these ideas in relation to currently available products and services, the strategic goals of the organisation and the general mood and readiness of the targeted consumer to adopt the new product or service. Entrepreneurial success is linked to the long-term sustainability of a given business idea, rather than being based on quick-fix solutions that might drain the project and its participants of time, energy, enthusiasm and resources.

People, their talent and experience matter to the success or failure of entrepreneurial ventures. The best predictor of future performance is past experience.[26] Diverse skills and experiences of the leaders are critical to the long-term success or failure of the proposed new business or service. Moreover, venture capitalist or banks that lend money to support entrepreneurial ventures will assess the experience of the leaders to determine the relative risk of the long-term success and payoff. The leadership team can come from the entrepreneur's circle of colleagues and contacts or from the larger organisation. In the early days of a venture it may be possible to accomplish great success with the skills of a few people. As the entrepreneurial venture grows it will be necessary to extend and grow the leadership team's skill set through hiring or investments in training. At some point in the venture's lifecycle the leaders will need to seek advice from or employ a strong team of outsiders such as accountants, lawyers or experienced board members.[9]

While entrepreneurs may act without sufficient resources in hand, attention to financial issues is a critical component in entrepreneurial success. Money is a tool to achieve and sustain the entrepreneur's vision for a new product or service. The mission of healthcare delivery organisations to care for the sick or most vulnerable of society has generated a number of misperceptions about financing these activities. Healthcare professionals and the organisations in which they work are guided by a strong value system of service and social solidarity to provide these vital services to all who need them. Historically, hospitals and other healthcare delivery organisations have been organised as not-for-profit or state-run enterprises. The not-for-profit designation is related to an organisation's tax status and not its need to be a financially healthy and viable enterprise. The slogan 'no margin no mission' provides a simple reminder that all organisations need to generate earnings in excess of their expenses to carry out their mission or reason for existence. For example, the HCP who establishes a job retraining and employment service for people recovering from alcohol or drug addiction will require money, space and staff to deliver this service. These resources can come from donations, in-kind arrangements for rent and utilities or government grants. While income generated from donations and other voluntary sources should be welcomed, in the long term it will not lead to sustainability and self-determination of the venture. An over-reliance on in-kind or donated sources revenue will ultimately lead the venture to close.

Starting and growing a new venture to sustainability requires both sufficient funding and an appropriate matching of resources to deliver products or services. Effective financial/resource management and spreading financial risks among the involved stakeholders are key factors associated with entrepreneurial success.[27,9] Entrepreneurial ventures may be funded from a number of sources including: personal savings, relatives, banks, professional investors (venture capitalists), employees, suppliers, government-sponsored agencies, strategic partnerships or the sale of stock.[28] The range of resources available to an entrepreneur will depend on whether they are establishing an independent venture or working within the boundaries of an existing organisation. A detailed description of new venture financing is beyond the scope of this chapter but Timmons[29] provides a detailed overview of financing options and methods for interested entrepreneurs.

Finally, entrepreneurial activity is distinguished by the pursuit of profits that are generated by the entrepreneur's ability to sell new goods or services at a price that is higher than the cost of production. Entrepreneurial profits are returned to the venture in the form of revenue for sustained growth, to the entrepreneur in the form of stock options or other financing methods, and ultimately to society in the form of an innovation that has an impact of daily life.[24,30] Economist Joseph Schumpeter[31] first described the process of shifting resources from a lower value to a higher value by individual action. Known as creative destruction, this process is viewed as a core element of entrepreneurship. Through the process of identifying opportunities and changing the pattern of production within a market, sector or industry the entrepreneur changes both the standard of competition (how organisations differentiate their goods and services to consumers) and consumer expectations. Interestingly, creative destruction is a cyclic phenomenon where the innovating organisation has the incentive to invest the majority of its resources in the product or service that created the new standard and may lose flexibility and foresight to see the next innovative idea.[32]

Creative destruction in healthcare includes shifts in the roles of professionals and institutions. For example, as part of the modernisation of the UK National Health Service (NHS) nurses and AHPs are taking on consultant roles to treat and manage diseases that used to require a physician's care. Labour shortages, advanced education, new medical technologies and policy changes have created an environment where specialist physicians can concentrate on treating the most critically ill and nurses and AHPs have been able to assume new roles to match their skills and expertise. The displacement of the specialist and subspecialist physicians as the main service provider enables less expensive professionals to do progressively more sophisticated things in less expensive settings. Consumers and ultimately society win because healthcare services are offered in more convenient settings, with improved quality and lower costs.[33]

Table 13.1 Leadership styles: entrepreneurial management vs administrative management styles

Attitude toward . . .	Administrative management	Entrepreneurial management
Organisational resources and capabilities	Resources and capabilities should be protected	Resources and capabilities should be valued but challenged
The organisation's business and purpose	Definitions as relatively enduring	Definitions should be periodically re-examined
Business strategy	Play the game better than competitors	Play the game better than competitors or play your own game
Organisational architecture	Designed to optimise implementation of the strategy	Designed to allow for strategic flexibility
Meeting customer/client needs	Stay close to the customer	Stay close to the customer, but also invent promising innovations that do not currently meet expressed needs
Entrepreneurial activity within the organisation	Entrepreneurial activity should follow strategy	Entrepreneurial activity should lead as well as follow from strategy
Organisational learning	Institutionalise knowledge to avoid having to relearn business lessons	Institutionalise a questioning attitude such that learning and unlearning can coexist

To summarise, at its heart entrepreneurship meets a need in the market and by extension society. Resources are obtained, deployed and managed in an effective manner so that the venture grows to the point of reaching a sufficiently large number of people who will benefit from the purchase or use of the new product or service. As an individual the entrepreneur values change and is skilled at creating a vision and selling this vision to others who are willing to assume risk (i.e. financial, time, reputation) for the success or failure of the proposed new venture. Finally, the entrepreneur exercises leadership in bringing together a diverse set of people with varying interests and skills to bear upon filling a market need or solving a particular problem. These relationships are depicted in Table 13.1.[34]

Social entrepreneurship

Social entrepreneurship can be traced to prominent Victorians such as William Lloyd Garrison and Florence Nightingale who recognised the gap between social classes resulting from the economic gains and losses of the Industrial Revolution.[35] These early leaders marshalled resources to focus on changing social conditions with the goal of elevating all members of society to a common denominator of employability and health. Throughout the twentieth century entrepreneurial efforts in the social or citizen sector have been in the form of government or philanthropically funded projects or services. Recent changes in the economic-political landscape have created a context for focused initiatives aimed at solving a number of seemingly intractable social problems. Among the western industrialised economies, the Labour government has been a leading proponent of stimulating social entrepreneurs to solve social problems with the same vigour as business entrepreneurs seek wealth creation. The White Paper *Our Competitive Future: building the knowledge driven economy* and the Millennium Awards programme evidence this commitment. While the government's policy could be viewed as an exemplar, the rise in social entrepreneurship activity over the last 20 years has been chronicled in the six main geographic clusters of: India and Bangladesh, Latin America, Eastern and Central Europe, Africa, China, and North America.[36]

For the purpose of this chapter, social entrepreneurs and entrepreneurship are defined as 'people who realise where there is an opportunity to satisfy some unmet need that the state welfare system will not or cannot meet, and who gather together the necessary resources (generally people, often volunteers, money and premises) and use these to make a difference'.[34] Social entrepreneurs focus their talent on solving social problems such as: why are children not reading? Why is pollution increasing? Why are technologies or services not being accessed equally?[36] Social entrepreneurship is distinguished from traditional business and economic entrepreneurship on the one hand and purely social initiatives on the other hand. The unique focus of social entrepreneurship is on solving problems – such as sustainable easing of the constellation of health, education, economic, political and cultural problems associated with long-term poverty – often demanding fundamental transformations in the political, economic, and social systems that underpin the current stable state.[37]

In both practice and in academic writings social entrepreneurship has taken on three main meaning and areas of activity.[37] First, social entrepreneurship can be viewed as combining social commercial enterprises with social impacts. In this sphere, entrepreneurs use business skills and knowledge to create enterprises that accomplish social purposes, in addition to being commercially viable. This type of entrepreneurial action has been used by both not-for-profit and for-profit organisations. A not-for-profit may create a commercial subsidiary and use it to generate employment or revenues that service their social purposes; for-profit organisations may donate some of their profits to organise their activities to serve social goals. One prominent example of this form of social entrepreneurship is the The Bill and Melinda Gates Foundation. The Foundation focuses its activities on promoting greater equity in global health, education, public libraries and support for at-risk families in Washington State and Oregon.

The second area of social entrepreneurship activity emphasises innovating for social impact. Social entrepreneurs working under this model are concerned with changing social arrangements and creating innovations that solve specific social problems. These entrepreneurs focus on creating innovations, building new social arrangements, and mobilising resources in response to those problems. The emphasis in this model is more on solving the problem than responding to an unmet market need or satisfying other commercial criteria. The Green Belt Movement (GBM) is one example of this type of social entrepreneurship.

Founded in 1977 by Wangari Maathai and the National Council of Women in Kenya, the GBM organises small groups of poor community members in both rural and urban settings to grow, plant, and care for trees in 'greenbelts' on public and private land. To date the GBM has mobilised over 6000 groups in poor villages and urban areas in Kenya to plant over 20 million trees. The GBM mobilises community action by emphasising self-determination, equity, improved livelihoods and environmental conservation.[37] In 2004 Wangari Maathai was recognised for her vision and determination with the Nobel Peace Prize.

The third area of activity for social entrepreneurs is to catalyse social transformation well beyond the solutions of the social problems that were the initial focus of concern. In this model small changes in the short term are used to create large changes in the long term. Social entrepreneurs operating under this model need to understand not only the immediate problems but also the underlying social system and its interdependencies to affect long-lasting change.[37] The Castleford Community Learning Centre, founded by Margaret Handforth in 1984, is an example of this type of social entrepreneurial action. This venture was founded during the coal miners' strike of the early 1980s in South and West Yorkshire. Castleford was one community especially hard-hit by the prolonged strike action and eventual closing of the mines by Prime Minister Margaret Thatcher. Originally called the Castleford Women's Centre this venture was started by a small group of miners' wives to organise pickets and soup kitchens. For many of these women, these activities helped them to realise their full potential. In the midst of crisis and 'in those dark days women who had been seen and not heard for most of their lives discovered that they had a voice and could use it to create a better future for themselves and others'.[34] From the specific purpose of sustaining families affected by the strike action, the organisation has evolved into a voluntary sector open college that provides training and facilities for all members of the local community. The Centre has plans to expand its activities to include a residential college and outdoor sport training.[34]

The contemporary wave of social entrepreneurs see themselves as leaders of viable businesses that happen to have a mission of solving social problems. The most successful social entrepreneurs are creative and savvy in applying a range of business and management techniques to create robust and viable enterprises. J. Gregory Dees,[38] a leading scholar in this area, points out that a new pro-business zeitgeist has made for-profit initiatives acceptable in the non-profit (i.e. charity) world. One strategic leadership challenge for not-for-profit or other socially focused ventures is to retain focus on mission-related objectives while exploring all strategic options to provide the most effective products and services. Dees[38] developed the social enterprise spectrum to differentiate between activities that are purely philanthropic on the one hand and purely economic on the other (*see* Figure 13.1).

Purely philanthropic, purely commercial

The social enterprise spectrum is a framework for strategic decision making that can be used by not-for-profit leaders to understand and assess strategic options and key issues when seeking various sources of earned income such as commercial funding or revenue-generating market-based activities. The key

Purely philanthropic ◄─────────────────────► Purely commercial

	Appeal to goodwill Mission driven Social value	Mixed motives Mission and market driven Social and economic value	Appeal to self-interest Market driven Economic value
Motives, methods and goals			
Beneficiaries	Pay nothing	Subsidised rates, or mix of full payers and those who pay nothing	Market-rate prices
Capital	Donations and grants	Below-market capital, or mix of donations and market-rate capital	Market-rate capital
Workforce	Volunteers	Below-market wages, or mix of volunteers and fully paid staff	Market-rate compensation
Suppliers	Made-in-kind donations	Special discounts, or mix of in-kind and full-price donations	Market-rate prices

Figure 13.1 Social enterprise spectrum

stakeholders identified in the framework include beneficiaries, capital, workforce and suppliers. Moving from left to right on the continuum a not-for-profit organisation could have six main options to improve the efficiency and effectiveness of the organisation.

1 **Full philanthropic support:** After exploring all of their options the leaders may decide that no potential sources of earned income are appealing given the organisation's mission and values. In this model the goal is to find the right mix of cash donations, in-kind donations and volunteer labour.

2 **Partial self-sufficiency:** In this option the sources of earned income will only cover part of the necessary operating expenses even when taking volunteer labour and in-kind donations into account. Therefore the organisation will need to develop some sort of subsidy either in the form of grants, user fees, or donations to cover the remaining operating expenses.

3 **Cash flow self-sufficiency:** A midrange option along the continuum is to generate revenue from commercial activities, but minimise the operating costs typically associated with these activities. Earned income is used to cover out-of-pocket expenses, like buying supplies, but there is still a

reliance on non-cash philanthropic activities like volunteer workers, donated office space or government grants and other below-market rate sources of income.

4 **Operating expense self-sufficiency:** In this model the not-for-profit venture is able to earn enough income to cover all operating expenses. Not many not-for-profit ventures reach this level of financial independence from philanthropic sources. In the start-up phase typically there will be the need for some form of subsidy. Leaders will need to determine at what level and for how long to subsidise the venture. There may come a point where the venture may have to be discontinued if mission and finance-related goals cannot be met.

5 **Full-scale commercialisation:** At this end of the continuum the organisation is fully commercial when revenue covers all costs at market rates, including the market cost of capital without any philanthropic subsidy even for start-up costs. Furthermore, the not-for-profit is able to attract new investment for expansion. Very few not-for-profit organisations are able to achieve full-scale commercialisation. One potential difficulty with this model is balancing mission-driven objectives with changes in the market or environment. Oftentimes, these organisations will be converted to for-profit ventures so that there is more flexibility in the types of financing available to fund activities.

6 **Mixed enterprise:** Many not-for-profit organisations are multi-unit ventures that run with different financial goals and funding structures. It is possible to adopt a blended approach using the five models described above to balance the organisation's mission with revenue requirements to offer their products and services for the greatest social impact.

Another interesting strategic tool used to satisfy the dual missions of community development and business innovation is public–private partnerships. In recent years, public–private partnerships have emerged as a mechanism to engage business (public sector organisations) to take on increased responsibility for the communities in which they operate. In Europe, these partnerships are an important example of how the traditional role of government as employer and service provider is changing.[39] On the one hand, governments are unable to finance the costs of providing public services and on the other hand more business leaders are focusing on the role of business in society. In recent years, healthcare and education have been two testing grounds for public–private partnerships. Many of these projects entail private sector financing or physical plant management contracts for new hospitals or schools, such as the English National Health Service's Public Financing Initiative (NHS Trust PFI).[39] The focus of many of these public–private partnerships is on contractual relationships between the private sector and the public sector for the provision of services. Another form of public–private partnership is corporate volunteer programmes in which employees may donate money to charitable causes or have a team building project to paint the local school.[40]

One overlooked benefit of public–private partnerships is the development of joint ventures that create profitable and sustainable change for both parties. In this expanded model, which can be called corporate social innovation, there is an exchange of competencies and expertise between individuals working in both sectors. Companies view community needs as opportunities to develop ideas and demonstrate business technologies, to find and serve new markets, and to solve long-standing business problems. The communities, on the other hand, gain exposure to and ultimately the transfer of the unique skills and capabilities of business and in the process may get new approaches that point the way to permanent and sustainable changes.[40]

Developing robust public–private partnerships is difficult work due mainly to differences in culture, mindsets and ways of working typically associated with the two sectors. These differences aside, it is possible to lead and manage partnerships that share the common objective of sustainable community or social change. In her study of successful community-enhancing public–private partnerships Harvard Business School Professor Rosabeth Moss Kanter identified six characteristics of successful partnership.[40]

1 **A clear business agenda:** The project should clearly demonstrate how the business agenda relates to a social need. What are the wins and who gains what in the project need to be clearly identified and communicated.

2 **Strong partners committed to change:** Strong partnerships based on commitment by both parties to bring about change are a necessary ingredient. Partners from business will need politicians and other visible community leaders to connect key constituents and provide legitimacy.

3 **Investment by both parties:** Investment builds mutuality and a sense of shared risk in the success of the project. Joint investment in the form of money, labour, technology and other resources improves the sustainability of the project, especially when funds from business taper off.

4 **Rootedness in the user community:** The project must be relevant to the needs of the community and members of the project team need to work in the community organisations or with targeted beneficiaries.

5 **Links to other organisations:** Sustainable change is created with the skill and expertise of multiple players within the broader community. Each of the core partners involved in a project should call upon external collaborators who possess skills or expertise to support the goals and objectives of the project.

6 **A long-term commitment to sustain and replicate the solution:** A key goal of a corporate social innovation project should be developing the project to the point of self-sufficiency in the host organisations as well as being able to roll out the model to as many other organisations or communities as possible.

To summarise, social entrepreneurship is concerned with addressing and solving seemingly intractable social problems that are created by gaps in the state welfare system. A distinguishing feature of the contemporary generation of social entrepreneurs is the use of management and financing tools and techniques to build sustainable mission-focused ventures that benefit society's most vulnerable or marginalised. This section presented an overview of three current models of social entrepreneurship; described the social enterprise spectrum, a strategic decision-making tool that can be used to assess options for earned income; and concluded with a brief overview of public–private partnerships that focus on corporate social innovation and offered techniques to improve the management and outcome of these projects. The final section of this chapter will present the key tool of entrepreneurship – the business plan.

Tool kit for practice

Business plans: bringing ideas into action

One of the key tools of the entrepreneur is the business plan. A good business plan is a selling document that conveys the excitement and promise of your business/new venture idea to any potential stakeholders or backers.[41] A business plan serves three main functions. First and foremost it is a document that enables an entrepreneur to convert an idea into a viable enterprise by thinking through all facets of a new venture. The process of putting a business idea onto paper lets you determine the consequences of different strategies as well as the human and financial requirements of a venture. Second, the business plan is a useful tool to conduct a systematic and comprehensive evaluation of a new venture. The process of writing a business plan serves as a reality check to anticipate risks associated with the proposed new venture. In the development and early implementation stages of the new venture the business plan is used to manage and control activities. Finally, the business plan is a document that is presented to investors – be they the senior management team of your organisation, bankers, or venture capitalists – to sell your business idea and secure funding.

Do you really need to write a business plan? That is a key question. Fundamentally, a business plan will enable you to address the motivations or concerns of the key stakeholders needed to make the proposed venture a success. Gumpert[41] identifies a number of reasons for taking the time, effort and resources for writing a business plan.

1 **To sell yourself on the business or venture idea:** Because entrepreneurial action carries a certain element of risk a business plan can serve as a useful 'reality check'. In the beginning oftentimes the entrepreneur needs to convince himself or herself that the risk of starting a new venture will be worth the time, resources and effort.
2 **To obtain bank financing:** At some point in the life of the venture it will be necessary to obtain a loan or secure funding to sustain operations. In recent years bankers have become more risk averse in loaning money and therefore a coherent and well argued business plan increases the probability of securing bank financing.
3 **To obtain investment funds:** Venture capitalists, or professional investors, make investments into promising entrepreneurs and their business ideas. A business plan is a necessary step in the screening process to gain access to venture capital funding.

4 **To arrange strategic alliances:** Increasingly, small ventures join with larger organisations to gain access to established marketing, distribution and research capabilities or access to clients who will use the entrepreneur's product or service. In the early phase of strategic alliance discussions a well-crafted business plan can improve the entrepreneur's attractiveness to the larger organisation.

5 **To obtain large contracts:** A business plan can be used to show a potential client the new venture's capacity to deliver the specification of a contract. Moreover, a good business plan will contain detailed projections on the number of people who will want to use the entrepreneur's product or service as well as the expected revenues. Market and financial projections help the entrepreneur show that they plan on being around in the future and are a good bet.

6 **To attract key employees:** One of the biggest obstacles facing small and growing companies is attracting key employees who are willing to take the risk of joining a new venture. A well-written business plan can help the entrepreneur to reassure potential employees that all the key risks and plans for addressing them have been thought through. In this instance, a business plan also can be used to promote a potential employee's understanding of the venture as well as convey the culture and rationale for starting the venture.

7 **To complete mergers and acquisitions:** Mergers and acquisitions both large and small are a useful strategy to gain access to customers/clients, distribution channels, marketing or technologies. A well written business plan lets the management teams know where the venture is heading and how goals and objectives fit together.

8 **To motivate and focus your management team:** As the new venture grows and becomes more complex, the business plan helps to focus attention to the venture's key goals. In this instance the business plan becomes a roadmap that outlines where the venture wants to go and how it will get there over a period of time.

Components of a business plan – for entrepreneurial action

Editors' note

Tia Gilmartin presents many important aspects of a tool kit for developing business plans in the context of entrepreneurial action for social change. The business planning process in which AHP managers in the NHS are likely to be involved differs in some aspects from the entrepreneurial model. The typical NHS business planning process will be explored by the editors in detail in a later volume in the series – *Managing Money, Measurement and Marketing*.

Typically, business plans follow a standard format and can range from 10 to 40 pages in length. A *summary business plan* is approximately 10 pages in length. This format has gained popularity in recent years. The summary business plan is used in the early phases of testing out interest in a new idea with key stakeholders or can be included with bank loan applications. *A full business plan* typically ranges from 10 to 40 pages and provides a detailed description of the business idea. This format is most useful when trying to secure large amounts of financing or when searching for corporate strategic alliance partners. Another format is an operational business plan, which may be more than 40 pages in length. This type of plan is used when a company is growing quickly and the management team needs to think through and focus on a number of contingencies and risks associated with running the business.

Typically a business plan is organised into the following sections.

- **Executive summary:** The executive summary should be clear, exciting and effective as a stand alone overview of the proposed product or service.
- **The company, products and services:** This section presents information on the product or service in terms of the targeted professionals, purchasers or clients, uses, functions, features and benefits, the underlying technologies and the current stage of development of the product or service. Legal issues related to the proposed venture are addressed in this section.
- **The market and strategy:** This section is used to describe the opportunity for the proposed new venture. This section contains information on the clients, collaborators, competitors and sector dynamics in terms of their strengths, weaknesses, threats and opportunities in relation to the proposed new product or service. This section also explains how the entrepreneur will 'make it happen'.
- **Marketing and operations:** The plans for how the entrepreneur intends to produce and deliver the proposed product or service. This section should include information on product costs, operating/production complexity, required resources, distribution channels and marketing and sales strategies.
- **Management team and organisation:** The strength and experience of the management team is a key ingredient for the success of a proposed new venture. This section should include information on the backgrounds of the project champions and the core project team, their skills and abilities to execute the business plan. Key personal needs, the roles of key project team members and the role of outside council (if any) are described in this section. Staffing requirements and organisational structure in terms of responsibilities and reporting relationships are included in this section.
- **Milestones and key events:** The purpose of this section is to present a realistic schedule of events, their anticipated timing and interrelationships necessary to develop and launch the proposed new venture. This section is used to identify and discuss critical events and their impact on the business plan. A contingency plan is also included to show how the management team will respond to the anticipated key risks.
- **Financial section:** This section provides a summary of the financial requirements for the proposed new venture. Typically, detailed cash flow projections on a monthly basis for years 1 and 2 and quarterly projections for years 3 to 5 are presented.

Table 13.2 Business planning summary

Business plan component	Key topics
Product or service	• What is the potential in terms of people or organisations wanting to use the proposed product or service? • How many people will buy/use the proposed product or service? • How will the proposed product or service benefit users (e.g. community, patients/clients, healthcare professionals, managers, organisations)? • Describe the technology/service in terms of the benefits in a way that the 'lay' reader can understand • Describe where the product or service is in its development. When will it be ready to use? • How will the community be affected by the proposed clinical product or service?
Markets and strategy	• Are there other groups developing similar technologies, products or services? • If so, what are the features of these services or technologies? • How does your proposed technology, product or service differ? • What are the dynamics of the sector/health community/economy? • What are the strengths, weaknesses, threats and opportunities of your proposed product or service in comparison to other organisations/groups? • Describe how you will get your proposed product or service idea into reality.
Marketing and operations	• Describe how the proposed product or service will be distributed. • Describe how the proposed product or service will be advertised and promoted. • What are the production costs of your proposed product or service?
Management and operations	• What are the roles and responsibilities of the project champions and project team? • Who are the key leaders, what is their experience with similar projects? • Does the project team have training or learning needs to support the success of the proposed project? • Describe the functions of outside supporting professional services, if any. • What are the reporting relationships between key project team members?

Table 13.2 (*cont.*)

Business plan component	Key topics
Financial implications	• How many units of the service or product need to be sold/used to cover costs (break-even point)? • How many units of the product or service need to be sold/used to make a profit? • What are the resource requirements (funding, personnel costs, facilities, etc.) to develop and produce the proposed product or service? • How do the costs of operation balance against projected revenues from product or service sales/utilisation?
Legal implications	• Who will provide the product or service and who, ultimately, will be responsible? • Are there issues related to training or qualifications to deliver the proposed product or service? • How will contracts be created and how will payments be collected? • Are there issues related to information sharing or informed consent?
Milestone events and key risks	• Discuss potential problems with the proposed product or service. • Are there dependencies associated with the operation of your proposed product or service? • Provide a realistic time line of activities needed to develop and implement your proposed product or service.

Adapted from Covin and Slevin[44]

• **Proposed company offering:** This section of the business plan is used to assess the economic value of the proposed new venture and outlines the return on investment, the terms of payment for selling the venture, as well as exit strategies that the entrepreneur will use.

Table 13.2 provides a summary of key content and questions that should be answered in each section of the business plan. A good business plan is written in a crisp, focused and engaging style, flows logically and contains relevant statistics, studies and examples to build the case for why the proposed new venture fills a need in the market. There are a number of useful books and software packages available to support the writing and development of a successful business plan. During the writing process it is also a good idea to get an opinion from an outsider who will give you a frank critique of the logic and flow of the business plan. And finally, write, rewrite and write again. A good business plan will take many drafts and iterations to become a polished selling tool.

It is important to remember that a business plan is a document to sell your new venture idea to potential partners or investors. The key idea of the new venture may need to be packaged in a way that resonates best with the group to whom you are trying to sell your idea.[42] For example, when meeting with the board members or bankers, the key message should focus on why the proposed product or service is a good investment, the financial projections and potential benefits to the organisation and the target clients/consumers. When meeting with other healthcare professionals, the message should focus on health outcomes, clinical expertise or the quality of care.

Common pitfalls in business plan writing

Like any written document, there are good business plans and there are not so good business plans (*see* Table 13.2). Some common mistakes associated with the writing of business plans include the following.

- Too complex (KISS: 'keep it simple smartie').
- Too technical (KISS it again. Can your grandma understand your idea?).
- Too few facts or too many irrelevant facts.
- Entrepreneur-centric – there is too much focus on how great the entrepreneur is and not enough information about the product, service or how clients/consumers will benefit.
- Product- or service-centric – there is too much focus on the technical aspects of the product or service.
- Little or no knowledge of intended customers or clients.
- Unrealistic assumptions or no assumptions.
- Boring executive summary.

Assessing opportunities

Successful entrepreneurs are able to identify and screen winning business ideas. While ideas for new businesses are plentiful, identifying opportunities that fulfil an unmet market need is a complex and iterative process. External screening requires systematic analytical consideration of issues such as market growth potential and the size of the market that the new venture is likely to serve, and the economics. Internal screening, by contrast, involves careful examination of the idea in terms of its personal attractiveness and the extent to which the entrepreneur has the experience, know-how and mindset required to carry out the idea successfully.[9]

External screening: is the market ready for your idea?

- Is your idea unique? Can it be easily copied?
- Have you tested your product or service on some test clients? Will they spend money on it?
- Is the service or product easily understood by clients, funders, lawyers and other professionals?
- What is the market? Its segments? How will you enter and reach the market of potential clients?
- What are the production costs? What is the break-even point? Return on investment?

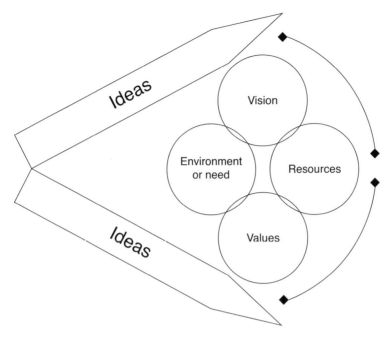

Figure 13.2 A model of entrepreneurship. From: Thompson *et al*[34]

Internal screening: improving the value of your idea

Can you strengthen your idea by enhancing its:

- simplicity
- convenience
- risk (reduce risk of failure and liability)
- image
- environmental friendliness
- customer/client productivity?

Conclusion

This chapter focused on principles and practices of entrepreneurship in general and social entrepreneurship in particular. In their roles as individual practitioners, leaders and managers, HCPs possess the knowledge, skills and insights to create new contexts for health and healthcare. Greater familiarity with key concepts and techniques of entrepreneurship will enable HCPs to identify opportunities, package new service ideas in a persuasive manner, and play a role in transforming the current health and social care system. The time to act boldly to solve some of society's intractable social problems is now and look at new models of entrepreneurship (*see* Figure 13.2).

Key points

- Entrepreneurship is the means by which innovation in the form of new products, services or organising patterns is identified, developed and brought into being.

- The driving forces of entrepreneurship are ideas, money and people.
- Entrepreneurship is distinguished by the willingness to act boldly, sometimes without resources in hand, and to assume risk for the success or failure of a new venture.
- Social entrepreneurship is concerned with solving problems associated with long-term poverty that often demand a fundamental transformation in current political, economic and social systems.
- Social entrepreneurs solve problems in three ways: combining social commercial enterprises with social impacts; innovating for social impact; catalysing social transformation.
- A business plan is the key tool that enables the entrepreneur to bring his or her idea into reality. Business plans are used to think through all facets of a new venture, to conduct a systematic and comprehensive evaluation of a new venture, and to secure funding from investors.
- Greater familiarity with key concepts and techniques of entrepreneurship will enable healthcare professionals to identify opportunities, package new service ideas in a persuasive manner, and play a role in transforming the current health and social care system.

References

1 Crown Office. *Our Competitive Future: building the knowledge-driven economy*. London: Crown Office; 1998.
2 Organization for Economic Cooperation and Development (OECD). *Fostering Entrepreneurship*. Paris : OECD; 1998.
3 Reynolds P, Hay M, Camp M. *Global Entrepreneurship Monitor: Executive report*. Kansas City: Kauffman Centre for Entrepreneurial Leadership; 1999.
4 Reynolds P, White S. *The Entrepreneurial Process*. Greenwich: Greenwood Press; 1997.
5 Aldrich H, Zimmer C. Entrepreneurship through social networks. In: Sexton D, Smilor R, editors. *The Art and Science of Entrepreneurship*. Cambridge: Ballinger; 1986.
6 Brenkert G. Entrepreneurship, ethics and the good society. *Business Ethics Quarterly*. 2002; **3**: 5–43.
7 Whitehead J. Remember, rebuild, renew. *Columbia Entrepreneurship Update*. 2003; **8**(1): 3.
8 Drucker P. *Innovation and Entrepreneurship*. New York: Harper Collins; 1985.
9 O'Connor E, Fiol M. *Reclaiming Your Future: entrepreneurial thinking in health care*. Florida: American College of Physician Executives Press; 2003.
10 Saxe-Braithwaite M. Nursing entrepreneurship: instilling business acumen into nursing healthcare leadership. *Nursing Leadership*. 2003; **16**(3): 40–42.
11 Gilmartin M, Freeman R. Business ethics and healthcare: a stakeholder perspective. *Health Care Management Review*. 2001; **27**(2): 52–65.
12 Pinchot G. *Intrapreneuring*. Harper Collins, New York; 1985.
13 Stevenson H, Jarillo J. A paradigm of entrepreneurship: entrepreneurial management. *Strategic Management Journal*. 1990; **11**: 17–27.
14 Greiner P. The function of social entrepreneurship in the UK. Paper presented at ISTR Conference, July, Cape Town, South Africa.
15 Carpenito L, Neal M. Nurse entrepreneurs: who are they, what do they do, and what challenges do they face? In: McCloskey J, Grace H, editors. *Current Issues in Nursing*. 5th ed. St Louis: Mosby; 1997.
16 Wilson A, Averis A, Walsh K. The influences on and experiences of becoming nurse entrepreneurs: a delphi study. *International Journal of Nursing Practice*. 2003; **9**: 236–45;.

17 Roggenkamp S, White K. Four nurse entrepreneurs: what motivated them to start their own business. *Health Care Management Review*. 1998; **23**(3): 67–75.

18 McCline R, Bhat S, Baj P. Opportunity recognition: an exploratory investigation of a component of the entrepreneurial process in the context of the health care industry. *Entrepreneurship Theory and Practice*. 2000; **Winter**: 81–94.

19 Rozier C, Thompson M. Female entrepreneurs in a female-dominated profession: an exploratory study. *Journal of Developmental Entrepreneurship*. 1998; **3**(2): 149–63.

20 Sanders E, Kigma M. *Handbook on Entrepreneurial Practice: nurses creating opportunities as entrepreneurs and intrepreneurs*. Geneva: International Council of Nurses; 2003.

21 Gartner W. 'Who is the entrepreneur' is the wrong question. *American Journal of Small Business*. 1988; **12**(4): 1–32.

22 Singh R. A comment on developing the field of entrepreneurship through the study of opportunity recognition and exploitation. *Academy of Management Review*. 2001; **26**(1): 10–12.

23 Timmons J. Opportunity recognition. In: Bygrave W, editor. *Portable MBA in Entrepreneurship*. 2nd ed. New York: John Wiley & Sons, Inc; 1997.

24 Shane S, Venkataraman S. The promise of entrepreneurship as a field of research. *Academy of Management Review*. 2000; **25**(1): 217–26.

25 Kim C, Mauborgne R. Knowing a winning business idea when you see one. *Harvard Business Review*. 2000; **78**(5): 129–38.

26 Ownes W. Background Data. In: Dunnette M, editor. *Handbook of Industrial Psychology*. Chicago: Rand McNally College Publishing; 1976.

27 Kihlstrom R, Laffont J-J. A general equilibrium entrepreneurial theory of firm formation based on risk aversion. *Journal of Political Economy*. 1979; **87**(4): 719–48.

28 Bygrave W. *Portable MBA in Entrepreneurship*, 2nd ed. New York: John Wiley & Sons, Inc; 1997.

29 Timmons J. *New Venture Creation: entrepreneurship for the 21st century*. Chicago: Irwin Press; 1999.

30 Boschee J. Social entrepreneurship. *Across the Board*. 1995; **32** (3): 20–25.

31 Schumpeter J. Entrepreneurial profit. In: Krueger N, editor. *Entrepreneurship: critical perspectives on business and management*. London: Routledge; 2002.

32 Christensen C, Overdorf M. Meeting the challenge of disruptive change. *Harvard Business Review*. 2000; **March–April**: 67–76 (reprint R00202).

33 Christensen C, Bohmer R, Kenagy J. Will disruptive innovations cure health care? *Harvard Business Review*. 2000; **September–October**: 1–11 (Reprint R00501).

34 Thompson J, Alvy G, Lees A. Social entrepreneurship – a new look at the people and the potential. *Management Decision*. 2000; **38**(5): 328–38.

35 Mair J, Marti I. *Social Entrepreneurship: what are we talking about? A framework for future research*. Working Paper, IESE Business School, University of Navarra.

36 Drayton W. The citizen sector: becoming as entrepreneurial as competitive business. *California Management Review*. 2002; **44**(3): 120–32.

37 Alvord S, Brown L, Letts C. *Social Entrepreneurship: leadership that facilitates societal transformation – an exploratory study*. Working Papers, Centre for Public Leadership, Harvard University; 2004.

38 Dees G. Enterprising nonprofits. *Harvard Business Review* 1998; **January–February**: 55–67.

39 Grimshaw D, Vincent S, Willmott, H. Going privately: partnership and outsourcing in UK public services. *Public Administration*. 2002; **80** (3): 475–502.

40 Kanter RM. From spare change to real change: the social sector as beta site for business innovation. *Harvard Business Review*. 1999; **May–June**: 123–32.

41 Gumpert D. Creating a successful business plan. In: W Bygrave, editor. *Portable MBA in Entrepreneurship*. 2nd ed. New York: John Wiley & Sons, Inc; 1997.

42 Howard-Grenville J, Hoffman A. The importance of cultural framing to the success of social initiatives in business. *Academy of Management Executive*. 2003; **17**(2): 70–86.

43 Zott C. *Entreprenurial Finance and Venture Capital*. Session 2: Business Plan. INSEAD Course Materials; 2003.

44 Covin J, Slevin D. Entrepreneurial imperatives of leadership. In: M Hitt *et al.*, editors. *Strategic Entrepreneurship: Creating a New Mindset*. Oxford: Blackwell Publishers; 2002.

Further reading

Economy P, Emerson J, Dees G. *Strategic Tools for Social Entrepreneurs: enhancing the performance of your enterprising nonprofit*. New York: John Wiley and Sons; 2002.

Brinckerhoff P. *Social Entrepreneurship: the art of mission–based venture development*. New York: John Wiley and Sons; 2000.

Vaughn D. *Financial Planning for the Entrepreneur*. New Jersey: Prentice Hall; 1997.

Websites for social entrepreneurship

www.missionbased.com: a website that offers a range of free organisational self-assessment tools for leaders and managers of not-for-profit enterprises.

www.joshuaventure.org: a number of resources for networking and education and training in principles and practices of social entrepreneurship are highlighted on this website.

www.unltd.org.uk: sponsored by the Millennium Awards Trust, Unltd; the Foundation for Social Entrepreneurship is a charitable organisation that promotes social enterprise across the United Kingdom.

www.sse.org.uk: the School of Social Entrepreneurs is a network of schools across the United Kingdom dedicated to training and connecting social entrepreneurs. The SSE trains social entrepreneurs to grow and replicate community-based development projects.

www.cdx.org.uk: formerly known as the Standing Conference for Community Development (SCCD), CDX is a UK-wide organisation for community development. The mission of CDX is to bring people together, share expertise, inform policy and develop resources for tackling inequality and social justice.

Chapter 14

Cultural issues and management

John Swain and Sally French

Introduction

The topic for this chapter is, of course, vast and the whole arena so complex that we need to begin by outlining a particular focus and scope for our discussions. The term culture is the obvious starting point and as so often in the social sciences there is little unanimity when it comes to what might seem a fairly basic term. From a management viewpoint, however, Schein[1] defines culture as:

> A set of basic assumptions – shared solutions to universal problems of external adaptation (how to survive) and internal integration (how to stay together) – which have evolved over time and are handed down from one generation to the next.

Schneider and Barsoux[2] suggest that this definition directly addresses key challenges facing managers, and indeed this is evident in the phrases 'how to survive' and 'how to stay together'.

A culture then is a shared set of values and attitudes derived from and giving meaning to membership of and belonging to groups, and by implication non-membership of and non-belonging to other groups. We recently conducted an evaluation of user involvement in a large traditional charity organisation. In the feedback to a draft of the final report one member of the management team was critical on, at least, two grounds. First was that it differentiated service users from service providers in the analysis of the findings, on the grounds that this was divisive. Second that she as a member of the management team had been 'lumped with' service providers, a group from whom she clearly wished to be differentiated. Culture, then, relates to identity and how we define who we are, and equally who we are not.[3] In our work in the area of disability studies, we have experienced this in many manifestations expressed in different ways. Non-disabled people can, for instance, affirm their identity as 'not one of those', that is a member of a group identified as being disabled – as 'other'. But also disabled people can positively affirm their identity as 'not one of those', that is not a non-disabled person, and in so doing challenge stereotypical views of disabled people as 'tragic'.

In this chapter we shall explore the broader social context of management that this concept of culture engages. Central to our analysis is the inequality of power, locating culture within its socio-economic, political and historical context.[4] One layer of power is provided by the wider social relationships in which everyone in health and social care – service users, service providers and managers – is embedded. In this broader social context of management, there are significant and constantly changing differences in power between people belonging to different groups embedded in different cultures. Some groups have greater power, resources, status and better health. Other people can face discrimination – including members of ethnic minority groups, disabled people and older people – in a variety of areas including access to required services.

In the context of management, leadership and development in the Allied Health Professions, women, members of ethnic minority groups and disabled people experience discrimination such as gaining promotion to management positions. For instance, the NHS, like other organisations and institutions, has a history of discrimination in its employment practices. Though full and accurate data is difficult to obtain, research into the experiences of black women health workers has identified many areas of discrimination. For instance, one survey found that 4 out of 534 chairs of health authorities and trusts were from black and ethnic minority communities – and only one of those was a woman.[5] More recently, one review documents some evidence that the position of black and ethnic minority women managers may be worsening.[6] Atkins *et al*[7] provide evidence that a similar situation still pertains in healthcare. For example, they report on a survey by the Chartered Society of Physiotherapy in 2002 where 98% of physiotherapists described themselves as white.

This chapter, then, is about diversity and difference and how this is realised and expressed in power relations within healthcare. We look first at inequalities in health and healthcare; then at interactions and communication across cultures constructing such inequalities; and finally at the promotion of cultural awareness, knowledge and sensitivity within healthcare management.

Inequalities in health and healthcare

The notion of social divisions is broad and correlates with other concepts in social theory, including hierarchies, equality/inequality, culture, poverty, and identity. The central, controversial issues pertain to commonalities, which are shared across a group of people within a culture or a society, and diversities within a group, culture or society. We all have multiple identities – male/female, black/white, young/old, heterosexual/homosexual – and potential identities whether or not we choose to embrace them.[3] The outermost layer affecting our health concerns general socio-economic, cultural and environmental conditions. This includes the economic state of the country, the level of employment, the tax system, the degree of environmental pollution and our attitudes, for example towards women, ethnic minorities and disabled people.[8]

It is clear that these factors all interact and influence each other. If the economic state of the country is favourable, for example, people are likely to have more disposable income which may improve their health by allowing them to buy good quality food and housing of a better standard, engage in leisure pursuits, give their children more opportunities and enjoy relaxing holidays to reduce stress. Similarly, if a person is attempting to give up using illegal drugs, success is more likely if community support is strong and if government is willing to act by setting up and financing supportive policies. As Whitehead[9] states:

> If one health hazard or risk factor is focused upon, it is important to examine how it fits in with other layers of influence and whether it

could be considered a primary cause or merely a symptom of a much larger problem represented in some other layer.

In the context of our present discussion, a key question is whether health is randomly distributed: can illness strike anyone at any time irrespective of her or his income, ethnicity or gender? The overwhelming evidence suggests an unequal distribution. In most countries of the world there are large inequalities in health, with those people with the lowest socio-economic status having the worst health. Certain groups within society such as women, old people, people from ethnic minorities and disabled people are also disadvantaged partly because of their over-representation in the lower socio-economic groups. There are also regional variations in health status.[10,11] Furthermore, in Britain as in most countries of the Western world, these inequalities are increasing.[12,11] Benzeval et al[13] state that:

> It is one of the greatest contemporary social injustices that people who live in the most disadvantaged circumstances have more illness, more disability and shorter lives than those who are more affluent. In Britain death rates at most ages are two to three times higher among the growing number of disadvantaged people than they are for their better off counterparts. Most of the main causes of death contribute to these differences and together they can reduce life expectancy by as much as eight years.

Inequalities in health exist regardless of the way in which socio-economic class is measured and at all stages of the life span.

Despite the various influences on our health, the evidence overwhelmingly suggests that broad social factors concerning housing, income, educational level, employment and social integration are far more important than our individual behaviour or medical practice and advances. As Benzeval et al[13] commented, that evidence shows quite convincingly that the more we increase our understanding of the determinants of health, the more inescapable is the conclusion that a person's health cannot be separated from the social and economic environment in which they live and work.

There is often a vicious circle in operation that can continue over generations. Benzeval et al[13] comment:

> There is a body of evidence that poor socio-economic circumstances are highly correlated with low levels of educational attainment. In turn, the lack of educational qualifications increases the probability of unemployment and poverty in adulthood which are associated with poor health outcomes.

People of the lowest socio-economic status are at far higher risk, not only of physical illness and early death, but also of accidents, premature births, mental illness and suicide.[11] There is a clear relationship between health and income that is well-established and widely acknowledged. Beyond this, however, the usefulness of a simple cause–effect relationship between one risk factor and one type of disease has been extensively questioned.[7] Kendell[14] suggested that in medicine, as in physics, specific causes have given way to complex chain of event sequences in constant interplay with one another. The very idea of 'cause' has become meaningless, other than as a convenient designation for the point in this chain of event sequences at which intervention is most practicable.

A multifactorial explanation of ill-health is predominant in reviews and analyses of research. Helman[15] lists 25 cultural factors that can be causal, contributory or protective in relation to ill-health. Important here is the notion that cultural factors, diet being an obvious example, may protect against ill-health as well as being a possible risk factor. Taking diet as the example, the relationship between health/ill-health and cultural factors is diffuse and complex. This includes how food is prepared, stored and preserved; the utensils used in cooking and storing food; whether food routinely contains contaminants; whether food is symbolically classified into 'food' and 'non-food', 'sacred' or 'profane' food irrespective of nutritional value; whether vegetarianism or meat-eating is the rule; and whether special diets are followed during pregnancy, lactation, menstruation and ill-health.

The general health of people from black and ethnic minority communities in Britain is poorer than the indigenous white Anglo-Saxon population. Smaje[16] suggests five cultural factors as playing a role in multifactorial causality: genetics; migration; material disadvantage; lifestyle, social networks and kinship; and racism. In relation to genetics, there are a number of disorders that mainly affect people from specific ethnic minority groups. Sickle cell disorder, for instance, is Britain's most common genetic illness, affecting about 15 000 people. It largely affects African and African-Caribbean people, though is also present in people of Mediterranean, Asian and Arab origin.[17] Anionwu and Atkin also make the point that sickle cell anaemia is under-resourced when compared with cystic fibrosis, the most common genetic disorder affecting white people.[17]

Most government initiatives to improve people's health in Britain have focused on strategies to change individual behaviour, often adopting a 'victim blaming' stance. It is now known, however, that our behaviour is to a large degree determined by our social circumstances.[18] If drug users are returned to the community without support following successful treatment, for example, they are likely to drift back to their old way of life with the people they know and trust.[19] This is not to suggest that personal approaches are never beneficial. Personal empowerment, through assertiveness training for example, can be helpful, especially if it is linked with social support and evidence of positive change.[11]

There is no obvious correlation between healthcare and health status in any population; indeed the health service has sometimes been referred to as an 'ill health' service as it tends to respond when the damage has been done. Benzeval *et al*[13] suggest:

> There is little evidence that variations in the quantity and quality of health services between advanced industrial countries make a sub-stantial difference to crude measures of health such as national mortality rates . . . Levels of well-being and life expectancy are more closely related to the availability of decent social security, housing, employment and education than health care.

This is not to imply that inequalities in health and healthcare facilities should be tolerated. Healthcare should be distributed in accordance with need. There is evidence, for example, that the up-take of immunisation, birth control, antenatal care and screening is low among poor people. This is due to a range of factors that were summed up by Tudor Hart[20] in his notion of the 'inverse care' law. People with low incomes find it harder to access healthcare premises because of social isolation and lack of facilities such as a car. It is also the case that the areas in which they live tend to have poor facilities and that health professionals tend to give them less time and attention than people who are perceived to be culturally similar to themselves.[10]

There are still many people in Britain who do not fully benefit from the facilities of the NHS. People from ethnic minorities are not well served nor people with learning difficulties.[21] This is due to a variety of factors that include poor communication, racism, disablism and lack of cultural sensitivity. Fox and Benzeval[22] argue:

> Access to health services cannot be taken for granted especially in the most disadvantaged communities. There is still much to be done to ensure that services are provided in appropriate locations, that user charges do not deter people from expressing legitimate needs and that cultural diversity is not ignored . . . people must be involved in helping to identify their own needs and services must be provided in ways that users themselves recognise as legitimate.

Fox and Benzeval[22] believe that an important role of the NHS should be to encourage social equity across all public departments and policies that have an impact on health. The enactment of such a change would involve an increase in services such as outreach, the mobilisation of self-help groups and community action and empowerment. At a broader level it would mean involvement in areas such as housing, employment, education, leisure and community regeneration.[23] Such a development would move AHPs from their role as clinical practitioners dealing with the consequences of ill health, to the broader arena of health promotion and political activism.[24]

The documented views of black disabled people consistently speak to experiences of segregation and marginalisation within services. For instance, in their research into the views and experiences of young black disabled people, Bignall and Butt[25] report feelings of segregation due to racism in settings segregated due to disablism. Summarising the evidence from several studies, Butt and Mirza[26] state:

> The fact that major surveys of the experience of disability persist in hardly mentioning the experience of black disabled people should not deter us from appreciating the messages that emerge from existing work. Racism, sexism and disablism intermingle to amplify the need for supportive social care. However these same factors sometimes mean that black disabled people and their carers get a less than adequate service.

In their study of young black disabled people's experiences and views, Bignall and Butt[25] conclude:

> Our interviews revealed that most of these young people did not have the relevant information to help them achieve independence. Hardly any knew of new provisions, such as Direct Payments, which would

help with independent living. Most people did not know where to get help or information they wanted, for example, to move into their own place or go to university.

It is clear that managers of healthcare services need a very broad perspective on the meaning of health, illness and disability as well as an appreciation of how age, gender, ethnicity and other social divisions can impact on health and the healthcare received. A biomedical approach is clearly not sufficient in the management of healthcare services today.

Communication and interpersonal interaction

At this point we reach the central cultural issues from the viewpoint of management. In terms of 'how to survive' and 'how to stay together', the problem can be defined and solved in terms of the quality of communication and interaction. This leads to the stance that listening to service users' views and providing accessible information addresses cultural issues. Within the analysis in this chapter, however, processes of communication and interpersonal interaction need to be understood within the construction of broader power relationships and also within an understanding of the complexity of the interaction processes.[27] Schneider and Barsoux[2] suggest:

> Organisations must process information in order to make decisions, to communicate policies and procedures, and to co-ordinate across units. Yet what kind of information is sought or heeded, how information circulates, and what information is shared with whom, are likely to reflect cultural preferences for hierarchy, formalisation, and participation.

Language, in terms of cultural issues, is often seen as the main barrier to effective service provision. It is, therefore, assumed that an adequate supply of leaflets in appropriate languages and an adequate number of interpreters would solve the problem. Whilst the accessibility of information is crucial, communication consists of more than language skills and literacy. The research suggests that even among British-born English-speaking Asians, there is considerable lack of knowledge of what services are on offer. Research by Banton and Hirsch[28] bears out the findings of previous research. They propose:

> Communication problems are identified in all work in this area. Such problems are partly to do with language differences, but also arise from the separate lives led by different ethnic groups in our society and the consequent unlikely coincidence of communications about services arising through informal contacts.

Perhaps the most consistent recommendation from research has been the necessity for the direct involvement of disabled clients, including black disabled clients, in the planning of services.[29] Again this needs to be understood within the context of multiple discrimination. Concluding their study with Asian deaf young people and their families, Jones, Atkin and Ahmad[30] state:

> . . . identities are not closely tied to single issues and young people and their families simultaneously held on to different identity claims. To this extent, it is not a question of forsaking one claim for another and choosing, for instance, 'deafness' over 'ethnicity', but to negotiate the space to be deaf and other things as well. It is only through addressing these tensions that services will adequately respond to the needs of Asian deaf people and their families.

Hill[31] drew attention to the extremes of oppression faced by black disabled people. She stated that the cumulative effect of discrimination is such that black disabled people are 'the most socially, economically and educationally deprived and oppressed members of society'.

Comparable analyses of the experiences of the interaction of other social divisions, for instance disabled and old, disabled and female, disabled and gay or lesbian, and disabled and working-class, indicate that there are parallels. For instance, in the most extensive research into the views and experiences of disabled lesbians and bisexual women, there was evidence that they felt marginalised by lesbian and gay groups.[32] Bhavnani[33] has pointed out that black women's experience cannot always be assumed to be different from white women, black men or white men in all contexts. The interplay of factors such as 'race', gender, class, age and disability creates a multiplicity of discrimination. These may, in some contexts, suggest similarities with, as well as differences between, white women and black and white men.

Modood[34] has traced the complex changes in patterns of ethnic identity for second and third generation members of minority ethnic groups in Britain. He suggests that identities are more consciously chosen, publicly celebrated, debated and contested.

Another more recent addition to the list of groups with fragmented identities whose interests are not fully addressed by single issue movements is disabled refugees and asylum seekers who 'constitute one of the most disadvantaged groups within our society'.[35] Roberts goes on to propose that disabled refugees and asylum seekers are 'lost in the system' because both the disability movement and the refugee community focus their attention on issues affecting the majority of their populations and fail to engage adequately with issues which affect a small minority.

People from ethnic minorities are often living in poverty which has an impact on their health. Two studies of the families of Asian people with learning difficulties,[36,37] for instance, provided evidence of high levels of poverty with 69% of families having no full-time wage earner, and half of the families being on income support. Significant language barriers were found in the same studies. Ninety five percent of carers had been born outside of Britain and only a minority could speak or write English.[38]

However, there are dangers in such statistics. First, they can feed presumptions and stereotyping which belie diversity. In her study of Asian parents, for instance, Shah[39] found that the majority of parents had a good command of English and, for some, English was their first language. She also cites language barriers as an example of preconceived notions of discrimination experienced by Asian families. Second, there is a danger of oversimplifying language barriers. As the Black Perspectives Sub-group points out,[40] language is 'about freedom of expression, release of emotion, cultural identity and shared values' and a common language is no guarantee of shared understanding. At the attitudinal level of institutional discrimination, there is a lack of understanding among the majority population concerning the life style, social customs and religious practices of people from ethnic minority groups.[41] Discrimination has been rationalised through misconceptions that, for instance, black families prefer 'to look after their own'.[42]

Turning to the implications for the management of healthcare, they are most readily conceived under the umbrella of inclusion. 'Inclusion' has been viewed by many as a process of social change, rather than a particular state[43] and this can be seen to apply equally to communication and relationships.

> But without a vision of how things should and ought to be, it is easy to lose your way and give up in the face of adversity and opposition . . . we all need a world where impairment is valued and celebrated and all disabling barriers are eradicated. Such a world would be inclusionary for all.
>
> Oliver and Barnes[44]

Reviewing research evidence in the more specifically relevant arena of communication and health in a multi-ethnic society, Robinson[45] states:

> The review strongly indicates that the development of effective strategies to overcome 'communication barriers' requires context-sensitive, needs-led initiatives.

To develop this conceptualisation, this vision of an inclusive communication environment, we shall conclude this chapter by tentatively offering some general principles based on our discussion that we hope will be useful to managers.

1 Participation

Priority needs to be given to the participation of service users in the planning and evaluation of changing policy, provision and practice in developing inclusive communication. The onus is on service providers to face the challenges of enabling true participation of service users in decision-making processes, recognising that service users need to participate in different ways. These include the democratic representation of the views of organisations of service users. Participation also includes as wide a consultation process as possible. Service users often continue to be treated as passively dependent on the expertise of others yet control seems to have become increasingly central to social change for service users.

> Users should have more power. Until you give users real power, real control we'll get nowhere . . . there's an awful lot of people with a lot of vested interests. The more we shout about rights the more people get afraid. I'd like to see therapy training following the social model rather than the medical model. The only way to do it is to get much more input from disabled people into the training.
>
> French[46]

2 Accessible communication

The issues around language and ethnicity are complex but there are many examples of good practice. The Sandwell Integrated Language and Communication Service in the West Midlands involves a range of local health organisations – health authorities, NHS Direct, primary care groups, local authorities and voluntary agencies – working together to provide a pooled resource for spoken, written and telephone translation and interpreting, as well as sign language interpreters.[47] Accessibility of communication, however, needs management beyond such a resource, including training for staff on using interpreters. The provision of written information in a range of languages must ensure that translations meet the information needs of black and ethnic minority communities and are culturally relevant. There are, of course, many social factors within the diversity of the needs of people from black and ethnic minority communities. As Dominelli[48] argues, for instance, 'translation services should be publicly funded and provide interpreters matched to clients' ethnic grouping, language, religion, class and gender'.

Much is known about the accessibility of information based on the views expressed by disabled people. Clarke[49] offers wide-ranging recommendations which cover such things as alternative formats. He states 'the following formats should be available – large print, large print with pictures and symbols, Braille, computerdisc containing the file in plain text format, accessible websites, audiotape, videotape with plain, spoken language, audio description and British Sign Language'.

For some people, particularly those with communication disabilities, the issue of time can be crucial to an inclusive communication environment. For people with communication disabilities a slower tempo can be the only accessible pace to ensure understanding. Two participants within the research by Knight et al[50] explain:

> I would rather repeat myself ten times than have someone finish a sentence for me. This is why I won't use a communication aid.

> I prefer to speak for myself and I would rather repeat myself several times than have someone say they understood me when they did not.

Along similar lines, Pound and Hewitt[51] emphasise that the speed of communication and the length of meetings need careful consideration if people with communication impairments are to be included successfully.

3 Diversity and flexibility

Douglas, Komaromy and Robb[47] point to some of the complexities when attempting to respect diversity and provide flexible services:

> Interpreting is extremely complex in that interpreters must ensure that the patient or client easily understands the language they use. Again other factors, such as class, region, religion and geography, may impinge on the process of interpreting and communication – such that just speaking the same language may not necessarily mean the same understanding will follow.

A disabled client provides the foundation for this by questioning the focus on 'normality', rather than being flexible and taking the client's perspective into account.

> What concerns me most of all is this focus on trying to make me 'normal'. I get that from all the therapists. I get a lot of referrals of 'this may help' and 'that may help'. They had a massive case conference before the adaptations – it was a case of 'how normal can we make her first? Are the adaptations necessary?'
>
> French[46]

The lists of recommendations for communication access, as produced by Clark[49] and others, clearly challenge the imperatives of normality and emphasise the diversity of communication styles and formats. Nevertheless, there are diverse needs even within specific groups of people with impairments, which again puts the emphasis on listening to and control by individual people. Sally French, as a person with a visual impairment, has found, for example, that she is often presented with large print even though it is the depth, font and colour contrast that are more important to her and that she would rather use a magnifying glass if the print is small than have paper of an unwieldy size.

4 Human relations

Communication is constructed and embedded in relationships between people. The notion of personal relationships can be seen as irrevocably intertwined with communication. Communication is a means of expressing a relationship; it constitutes the initiation, maintenance and ending of a relationship; and it is the medium and substance through which the relationship is defined and given meaning. A disabled client offered advice to therapists on the basis of her experience:

> Forget you're a therapist – just be yourself. I don't mean forget all your training – but be yourself. Don't be afraid of showing the real you because that's what makes people respond, when they're ill they respond more easily if the therapist is being real.[46]

5 Use of inclusive language

In part this reflects the idea that language controls or constructs thinking. Sexism, ageism, homophobia, racism and disablism are framed within the very language we use. This has been characterised and degraded by some people as 'political correctness', often with reference to examples that seem trivial or fatuous (for example being criticised for offering black or white coffee). Use of language, however, is not simply about the legitimacy of words or phrases – what we are allowed to say or not say. As Thompson[52] explains, language is a powerful vehicle within interactions between health and social care professionals and clients. He identifies a number of key issues.

- **Jargon:** the use of specialised language, creating barriers and mystification and reinforcing power differences.

- **Stereotypes:** terms used to refer to people that reinforce presumptions, for example disabled people as 'sufferers'.
- **Stigma:** terms that are derogatory and insulting, for example, 'mentally handicapped'.
- **Exclusion:** terms that exclude, overlook or marginalise certain groups, for example the term 'Christian name'.
- **Depersonalisation:** terms that are reductionist and dehumanising, for example 'the elderly', 'the disabled' and even 'CPs' (to denote people with cerebral palsy).

In this light, questions of the use of language go well beyond listing acceptable and unacceptable words to examining ways of thinking that rationalise, legitimise and underline unequal professional–client power relations.

Managing the communication environment within healthcare is clearly a central and very complex task for all managers with regard to patients, clients and staff at all levels. Communication beyond listening, however important that may be, is required. Managers need a full appreciation of cultural identity if the services they provide are to respect every person as a unique individual with skills, insight and knowledge to bring to the professional-client encounter.

Managing anti-discriminatory practice

The management of cultural issues challenges the underlying structures and processes of management. There is no set of management practices that can be shipped into an organisation or institution, to empower or emancipate people who are disempowered. Considering the concept of 'citizenship', the analysis we have developed in this chapter challenges:

> Explanations that blame poor health on cultural lifestyle factors and acknowledges the ways in which disadvantage is socially produced and exacerbated by citizenship status.
>
> Papadopoulos, Tilki and Taylor[53]

Anti-discriminatory practice recognises the difference of class, sexual orientation and other social divisions as part of the warp and weft of individual differences. The management of cultural issues can, therefore, be framed in the management of anti-discriminatory practice.

'Managing diversity' puts the emphasis on the organisation rather than the ostensible needs of minority groups.

It embraces all employees and potential employees, not just personnel and human resources staff, and requires a commitment from everybody. Managing culture concentrates on the culture of the organisation and its objectives. Managers are particularly required to take the lead in equality strategies and to improve the skills of staff so they can contribute to the organisation by their own personal development.[53]

This is again a diverse set of notions that are defined in various ways. Indeed anti-discriminatory and anti-oppressive practices are often used as umbrella notions that incorporate challenging dominant ideologies and strategies for empowerment. Braye and Preston-Shoot[54] differentiate between anti-discriminatory and anti-oppressive practice, highlighting some of the issues. In their model, anti-discriminatory practice is reformist, and challenges inequality within officially sanctioned rules, procedures and structures. Specific strategies include: equal access to services; ethnically sensitive services; and consultation about services. Anti-oppressive practice, in this model, seeks more fundamental changes in power structures and specific strategies include: rebalancing power relationships between professionals and clients, with client control of services and resources; and identification and challenging of abuses of power experienced by clients. In most of the literature, however, the two terms are used interchangeably and draw on similar ideas.

Thompson[55] points out that 'establishing a basis of equality and social justice in service provision is no easy matter'. In the face of different forms of discrimination and multiple discrimination, and also the vested power interests that obstruct change, there can be no simple formula solutions to developing AHP practice. Successful change will depend on collective commitment and action.

Questioning dominant racist ideologies involves actively seeking awareness and understanding of our own racism and that of others; examining ways in which our attitudes, understandings and behaviour contribute to racism; and challenging and seeking to avoid cultural and racial stereotyping. Therapists wishing to challenge racism in their organisations need to begin along two lines suggested by Dominelli:[56]

> The first is that they subject their work to being monitored and evaluated by black people. The second is that they form anti-racist collectives with white people sharing their anti-racist objectives and develop ways of working together and supporting each other.

It is essential that the 'voice' of clients, individual and collective, directs the provision of appropriate and culturally sensitive services. This applies through listening to individual clients whose daily experiences are likely to be fundamentally different to the experiences of healthcare professionals. It also applies through the consultation of organisations of people, such as people with learning difficulties and people from black and ethnic minority communities, at every stage of service planning and implementation.

The employment of disabled, black and ethnic minority staff is of crucial importance. The discrimination faced by clients from minority groups can be faced too by members of staff and people from minority groups seeking employment, highlighting the importance of equal opportunity and anti-racist policies. There are many advantages to the employment of staff from minority groups. Black and ethnic minority staff, for instance, can communicate with clients in their own languages and can contribute to the evaluation of the adequacy of services, though it is important that such staff do not become restricted in their role to 'race experts'.[56]

'Ethnic matching' has been a widely debated and contested strategy in the management of provision of services for minority groups. Taking a specific focus on sickle cell anaemia and thalassaemic counsellors, for instance, Anionwu[57] argues that those involved in recruiting candidates to such posts should actively seek out applicants from relevant ethnic groups from their local community.

On a wider front, however, the issues are complex and multiple. Shifting the debate to disability, it can be argued that disabled service practitioners will have more sensitivity towards and a better understanding of the experiences of disabled service users. There are, however, questions relating to specific impairments: for instance the understanding and sensitivity of a service provider with a visual impairment towards service users with learning difficulties. From a service providers' viewpoint, another issue is the presumptions and career limitations of being channelled to work with particular groups of service users.

A major strategy used to change disabling behaviours and practices is equality training. Disability equality training (DET) was originally devised by disabled people themselves and pioneered by a small group of disabled women in London. In its strict sense DET originally referred to courses delivered only by tutors who had been trained by organisations of disabled people, in particular the Disability Resource Team in London and the Greater Manchester Coalition of Disabled People.[58] These organisations train disabled people themselves to be trainers. DET courses are not about changing emotional responses to disabled people but about challenging people's whole understanding of the meaning of 'disability'. The following are the stated aims of courses run by disabled trainers who have themselves been trained through the work of the Disability Resource Team:

> A DET course will enable participants to identify and address discriminatory forms of practice towards disabled people. Through training they will find ways to challenge the organisational behaviour which reinforces negatives myths and values and which prevents disabled people from gaining equality and achieving full participation in society.
>
> Gillespie-Sells and Campbell[59]

There are predominantly two types of disability training in practice: awareness and equality training. According to The Disability Rights Commission (www.drc-gb.org), the differences between the two are as follows.

- Awareness tends to 'focus on individual impairment' and 'will often involve simulation exercises'.
- Equality on the other hand explores the concept of the social model of disability and would be carried out by a disabled person 'well versed in the social model'.

DET uses discussion-based methods for teaching and learning rather than simulation and is devised and delivered by disabled people.

Organisations may be becoming increasingly aware of their role in providing customer care for all their customers and clients. The Department of Health guidance on care management and assessment states that, 'The most effective way of demonstrating the centrality of users' needs and wishes will be by consulting users and carers over the training programme and inviting them to contribute to the training itself'.[60] Awareness in Britain has been increased, in part, due to the Disability Discrimination Act (1995) and also due to the awareness raising initiatives being put in place by disabled individuals and disability groups.

There are dangers, however, in assuming that there has been progress. There is evidence to suggest that DET is not widely offered to professionals on an in-service basis.[61] Furthermore, experience suggests that courses offered under the umbrella of DET differ quite widely in terms of their aims, who delivers them and how they are delivered. DET is not necessarily delivered by trainers who have been trained by organisations of disabled people.

There are similar arguments and issues about the provision of race equality training for therapists. French and Vernon,[41] advocating race equality training, argue:

> Race equality training, when skilfully carried out by people from ethnic minority groups, can help people to become aware of their attitudes and behaviour in a relaxed and non-threatening environment.

As in disability there are different forms of training. Race awareness training resembles disability awareness training, while anti-racism awareness training corresponds to disability equality training. Anti-racism awareness training focuses on the social processes and racist power differentials existing between different ethnic minority groups, and links personal racism with structural racism. It also legitimates combining action aimed at eradicating racism with an appreciation of its effects.[48]

Turning specifically to the management of anti-discrimination practices and culture in organisational development, human resource management is clearly relevant. Storey[62] recognises four features. First is a culture of commitment. This has implications for selection and recruitment, training, supervision, appraisal and personnel issues generally. Second is the need to ensure that cultural issues are taken into consideration in formulating and implementing organisational strategy at all levels. Questions of equality and diversity should feature in strategic planning. Third, human resource management puts the emphasis on line managers, rather than specialists, having responsibility for managing diversity and cultural issues. Fourth is the development of specific techniques and processes for the human resource potential in addressing cultural issues. Overall, managing diversity engages with organisational culture and effective staff involvement.

Conclusion

The argument in this chapter has been that culture is important in the management of healthcare. Cultural issues need to be managed within the broader social and historical context of difference and diversity in healthcare and the power relations of 'how to survive' and 'how to stay together'. There are dangers in that:

> Culture becomes a rigid and constraining concept which is seen somehow to mechanistically determine people's behaviours and actions rather than providing a flexible resource for living, for according meaning to what one feels, experiences and acts to change.
>
> Ahmad[63]

Cultural issues cut across management in policy and practice and, we would suggest, are best conceptualised as a set of general principles. Drawing on the work of Connelly and Seden,[64] the following is a tentative list.

- Use a diversity of approaches, with flexibility as a key principle.
- Aim for small but cumulative change in an action-plan approach that is systematically monitored.

- Increase communication and contact between service users, to recognise a collective as well as individual voices.
- Increase direct communication between service users and managers, rather than through intermediaries.
- Ensure equality training, in understanding cultural issues as well as procedures, is provided for all staff, including new staff.

Cultural issues in management essentially challenge management culture. Managers have tended to hold on to power or vie with other powerful groups such as practitioners. In the modern NHS therapy managers need to work with patients, clients and staff to develop services that are responsive to the needs of all citizens in our diverse and complex society.

References

1 Schein EH. *Organisational Culture and Leadership*. San Francisco: Jossey-Bass; 1985.
2 Schneider SC, Barsoux J. *Managing Across Cultures*, 2nd ed. Harlow: Pearson Education Limited; 2003.
3 Woodward K. Questions of identity. In Held D, editor. *A Globalizing World: culture, economics, politics*, 2nd ed. London: Routledge; 2004.
4 Ahmad WI. *'Race' and Health in Contemporary Britain*. Buckingham: Open University Press; 1993.
5 National Association of Health Authorities and Trusts and the King's Fund Centre. *Equality Across The Board*. London: King's Fund Centre; 1993.
6 Bhavnani R, Coyle A. Black and ethnic minority women managers in the UK – continuity or change? In Davidson MJ, Burke RJ, editors. *Women in Management: Current Research Issues Volume II*. London: Sage; 2000.
7 Atkins K, French S, Vernon A. Health care for people from ethnic minority groups. In: French S, Sim J, editors. *Physiotherapy: a psychosocial approach*. 3rd edn. Oxford: Butterworth-Heinemann; 2004.
8 Smith B, Goldblatt D. Whose health is it anyway? In: Held D, editor. *A Globalizing World: culture, economics, politics*, 2nd ed. London: Routledge; 2004.
9 Whitehead M. Tackling inequalities: a review of policy initiatives. In: Benzeval M, Judge K, Whitehead M, editors. *Tackling Inequalities in Health: an agenda for action*. London: King's Fund; 1995.
10 French S. Inequalities in health. In: French S, editor. *Physiotherapy: a psychosocial approach*. 2nd ed. Oxford: Butterworth-Heinemann; 1997.
11 Talley J. Change, diversity and influence on patterns of health and ill health. In: French S, Sim J, editors. *Physiotherapy: a psychosocial approach*. 3rd ed. Oxford: Butterworth-Heinemann; 2004.
12 Department of Health. *The National Health Inequalities Targets*. London: Department of Health; 2001.
13 Benzeval M, Judge K, Whitehead M. Introduction. In: Benzeval M, Judge K, Whitehead M, editors. *Tackling Inequalities in Health: an agenda for action*. London: King's Fund; 1995.
14 Kendell RE. *The Role of Diagnosis in Psychiatry*. Oxford: Blackwell; 1975.
15 Helman CG. *Culture, Health and Illness: an introduction for health professionals*, 4th ed. Oxford: Butterworth-Heinemann; 2000.
16 Smaje C. The ethnic patterning of health: new directions for theory and research. *Sociology of Health and Illness*. 1996; **18**(2), 139–71.
17 Anionwu E, Atkin K. *The Politics of Sickle Cell and Thalassaemia*. Buckingham: Open University Press; 2001.

18 Hollway W. What is human nature? In: Held D, editor. *A Globalizing World: culture, economics, politics.* 2nd ed. London: Routledge; 2004.

19 Walmsley J, Heller T. Accessing Community Services. In: Block 3, Unit 10, Care and Communities. *Understanding Health and Social Care.* K100. Milton Keynes: Open University; 2003.

20 Tudor Hart J. The inverse care law. *The Lancet.* 1971; 1: 405–12.

21 Shaughnessy P, Cruse S. Health promotion with people who have a learning disability. In: Thompson J, Pickering S, editors. *Meeting the Health Needs of People Who Have a Learning Disability.* London: Baillière Tindall; 2001.

22 Fox J, Benzeval M. Perspectives on social variations on health. In: Benzeval M, Judge K, Whitehead M, editors. *Tackling Inequalities in Health: an agenda for action.* London: King's Fund; 1995.

23 Ewles L, Simmett I. *Promoting Health: a practical guide,* 5th ed. London: Baillière Tindall; 2003.

24 French S, Swain J. Overview – culture and context for promoting health through physiotherapy practice. In: Scriven A, editor. *Health Promoting Practice: the contribution of nurses and allied health professions.* Basingstoke: Palgrave; in press.

25 Bignall T, Butt J. *Between Ambition and Achievement: young black disabled people's views and experiences of independence and independent living.* Bristol: Policy Press; 2000.

26 Butt J, Mirza K. *Social Care and Black Communities.* London: Race Equality Unit; 1996.

27 French S, Swain J. Disability and Communication: listening is not enough. In: Robb M, Barrett S, Komaromy C, Rogers A, editors. *Communication, Relationships and Care: a reader.* London: Routledge; 2004.

28 Banton M, Hirsch MM. *Double Invisibility: report on research into the needs of black disabled people in Coventry.* Warwick: Warwickshire County Council; 2000.

29 Butt J, Box L. *Supportive Services, Effective Strategies: the views of black-led organisations and social care agencies on the future of social care for black communities.* London: Race Equality Unit; 1997.

30 Jones L, Atkin K, Ahmad W I. Supporting Asian deaf young people and their families: the role of professionals and services. *Disability and Society.* 2001; 16(1): 51–70.

31 Hill M. Race and disability. In: *Disability – Identity, Sexuality and Relationships: Readings.* K665Y course. Milton Keynes: The Open University; 1991.

32 Gillespie-Sells K, Hill M, Robbins B. *She Dances to Different Drums: research into disabled women's sexuality.* London: King's Fund; 1998.

33 Bhavnani R. *Black Women in the Labour Market: a research review.* London: Equal Opportunities Commission; 1994.

34 Modood T. Culture and identity. In: Modood T *et al,* editors. *Ethnic Minorities in Britain.* London: Policy Studies Institute; 1997.

35 Roberts K. Lost in the system: disabled refugees and asylum seekers in Britain. *Disability and Society.* 2000; 15(6): 943–8.

36 ADAPT. *Asian and Disabled: A Study into the Needs of Asian People with Disabilities in the Bradford Area.* West Yorkshire: Asian Disability Advisory Project Team, The Spastics Society and Barnardos; 1993.

37 Azmi S *et al. Improving Services for Asian People with Learning Difficulties and their Families.* Manchester: Hester Adrian Research Centre/The Mental Health Foundation; 1996.

38 Nadirshaw Z. Cultural issues. In: O'Hara J, Sperlinger A, editors. *Adults with Learning Difficulties.* London: John Wiley and Sons; 1997.

39 Shah R. 'He's our child and we shall always love him' – Mental handicap: the parents' response. In: Allott M, Robb M, editors. *Understanding Health and Social Care: an introductory reader.* London: Sage; 1998.

40 Black Perspectives Sub-group. Black perspectives on residential care. In: Allott M. Robb M, editors. *Understanding Health and Social Care: an introductory reader.* London: Sage; 1998.

41 French S, Vernon A. Health care for people from ethnic minority groups. In: French S,

editor. *Physiotherapy: a psychosocial approach*. 2nd edn. Oxford: Butterworth-Heinemann; 1997.

42 Baxter C. Confronting colour blindness: developing better services for people with learning difficulties from Black and ethnic minority communities. In: T Philpot, L Ward, editors. *Values and Visions: changing ideas in services for people with learning difficulties*. Oxford: Butterworth-Heinemann; 1995.

43 Oliver M. *Understanding Disability: from theory to practice*. Basingstoke: Macmillan; 1996.

44 Oliver M, Barnes C. *Disabled People and Social Policy: from exclusion to inclusion*. London: Longman; 1998.

45 Robinson M. *Communication and Health in a Multi-ethnic Society*. Bristol: The Policy Press; 2003.

46 French S. Enabling relationships in therapy practice. In: Swain J *et al.*, editors. *Enabling Relationships in Health and Social Care: a guide for therapists*. Oxford: Butterworth-Heinemann; 2004.

47 Douglas J, Komaromy C, Robb M. *Diversity and Difference in Communication*. Unit 6 K205. Milton Keynes: The Open University; 2004.

48 Dominelli L. *Anti-Racist Social Work*, 2nd ed. Basingstoke: Macmillan Press; 1997.

49 Clarke L. *Liverpool Central Primary Care Trust Accessible Health Information: project report*. www.leeds.ac.uk/disability-studies; 2002.

50 Knight B, Sked A, Garrill J. *Breaking the Silence: identification of the communication and support needs of adults with speech disabilities in Newcastle*. Newcastle: CENTRIS; 2002.

51 Pound C, Hewitt A. Communication barriers: building access and identity. In: Swain J *et al.*, editors. *Disabling Barriers – Enabling Environments*. London: Sage; 2004.

52 Thompson N. *Promoting Equality*. Basingstoke: Macmillan Press; 1998.

53 Papadopoulos I, Tilki M, Taylor G. *Transcultural Care: a guide for health care professionals*. Dinton: Quay Books; 1998.

54 Braye S, Preston-Shoot M. *Empowering Practice in Social Care*. Buckingham: Open University Press; 1995.

55 Thompson N. *Anti-Discriminatory Practice*. 3rd ed. Basingstoke: Palgrave; 2001.

56 Dominelli L. *Anti-Oppressive Social Work Theory and Practice*. Basingstoke: Palgrave Macmillan; 2002.

57 Anionwu E. Ethnic origin of sickle and thalassaemia counsellors. In: Kelleher D, Hillier S, editors. *Researching Cultural Differences in Health*. London: Routledge; 1996.

58 Swain J *et al*. *Enabling Relationships in Health and Social Care: a guide for therapists*. Oxford: Butterworth-Heinemann; 2004.

59 Gillespie-Sills K, Campbell J. *Disability Equality Training: trainers guide*. London: Central Council for Education and Training in Social Work; 1991.

60 Department of Health, Social Services Inspectorate, Scottish Office, Social Work Services Group. *Care Management and Assessment: summary of practice guidance*. London: HMSO/Scottish Office, Social Work Services Group; 1991.

61 Swain J, Gillman M, French, S. *Confronting Disabling Barriers: towards making organisations accessible*. Birmingham: Venture Press; 1998.

62 Storey J. Human Resource Management: still marching on. In: Storey J, editor. *Human Resource Management: a critical text*. London: Routledge; 1995.

63 Ahmad WIU. The trouble with culture. In: Kelleher D, Hillier S, editors. *Researching Cultural Differences in Health*. London: Routledge; 1996.

64 Connelly N, Seden J. What service users say about services: the implications for managers. In: Henderson J, Atkinson D, editors. *Managing Care In Context*. London: Routledge; 2003.

Index